A Woman's Guide to
Building a Business

SMALL

BUSINESS

SAVVY

Norma J. Rist & Katina Z. Jones

Adams Media Corporation
Avon, Massachusetts

This book is dedicated to my son, Brian Rist, and to my daughter, Kristin Wolfe. They are the light of my life.

Also to my mother, Neva Tompsett,
who told me I could do anything.   —NJR

For Lilly, Madelyn, John, and our little wonder from China.   —KZJ

Published by
Adams Media Corporation
57 Littlefield Street, Avon, MA 02322. U.S.A.
www.adamsmedia.com

ISBN: 1-58062-568-1

Printed in Canada.

J I H G F E D C B A

Library of Congress Cataloging-in-Publication Data
Rist, Norma J.
Small business savvy : a woman's guide to building a business /
by Norma J. Rist and Katina Z. Jones.
p.   cm.
Includes index.
ISBN 1-58062-568-1
1. New business enterprises–United States–Management. 2. Small business–
United States–Management. 3. Women-owned business enterprises–
United States–Management. I. Jones, Katina Z. II. Title.
HD62.5 .R57   2001
658.02'2'082–dc21   2001046348

This publication is designed to provide accurate and authoritative information with regard to the subject matter covered. It is sold with the understanding that the publisher is not engaged in rendering legal, accounting, or other professional advice. If legal advice or other expert assistance is required, the services of a competent professional person should be sought.
—From a *Declaration of Principles* jointly adopted by a Committee of the American Bar Association and a Committee of Publishers and Associations
Front cover image courtesy ©International Stock.

This book is available at quantity discounts for bulk purchases.
For information, call 1-800-872-5627.

Contents

introduction

Strength in Numbers: Where to Start in Building the Business of Your Dreams

---

—— Secret 1 ——
You can have the business of your dreams.

Norma's Story
Women Helping Women: It All Starts with Support

As a small business consultant, I learned that owners of a small business have very little money to pay a consultant—but they really need information in order to create and grow the business of their dreams.

I was actively looking for a way to work with business owners in small groups. They pay a small amount and I receive a reasonable amount for my time, kind of like golf lessons that are cheaper when offered in a group setting. As I called on business owners in my community and talked with them about creating an owners' group—a board of advisors, a group of rather evenly matched entrepreneurs—to meet once a month and talk about challenges, I looked at my Day-timer and found that I had a week of car-pooling scheduled and couldn't easily set appointments and continue marketing my concept.

But I did decide that I *could* make phone calls—and that it might be interesting (and fun) to call a group of women owners and see if I could start an owners' group of women entrepreneurs.

I had a directory for Women's Network, a 20-year-old organization headquartered in Ohio that I knew well, having served on the board and as president many years ago. I spent that week, in between car-pooling my daughter and several of her schoolmates back and forth to school each day, phoning the women owners in the directory and asking them if they had any interest in an owners' group.

The most difficult part of this phoning was making a cold call. I dreaded every moment of it, but after talking for several minutes I began to make some new acquaintances and I loved talking with them. These women ran fascinating businesses, from graphic designer to laundry service, from writer to florist, gardener, and speech therapist. These women were interesting, excited about their businesses, and working hard.

The second most difficult thing about those phone calls was clearly defining the difference between a personal support group, most often called a networking group, and the kind of business advisory group that I planned to provide. Almost everyone belonged to a networking group and either liked it or really didn't like it. But this group would be different—it would discuss business in a confidential meeting with me as a facilitator and business coach.

The interested owners came to my conference room and attended what was to be the first Boardroom Group meeting. They learned what it was like to talk with eight other owners about challenges as well as opportunities.

It was a magical meeting—there was nothing else quite like it. Ideas were incredibly free-flowing, and the owners really wanted to help each other to succeed. They immediately began providing resources and solutions to each other. I facilitated the meeting and offered brief overviews of everything we will cover in this book, from business plan to exit plan.

Business friendships were developed. Soon the Boardroom Group women decided to continue meeting regularly, and we set a schedule.

Today, several Boardroom Groups meet in Northeast Ohio and many participants are the original members who have moved on to newer groups in order to mentor and inspire the hundreds of other women who are still in the beginning stages of starting their businesses.

Groups with an "Entrepreneurial Spirit"

One day I received a phone call from a business friend who knew that I now had several Boardroom Groups for Women. She was referring a woman owner to me, a woman who wanted help with her very small business. Carolyn McCullick, owner of Country Harvest Ceramics, called for an appointment and arrived with a large box of ceramics—great hand-painted teapots and statues and holiday decorations. She said that she wanted a "real business," a business that would pay her a salary. Carolyn seemed nervous and I spent almost an hour talking to her about her ceramics, her current customers, and how she started selling her products to give her time to relax and become comfortable so that we could talk about the future.

I am very down to earth and easy to talk to, so it was a surprise to me that someone was worried about an appointment with me; it turns out that she had never met with a consultant or a business owner before and was concerned about what I would ask her or what I would expect. Later, I learned that this valid concern was shared by many small business owners, owners who had a wonderful talent or expertise but didn't yet know the terminology and techniques to create the business of their dreams.

Almost three hours later, we had discussed the ways she could sell her ceramics: wholesale to gift stores or retail in her own store. We talked about the difference in pricing and how to establish a wholesale price that would permit a retail store to mark up the product enough to make a good profit.

We talked about positioning and how her products would be known. I gave her a list of three people to visit: a retail florist who might have some good ideas, and two other business owners who might give her ideas and a big dose of courage. I realized that I wanted her to succeed and that she needed to keep meeting and talking with other owners in order to begin to build her business.

This was the beginning of the Entrepreneur's Boardroom Group, except that in those days, I called it a "Spirit Group." I put together 13 women owners who wanted to learn about growing a profitable business, and we met evenings for six weeks.

Carolyn had her ceramics business. Jo Adamczyk, owner of Cards in the Mail, produced cards and mailings from a carefully maintained database for local business owners. Kathy Baker, owner of The Write Choice, was a writer. Marilyn Beal, owner of CanvasWorks, produced canvas tents and awnings. Kim Cockerham, president of A Winner's Choice, Inc., sold trophies and awards. Louise Giancola, owner of Tuffy Auto Service Center, was a new franchise owner. Scarlett Huttner, owner of Scarlett's Sewing Shop, and Pat Smith, owner of Custom Cushions, created custom sewn products. Carolyn Kastelic, owner of Greenward, designed and marketed environmentally friendly canvas bags. Freda Kramer owned Creative Computing and provided home-based data entry. Debbie Lingo-Donkowski, owner of Deli To Your Door, had four routes to sell homemade breakfast and lunch food to office employees. Diane Pullen was president of Grow-With-Me-Creations and produced embroidered products including bibs with a non-stain fabric. Betty Troccolo, owner of Sew and Sew, provided alterations.

I called this group a Spirit Group because I believed that it was spirit that would help them to continue the process of growth and profitability. The energy and spirit that these women brought to each fellow member of the group helped them to get through the tough times. Now, they had a group that appreciated their hard work—and a group that would celebrate even the smallest success.

I continued offering these training groups—one each month, for more than three years. Members wanted to continue meeting and another Boardroom Group was started.

Today, I meet with five of these groups in the Akron/Cleveland area, once each month for a half day. Many stories about these owners and others who followed will appear throughout this book. They are great entrepreneurs and are very much like those of you who are working hard to build the business of your dreams.

Katina's Story

Behind the Boardroom Group Walls:
What It's Like to Be in a Boardroom Group

In 1992, after putting in 22 years as one of General Cinema Beverage Division's first female controllers, Norma J. Rist, coauthor of this book, started Norma J. Rist CEO Consulting Inc. and Boardroom Groups for Women. Since that time, her companies have helped hundreds of women get their businesses going places.

So it was no coincidence that one day in 1992, a few months after I started my designer resume service, Going Places Self-Promotions, Inc., I got a phone call. "Congratulations on starting your business," said a woman's voice at the other end of the phone. "Now that you've started, do you know where you are going with your business? Have you got a plan that works?"

I wasn't sure how to answer. I mean, here I was, a new young mother and business owner who had, until now, never even thought of herself as an entrepreneur. I simply launched a business that I thought could help me earn more money as a writer—and provide me with positive cash flow in between book advances and freelance checks.

Then there was this voice, imploring me to delve further, to explore the possibilities that lay ahead of me with confidence and (gulp) a plan.

I finally answered, after much stammering and consideration. "Well, I don't exactly have a plan . . . um . . . I did try to use one from a book, but since I've invented a different format for resumes, I'm not really the same as a lot of other resume companies."

"Then you need to develop a marketing plan that targets your unique customers," said the voice. "I can help you with that. And, you can learn a lot from other women business owners who are struggling with the same issues and concerns."

Marketing plan? How was that any different from my so-called business plan? "Hmmm," I thought. "This could really teach me what I need to know."

So, I went to my first Boardroom Group for women business owners with that lovely, encouraging yet businesslike voice, which belonged to

Norma J. Rist. All I knew about her at this point was that other women I'd met in the community were flocking to her in order to launch or fine-tune their businesses. They were getting results—and I wanted to be a part of this energizing group that could help my business fly.

It was a wonderful experience for me, a crash course in business management topics such as target marketing and profit-and-loss. Until I joined a Boardroom Group, I had no idea what a P&L was; I only knew that it had some numbers and I was number-phobic. But when Norma explained that a P&L could tell me the story of how my business was doing—of where to increase spending and where to cut it when certain things weren't working—well, that made a whole lot of sense to me. Norma could put a whole lot of business ideas into a language I could understand—and benefit from later.

For once, I finally felt like I had earned the title of president of my company.

Now, five years later, I am able to fine-tune and steer my company in whatever direction suits my needs. They seem to change constantly, as my family grows and other opportunities present themselves. But I've learned that, as long as I know who my target market is and figure out the most inventive ways to get as many customers as I need each month to meet my goals, I can keep my business alive, healthy, and growing. I've written two books for entrepreneurs who are still in the thinking stage of their businesses, and I'm even helping my husband launch his new business. All of this because I met Norma, took the plunge, and went to my first Boardroom Group.

What are Boardroom Groups, and what do they do for women business owners?

Boardroom Groups are groups made up of a panel of 8 to 12 female entrepreneurs, each from a slightly different industry than the other. There are several groups running concurrently, with meeting times in the morning, afternoon, or evening. Plans in the near future call for an Internet-based "virtual" Boardroom Group—one you may consider joining after reading this book. (See the Appendix for Norma's Small Biz Coach online address.)

We act as an informal board of advisors for each other, a group of other women who are each members of our business "success team." We learn from the mistakes of others, and from their successes, too.

Most of all, we support each other's growth as respected members of a global business community. You'll become part of that community by reading this book.

You will watch the Boardroom Group women grow through their experiences, which are, in most cases, universal enough for us all to learn something from.

Maybe your business is like one of theirs. Maybe you began with the seed of a dream, or maybe you designed a business specifically to meet the demands and needs of your own lifestyle. Maybe you just want to be the one who calls the shots—and cashes the paycheck.

Whatever reason you started your business, you are now in the driver's seat. You are the president, owner, director, or CEO. And you have a responsibility to learn as much as you can possibly absorb to make your business better and better all the time.

A Labor of Love

Like many other women, if you are in the beginning phase of your business (the time from concept to the end of the second year), you are in a pivotal time period, since many businesses fail within their first two years. This is it—do or die.

We've learned that women who start a business of any kind have one common thread running through these businesses—each has been launched more as a labor of love than as a "potentially profitable venture" (the words a man might use to describe his new business).

Those who have begun their businesses from this kind of love really enjoy what they are doing—and particularly enjoy the nurturing process that takes place in the first two years of the business's growth. Women business owners are almost maternal toward their businesses, in a way that clearly separates them from their male counterparts.

What we have learned from the women entrepreneurs who have survived the nurturing phase of the first two years is that they are natural survivors—people who didn't throw in the towel when the going got tough. People who worked day after day solving the many problems that arrive daily on the phone, in their mail, standing in front of their desk. People who learned the process of solving challenges and looked forward to improving their operation and making it successful, no matter who said it couldn't be done. People who loved putting their time and talent into a new venture that would make something in the world better. They invested in themselves and in their new venture with renewed energy day after day—and they made it work.

Women business owners are becoming a new demographic on the economic horizon; a record 9.1 million businesses bringing in $3.6 trillion in revenues. The National Foundation for Women Business Owners (NFWBO) reports that in 1999, women-owned businesses employed more than 27.5 million people in the United States. Can we say we've "come a long way, baby"?

Female enterprises have greater longevity, too. NFWBO figures say three-quarters of women-owned businesses are still operating three years later, in spite of their owners' fears of not being taken seriously. Census reports and independent research shows that women own more than one-third of the businesses in the United States and they project that share to increase 40 percent by 2005.

What is contributing to this exciting trend? There are several forces that seem to be propelling women like you toward ownership at such a rapid pace. The downsizing of larger firms is pushing many midlevel female managers out. These women choose to fight their battles on a different playing field. They already know how difficult it was for them to make a name in a large company that may or may not have really valued their women managers. The thought of re-creating that battle again may be the last thing that appeals to them. They look at the opportunity to start a venture of their own as the easier course of action. And the truth is that it is not any harder to start a new company than it is to work for promotions, year after year.

Women at home also join this trend by looking for a part-time or a full-time opportunity to start a home-based business and combine their professional interests with a need to provide good parenting. They may actually be the largest group of new owners.

Technology, too, supports the small company; it lets small companies look and perform much like larger ones with advances such as the Internet that permit individual owners to have the professional image needed to compete with bigger and more established companies.

So what is the driving force inside the minds of all of these women who launch a new venture and keep working at it until it is successful—on their own terms?

Women tend to have a huge list of reasons that finally pushes them over the fence into their new ventures. At the top of the list is that they want to find a way to follow their own values, create a company where the environment is supportive and the rules are fair, where employees want to improve their performance and become an important part of the process. They want an atmosphere that is inviting and where everyone really enjoys their work.

After they have defined their own values, they want the opportunity to make their own mistakes, take their own risks, and receive their own rewards. This freedom is the greatest challenge of all.

Other important reasons that women start and grow their own companies include a desire to develop relationships in their own way; have flexibility of work time; gain respect in their industry; exercise control over future directions; provide service to their community; and have the opportunity to learn new things and to gain new confidence.

A Look Back: How It Used to Be

One woman business owner, an attorney named Gigi, tells the story of her seven-year-old daughter's fascination with the old television show, "Perry Mason." After watching an episode, her little one looked up at her, wide-eyed and incredulous. "I didn't know that men could be lawyers, too!" she said. It's a story we still laugh at.

But today's girls are growing up in an entirely different environment than we did. Even though we, the authors, are from different generations, we faced similar situations in the workplace.

Ours was a workplace of management by intimidation, of grown women being referred to as "the girls in the phone room." In both of our generations, women were given only a few career choices: teacher, nurse, and secretary. Or wife and mother.

Until quite recently, it was completely acceptable for a man interviewing a woman for a job to inquire as to her marital and reproductive plans. God forbid that any woman would dare seek to have both career and family—even though that's a choice men have never been asked to make.

Norma hid her pregnancies in order to protect her job. One day, a male coworker asked her how she was feeling, a sly attempt at getting her to admit her pregnancy. She replied, "I'm fine . . . how are *you* feeling?"

I once wrote for a manufacturing industry magazine. Often, I was the only woman in a room full of male engineers. The novelty of being one of the few women reporters took three years to wear off, not to mention having to listen to "honey" and "pretty thing" in nauseating repetition. The fact was, I was writing about appliance design and manufacturing, and I probably knew more about how to actually use appliances than any of the engineers did.

It's precisely that kind of working environment and management by intimidation that has, in the long run, led to more and more women entrepreneurs. Women are tired of climbing the corporate ladder, only to hit the "glass ceiling." They are tired of having lots of responsibility with little recognition or ownership of their ideas. They are tired of the balancing act of motherhood, career, and selfhood. Many are just plain tired, and are looking for easier ways to make a decent living—on their own terms.

Did you see yourself living under a glass ceiling? Did you start your business not only to pursue your dream, but also to escape the madness of twentieth-century management?

If so, you are not alone. In fact, worldwide, women-owned companies make up between one-fourth and one-third of the business population. According to the National Foundation for Women Business Owners (NFWBO), the number of women-owned enterprises is growing faster than the economy at large in many countries. From 1987 to 1999, the number of female-owned businesses has increased 103 percent!

Women-owned businesses are launching in every industry sector—even some of the traditionally male-dominated ones such as construction.

We are breaking down the barriers that previously kept us from pursuing our dreams. And, since women entrepreneurs are generally better at handling multiple tasks simultaneously (managing the juggling act of children, household, and business needs), we are proving that we're not too bad at it after all.

In fact, during World War II, women took over many of the businesses that enlisted men left behind so that they could fight in the war. The businesses were still there when the men came back—much to their surprise—and women learned for the first time that they could indeed do it all.

Creating Your Own Successes

We've talked about who we are and why we work with women business owners, but what do we know about you?

We know that the profile of the female entrepreneur is vastly different than that of their male counterpart. Women see their businesses as extensions of themselves and their families, while men tend to look at their families as "branch offices" of their business. Women are more team oriented and creative, while men are more methodical and procedural.

Are men inferior, then, when it comes to running exceptional businesses? On the contrary. Neither style of entrepreneurship is right or wrong, and both styles have much to offer each other in the way of insight and information.

If you fit the profile of the woman business owner, you are intelligent, hard-working, and persevering. You are honest to a fault, and will not let outside circumstances cause you to fail if you can possibly avoid it. A typical woman entrepreneur runs her business in spite of undermining efforts of family and friends.

Because of the direct honesty of women business owners, credibility is very important to them. Do you find yourself worrying about whether your clients and other business owners are taking you seriously? Are you making excuses about your business, feeling the need to explain to others that although you have a business and are trying to help it grow successfully, you are still managing to raise your children?

Women like those of you who have been in business anywhere from six months to five years or more have many of the same questions you do about running an exceptional business. They won't accept the status quo—they want answers to questions such as:

- How do I make a plan that suits my needs—and helps me accomplish what I want?
- How do I manage my business, and position it for future success?
- Where and how do I find the right team members to take my company where it needs to go?
- How do I give my customers what they want without giving away my product or service?
- How do I make smart purchases, and use technology to my advantage?
- How do I negotiate with suppliers and vendors to get the best deals possible?
- How do I "stay the course" once I've got all of these items under control?
- How do I know when to join forces with other business owners?
- How do I know when enough is enough?

But now that you know you are not alone in your pursuit of your entrepreneurial dream, that leads us to another interesting question: how can you define your own success? What will make you feel as if you've accomplished what you originally set out to do?

When we look at women entrepreneurs we know from the Boardroom Group, we see many different definitions of success. For some women, it's getting to a level of business where they have a solid team of employees and are making enough to pay everyone (even themselves). For others, success is more personal, based on the validation they receive as a credible professional or expert in their field. For still others, success can be growing their business to a point where it's profitable enough to be sold. Success is different for everyone.

Oddly enough, though, there are only a few women who actually base their success solely on monetary gain. Money is important to women, both in terms of financial independence and status, but it is not the be-all, end-all it tends to be for men. Women are more apt to feel proud of being able to help others achieve their financial goals through their businesses (i.e., employ people rather than focus on building their own wealth).

Where We Are Going from Here

Become a part of the growing international community of women biz owners. Connect with others who are experiencing the same joys, triumphs, and sorrows as you. Learn from their mistakes, and incorporate their winning ideas into your own business's blueprint for success.

As you read this book, you will begin making that connection. You will learn things you didn't before think possible. But most of all, you will become the woman entrepreneur you always wanted to be—an idea-generating, profit-making professional.

This book begins with a chapter on business plans. Some of you may already have one in place, but we would encourage you to take another look at it by reading this chapter and reviewing its major points. You might be missing something, as many of the Boardroom Group members did on their first try.

Some Boardroom Group members were well into their second and even third years of business—without a business plan. "We just thought it would all happen naturally," they protested. "We were sure that our businesses were so easy that they didn't require a plan. But that is a false sense of security. The truth is, we were afraid to commit to a plan because we were so unsure of our own ability to stick with it."

The Boardroom Group members who have stuck with it have done well for themselves. Each has earned the respect of others in the business community, and the strong network of women owners does a lot to support each other, both personally and professionally.

Throughout this book, you will feel a connection with these women and their challenges. You will see vignettes of these groups in the form of "Back to the Boardroom" mini-articles scattered throughout each chapter, and watch as these women struggle with the same issues and concerns as you.

The Idea Center items, also appearing throughout the book, will provide you with great tips and concepts to make your business run more smoothly—and more profitably—than ever before.

You Can Do It!

As a woman business owner, you truly have the opportunity to change the world. As a part of this group of incredible resources, you will contribute to changes that will improve the ways we do business—and the world as we know it. Your future and the future of small business is in your hands. We salute your courage and support your growth!

Remember as you think about your vision of the future—the dream of a small, energetic little company that fits perfectly into your life, adds to your financial security, and gives you such great pleasure—that there is no magic in making it happen. This book will bring you the experiences of hundreds of women who worked through lots of challenges to achieve their ownership goals. Norma's personal contact with hundreds and hundreds of women business owners provides insights and techniques to make each of your goals easier to achieve. Read the ideas, try the techniques—and keep putting one foot in front of the other without stopping. You can make it happen!

✦ IDEA CENTER ✦

Why Women Are Good at Small Business

Although men and women may approach business in a slightly different way, the growth of women-owned businesses over the past decade attests to the success of their nontraditional style.

• More than half of women business owners (53 percent) employ intuition or the "right-brain" instead of the "left-brain," which focuses on analysis, the processing of information methodically, and deducing procedures. Intuitive processes often allow someone to see opportunities that aren't readily apparent and to know if they are right without the use of reason and analysis.

• The way in which women business owners make decisions is more whole-brained than men's (i.e., it is more evenly distributed between the right-brain and left-brain). This allows someone to use creative analytical processes, a characteristic that is critical for a small business manager, especially in uncertain situations.

• Women business owners tend to reflect on decisions, and consider options and outcomes before taking action. In addition, women stop to gather information from business advisors and associates. The benefit here is the shared knowledge that is gathered through interpersonal interactive liaison.

• Women entrepreneurs describe their businesses in family terms and see their business relationships as a network. This "personal touch" is often what drives employee motivation and productivity. The downside is that they may lack policies and procedures that are clearly stated.

• Women have the ability to balance different tasks and priorities. In business for yourself or for someone else, the ability to be flexible and adaptable is a distinct advantage these days when everyone is expected to perform more duties.

• Women entrepreneurs tend to find satisfaction and success from building relationships with customers and employees, from having control of their own destiny, and from doing something that they consider worthwhile. We spend the majority of our lives at work. If our work and personal values are not in alignment, sooner or later we feel conflict. Women entrepreneurs have used this internal conflict as a motivation to create the life that they desire.

• Entrepreneurs in general are more similar to each other than they are to the working population in general. Compared to the general population, entrepreneurs tend to be more logical and analytical in the way they make decisions, no matter their gender.

Source: American Women's Economic Corporation, Stamford, CT; based on information gathered by the National Foundation for Women Business Owners and posted on the Online Women's Business Center.

⚐ IDEA CENTER ⚑

Checklist for Success:
Can You Be a Successful Entrepreneur?

Here are some questions you might ask yourself before embarking on a new business:

- Are you unhappy with your current situation—and ready for a change?
- Are you completely self-directed; that is, able to come up with and complete your own job requirements?
- Are you able to meet with and sell to many different types of people?
- Are you an expert planner—someone who can see not only the big picture, but every tiny line that created the big picture?
- Can you set and keep deadlines?
- Are you a clock-watcher, or someone who quickly loses track of time?
- Can you commit to projects and follow them through to completion every time?
- Are you adaptable and open to learning new ways of doing things?
- Do you have the mental and physical stamina you need to run your business?
- Are you afraid of risk?
- Do you have adequate savings to cover your first year's salary?
- Are you a positive person?

⚐ IDEA CENTER ⚑

What Kind of Business Should You Start?

It's been said that men start businesses to make money, and women start them to build relationships and create opportunities.

Every year, Norma and I go to women business owners' conferences, and every year they are getting larger and larger. More women than ever have designed businesses that revolve around their lives rather than eat up their lives.

Some feel the creative urge to begin a business after working for larger corporations and discovering ways to turn their former employers into their first, and main, customers. Some have started with a passion for a particular subject area, such as genealogy, and turned it into a business that helps people find themselves through their family trees.

Some have simply figured out that they could do the same thing as they had done for another company, and make as much as double their previous income.

Have you given much thought to the kind of business you really want to launch? If not, here are some terrific ideas to get you started:

- Airbrush artist
- Business plan writer
- Management consultant
- Marketing specialist
- Telemarketing service
- Word-processing service
- Computer consultant
- Graphic designer
- Computer trainer
- Internet marketing specialist
- Web site developer
- Advertising agency
- Desktop publisher
- Freelance writer/editor
- Public relations agency
- Child care referral service
- Day care service
- Career counselor
- Employee benefits consultant
- Executive search/placement agency
- Resume service
- Art consultant/broker
- Accountant
- Collection agency
- Financial planner
- Mortgage loan broker
- Retirement planner
- Tax preparation service
- Caterer
- Food delivery service
- Childbirth instructor
- Lactation consultant
- Framing service
- Interior designer
- Bridal/event consultant
- Genealogical service
- Massage therapist
- Fitness trainer
- Dog trainer
- Personal shopper
- Government contract consulting
- Dance instructor

- Mediator
- Real estate agent
- Party planner

- Travel agent
- Antiques dealer
- Catalog retailer

To learn more about each of these potential businesses and more, check out *Easy to Start, Fun to Run, and Highly Profitable Home Business*, by Katina Z. Jones (Adams Media Corp., 1997).

⚁ IDEA CENTER ⚃

Where the "Girls" Are

According to the National Foundation of Women Business Owners (NFWBO), the top ten states for women entrepreneurship (based on number of firms, number of employees, and sales generated) are: California, New York, Florida, Texas, Illinois, Pennsylvania, Ohio, Georgia, New Jersey, Washington, and Michigan.

The ten fastest-growing states based on 1992–1999 growth rates are: Georgia, Arizona, Washington, Delaware, Idaho, Nevada, New Mexico, Utah, Florida, and California.

First Things First:
Starting with a Solid Plan

Katina Z. Jones

―――― Secret 2 ――――
Your business plan is a living, breathing document
that will help your business grow and change.

When Norma and I attend women business owners' conferences, we are often amazed at how many women owners tell us that they've been operating without a plan.

Would you get into a car and start driving around aimlessly, not knowing where your destination was going to be? If you did, you'd find out in a hurry that you'd be wasting a lot of time and money spinning your wheels.

We've seen so many women owners doing exactly that–spinning their wheels–that we decided to include a chapter on business planning written for both new owners and experienced ones who haven't put enough time, energy, or thought into their business plan and wonder why they are not getting anywhere. How could you get anywhere when you're not sure where "there" really is?

Many women owners (and you may be among them) consider a business plan a long, tedious, and downright boring document to work on, so they cast it aside and operate their businesses in a shoot-from-the-hip mode. They make their decisions on an as-needed basis, then wonder why they have so many problems later on.

But the truth is, you don't need to make your business plan that intense. It can start off as a smaller, more compact outline detailing the who, what, when, and where of your business, like Norma's "cup of coffee" business plan, so named because it should be something you can write down while enjoying your morning cup of coffee.

Norma's "Cup of Coffee" Business Plan

- **Who:** Who am I, and what is my company all about? What are the values that create my business (and personal) identity? Who are my customers going to be, and where will they come from? Who are my competitors and how are they different from me? Who are the people who can help bring in additional business as "rainmakers," or people who talk up my business to others and therefore act as a referral base?
- **What:** What does my company specialize in? What am I offering as products or services? What will make people want what I have to offer? What is the benefit to customers who use my products or services?
- **Where:** Okay, you might decide to work from home, but would your future plans possibly include a move to an office? Or maybe you'll need a retail space from the get-go. Wherever it is, there you are, right?
- **When:** When do I plan to start the business, and what hours will I be available to service my clients? When do I expect certain growth periods to happen in the future? (For example: "I expect the first growth stage to occur in the final quarter of the first year. It will involve the launch of an Internet-only service for my clients.")
- **How:** How will your clients find you (on the Internet, in the phone book, through referrals)? How will you do business, as a

corporation or a sole proprietor? How will you accept payment (credit cards, payment plans, layaway for retail, etc.)? How will you get your products or services to your customers?

You can see how five easy questions can lead to many others. But all are important decision points for the development stages of your business. The best part is, once you've answered all of the above questions, you can erase the questions, and you'll have a simple, concise business plan already done!

If you decide to add on another segment or division to your business, you may need to do a separate business plan for that segment all over again.

Get used to thinking things out. It's really not as scary as it looks. I've found that it helps to not work on larger business plans all at one time. Breaking the plan into smaller segments that you can work on one day at a time can demystify the process and make it seem far less overwhelming to you.

The most important thing is not how your business plan looks, because it will always be in a state of change. It is a living, breathing document—one that will take on a life of its own once your business starts and your customers start telling you what they *really* want. All of the things you thought were absolutely critical in the early days of your business could look very different three or four years out. I keep copies of each of my own business plans, and they are always good for at least one laugh due to something I miscalculated.

That's why I always do what I call my "annual report," a document that evaluates my business plan annually in a simple, nonthreatening way. (See Idea Center in this chapter for more details about my annual report.) The annual report allows me an opportunity to acknowledge the schemes and strategies that didn't work out, and remove them from my future business plans in favor of fresh, new ideas that might stand a chance.

Putting Together a Plan That Works

There are literally hundreds of books and software programs available today to help you put together your first real business plan.

But this can be intimidating if you aren't really sure what a business plan is and why you need one. That's why we've decided in this book to take a few things into account when describing your planning options to you. For instance, you might be entirely new to the business world, and have an acclimation period that is generally longer than women who have worked in the business world before. Or maybe you have emotional decisions you need to make before embarking on your entrepreneurial path.

There are many kinds of business plans you can put together. The length and depth depends on your primary reason for putting it together: If you're asking for seed money to start or grow your business, a bank will be looking for as much documentation of your worthiness as possible. On the other hand, if you're simply using your business plan as your own internal management guide to running your business, you can write it in a much more casual (and loose) way, since it will likely be for your eyes only.

A business plan for a small, service-based company will look much different than one for a large product-driven corporation. But they all have some basic things in common, and you can use this outline as your starting point.

Basic Components of a Business Plan

PART ONE: THE EXECUTIVE SUMMARY

Okay, so maybe you're not an executive, but this is the piece that's purely about you and your business. It includes the title page and table of contents (if you have one), a definition or brief explanation of the business and a brief statement about yourself and your ability to run this business. This would be a good place to tell others why this business needs you as its leader.

PART TWO: A DESCRIPTION OF YOUR BUSINESS

This is the section where you tell a little bit about your initial concept for the business. Begin with the vision: what kind of business is this, and where do you ultimately see it going? If you have a service business, tell how your service works and what it offers to customers. If you are going to sell products, include a brief description of each. Talk about the industry, and how far you expect your market to extend.

PART THREE: MARKETING

The marketing section of your business plan can be the most fun, but also the most challenging piece of your business plan to write. It's fun to think of all the potential customers and how much they'll likely pay for your service or product, but to nail down a step-by-step strategy for attracting them is another story. This can be difficult, but not if you really know your market and understand how and why your customers buy. First establish the market size and demographics, then move on to your positioning statement. What about your business is different from all others like it? How will you put the word out that you are indeed different? (See Chapter 3 for more tips on positioning.) Next, talk about your pricing strategies, distribution channel, and sales potential. How are you going to get people to buy from you? That's the key to this section of your plan.

PART FOUR: COMPETITION

Okay, we've already touched on how your company is different from all of the others in the same category. Now let's get deeper into your competition: Who are they? Where are they? Are they able to secure enough customers? Do they charge (and get) a premium for their product or service? Would you buy from them? Why or why not? These questions must be answered in order for you to establish yourself in the marketplace. It will also help you to better compete against the other guys. Why are you stronger than any competition? Why are your chances for survival better than theirs?

PART FIVE: PRODUCT DEVELOPMENT

Here is where you lay out your business's production plans. Obviously, this section only applies to product-based businesses. Include a procedure plan, scheduling, budgets, personnel, and a risk assessment.

This is a critical part of a plan that is aimed at seed or growth money, because you need to show that you're a good risk because you've thought everything out in careful order.

PART SIX: OPERATIONS AND MANAGEMENT

This is the day-to-day, running-the-business plan. It should include details about your intended organization and structure, personnel, and overhead expenses you expect to incur while running your business. You will likely include the cost of your goods if you are going to sell products. The bottom line is, how will you operate and manage your business, and how much will it cost you to do so?

PART SEVEN: FINANCIALS

Well, you could make the argument that this business plan is just for your personal use and not for a banker—and therefore say that you don't need to run the numbers. But what if you don't do a projected income statement, a cash flow analysis, and a balance sheet? How will you know whether you're really making any money later on? Financial data is not just for the business plan that asks for bank money. It's as important for you as it is for any banker to see that you understand when you might turn a profit. Most financial sections of business plans also include a list of assets, liabilities, and personal equity. If you're confused, see your accountant for help in producing these reports. Or, read Chapter 5: Money Matters.

As you can see, there is no one-size-fits-all business plan. Everything depends on how well you've thought out every aspect of owning and operating your business. This is your time to shine—so take the time to do it right, and make sure that your commitment to your business comes through in each section.

Getting into the Right Frame of Mind

Have I talked you into planning yet? Do you feel ready to sharpen up your pencil (and your mind) and get down to this business of planning?

Margaret D'Anieri, owner of Acadia Business Resources, Inc. and a partner in Norma's Venture Group LLC (a five-day intensive workshop for new business launch), offers some criteria for practical business planning. In the materials she shares with women business owners in her presentations at conferences, D'Anieri calls the business plan your "roadmap" that provides you with the structure needed to achieve your goals.

She tells business owners that a solid business plan can also improve your focus and confidence while giving you the opportunity to learn about your business and its environment.

Finally, D'Anieri says that your business plan can be used to get financing from a bank should the need arise or as your business grows.

But where to start? Here are some things you should consider before applying words to a lofty business plan.

- Start at the beginning: Why are you doing this plan? Who is your audience? Is it just for you, or are you doing it for a business loan officer? Audience makes a big difference in how you write and present your plan.
- Take two steps back: Why are you in this business? What are your core values, and how do you want them reflected in your business? What is your vision, your mission, and your ultimate goal?
- Look at the process: Involve as many people (both inside and outside of your business) as you can. A facilitator such as a management consultant can make a huge difference in the outcome of your business plan—while keeping you accountable for creating one in the first place.
- Focus on marketing: Why should we buy from you, and why now? Does your message pass the "mom" test—in other words, will people other than your mom accept it? How will you find prospects? How do you know what they want?
- Check the numbers: How much will it really cost to run your business? Have you developed specific monetary goals, and how will you reach them each month? How did you arrive at your pricing? Have you any reserves set aside for emergency use?

I use a similar formula for creating the kind of thought process that should precede a business plan.

In my pre-business planning, everything begins from the vision. Why should this business exist in the first place, and how will it help people? In a service-based business, the benefit to the customer is what drives everything else. You can't make money from a business that hasn't considered what customers need and why you're the one to give it to them. With my business, the mission is clear: to empower individuals in career transition to reach new heights in their professional lives. The resume business, as many would see it on a superficial level, seems to be about a piece of paper, or an electronic document. But the reality is, people buy their self-esteem back when they buy one of my resumes.

Starting off with a vision is what will make your business strong and powerful to the outside world. There will be many others who do what you do—your vision is what sets you apart from the others.

SAMPLE BUSINESS/ MANAGEMENT PLAN FOR CONNOISSEUR DINING CONSULTANTS
Your Internet Link to Better Restaurant Management

Description: Connoisseur Dining Consultants, LLC, is a limited liability corporation that will be located at 380½ S. Main St., Suite B, Akron, Ohio 44311. The company is strategically located in the heart of the burgeoning downtown Akron restaurant scene.

Strategy Overview: Connoisseur Dining Consultants, LLC, is a restaurant management consulting firm aimed at improving the business processes and profitability of small to medium-sized independently owned restaurants. Connoisseur Dining Consultants acts as an advisor, helping restaurants become more profitable through surveys, "mystery shopping," and analysis of personnel, POs, information systems, and cost/pricing review.

Strategy Logic: Today's restaurateurs compete in a highly competitive marketplace. Since 1997 was the first year for independently owned restaurants to take a lead over chains, this target market makes good business sense, and would likely be the most in need of the assistance Connoisseur Dining Consultants can provide. Furthermore, Connoisseur would be the only restaurant management consultant in the Akron/Canton market—and the only one in all of Ohio to offer online products and services.

Business Development: Connoisseur Dining Consultants is in the start-up or launch phase of business as of January 1999. Business will formally be launched in March 1999. The business grew as a concept from one of the principals, John Yaceczko, Jr., who encountered many management-related questions from restaurateurs while installing specialized equipment for them.

Principals: Connoisseur Dining Consultants, LLC's first principal is John Yaceczko, Jr., Consultant, who has more than 30 years of experience in various realms of the restaurant industry, from back-of-the-house to executive-level management. Mr. Yaceczko has also worked for Business Data Systems as a Technician/Trainer in computer solutions for restaurants.

Writer/Creative Director Katina Z. Jones has 17 years of writing and editing experience, and has six books to her credit (three on entrepreneurial topics). Ms. Jones will be assisting Mr. Yaceczko with the production of his Web site and all management materials that can be purchased through Connoisseur Dining Consultants, LLC. In addition, Ms. Jones will create and distribute marketing materials pertaining to Connoisseur Dining Consultants, LLC, including press releases and publicity materials.

Concept: Connoisseur Dining Consultants, LLC, can develop a strong Internet presence as a viable, accessible business link for today's competitive restaurateur. Since few restaurant management consultants have an online presence, Connoisseur is automatically one step ahead of the competition.

Current Situation: Connoisseur Dining Consultants, LLC, will be launched entirely as a shoestring operation, sharing business expenses, etc., with Jones' Going Places Self-Promotions, Inc.

The Market: There are currently more than 500 independently owned restaurants in the Akron/Cleveland/Canton markets. None is currently using the services of a restaurant management consultant. Akron Beacon Journal food critic Jane Snow reports that she receives numerous inquiries from restaurant owners seeking management advice, and that they are often dismayed to discover that the nearest restaurant management consultant is located in Chicago.

Of these prospects, nearly all have office computer systems and many have Internet access. Since restaurant owners and managers work extremely long and unusual hours, it can be difficult for them to find answers to their problems quickly, easily, economically, and somewhat anonymously. This suggests enormous potential for an Internet-based consulting business, particularly one that allows downloading of manuals or tip sheets with a major credit card.

Market Segmentation: The market is broken down by category or type of restaurant, and possibly by size. For instance, a carry-out-only business may not need as many of Connoisseur Dining Consultants' services as a family-owned restaurant with two additional locations.

Consumer Analysis: The typical consumer of Connoisseur Dining Consultants will be a small to medium-sized restaurant owner or manager who is seeking quick, intelligent answers to business problems. The Connoisseur Report, a monthly e-mail newsletter containing helpful tips and business-generating ideas, will appeal most to these business owners. Also, the ability to have 24-hour access via e-mail—and be able to purchase and download information directly onto their computer at any moment of the day or night—

will be highly appealing. These online products and services will be less costly than having a consultant come into the restaurant for analysis; however, should the problem require such assistance, Connoisseur Dining Consultants, LLC, will make an on-site visit for a predetermined hourly fee.

Competition: Currently, there is no restaurant management consultant in the Akron/Canton area. Also, there are only a dozen or so nationwide who are online. Some of these firms have excellent Web sites, but no immediately accessible information, since everything has to be ordered and mailed.

Product Features/Benefits: The accessibility issue is of major importance to the success plan of Connoisseur Dining Consultants, LLC, since it offers the greatest opportunity for a wide-open, previously untapped market. Our products will help busy restaurant owners access useful management materials in an easy, affordable manner.

Positioning: Connoisseur Dining Consultants, LLC, will position itself as the only fully automated total restaurant management solutions available on the World Wide Web.

Advertising/Promotion: Connoisseur Dining Consultants, LLC, will promote itself through news releases to local newspaper and magazine food critics and other members of the local media. Also, business cards will be distributed by Mr. Yaceczko to all of his restaurant connections. There is much promotion through word-of-mouth, since the restaurant industry tends to be, in general, very tight-knit as a group.

Sales: Customers of Connoisseur Dining Consultants, LLC, will be able to purchase their downloadable documents directly from Connoisseur's Web site using a major credit card. Some orders can be printed out and mailed in to Connoisseur with a check and proper postage for physical mailing. Consulting services conducted on-site will be billed as 50 percent down to start the consulting, and 50 percent due upon finish date, at a rate of $150 per hour.

Research/Development: Connoisseur Dining Consultants, LLC, will continue searching for the best resources for restaurant owners and managers. Some Web sites may be listed in our "Links" section, pending their permission. Subscriptions to online publications about all aspects of the restaurant industry have already been established, and we will always do our best to stay current of all trends.

Operations: Major business functions will be carried out in conjunction with Going Places Self-Promotions, Inc., a business that Connoisseur Dining Consultants, LLC, will share office space with. A bank account will be established for Connoisseur at First Merit Corp. Legal assistance will be provided by attorney Kathryn A. Michael. Linda Trevorrow, CPA, of Benjamin & Trevorrow, Inc., will be the company's accountant.

Where to Get More Information for Your Business Plan

One of the toughest things about starting a business in the 1980s was the amount of time it took to conduct market research in the local library. You could put hours and hours into your research back then, only to find that the market was saturated in your area.

The Internet has changed that dramatically. Now, you can do all of your research online, at home in your pajamas. Simply plug in some keywords, and you can find out who else in the entire country has a business similar to yours—and you can get an immediate sense of how you are already different from them.

Several business directories are housed online, and you can even get credit information about certain companies for a small, per-item fee (see Dun & Bradstreet online, available through America Online's Business Resource Center; use keywords to search and find).

Use technology to your advantage. Seek out every Web site that even remotely appears to offer what you plan to offer. Learn from the best, and differentiate yourself from the rest. Print out a Web site that you think is attractive, and use the best things from every Web site as a guide for producing your own.

You can also access thousands of articles from newspapers and magazines worldwide—and articles can help fortify your business plan with expert opinion. This will help you explain why your business idea is a viable one, and how others are already successful in the same field. Many online sites offer links to experts right from the articles, so you can e-mail them for more details.

Web sites and online forums are also great sources for testimonials and feedback. I'll give you an example of what I'm talking about: A few years ago, when I was preparing a book proposal, I would do some market research simply by walking through a bookstore and checking Books in Print to see what else has already been written on the subject. If there were too many books like the one I was proposing, I knew it wouldn't stand a chance of selling. Now, I still do those two things, but I also wouldn't think of sending out a proposal before checking Amazon.com (*www.amazon.com*).

I do this for two big reasons: one is that I can now quickly assess everything that's been written about a particular topic, but the second reason is that I can read the "book reviews" posted by regular readers. These reviews tell me what the general public likes and dislikes about the other approaches to the topic—and that can help me shape a book that's more to their liking.

Be creative in your research. Visit online forums and "listen in" on your marketplace. If you want to sell cosmetics to young women, visit the teen forum and find out what they like and dislike. If you want to be a financial planner, go to the money discussion groups and see what they're worried about and talking about.

On the Internet, you have the best chance of putting your finger directly on the pulse of your market—and you could discover that they've been waiting all this time for a company like yours to help them solve their problems, make them happier or learn something new. Your business could be the "missing link"!

⊿ IDEA CENTER ⊿

Decisions, Decisions:
Choosing Your Business Structure

Here's a quick guide to the various forms of business ownership. Note that many women begin as a sole proprietorship and wind up as a larger company, so you may choose a different structure as your business progresses.

• **Sole proprietorship:** In this form of ownership, you are the only owner of the company, and are therefore personally liable for everything pertaining to the business. Any debt you incur is considered your personal debt, even if you have separate bank accounts and operate your company under a different name. You and the business are inseparable in the eyes of business law. Still, when you're just starting out, this is a great way to operate your business until it starts to make big money.

• **Partnership:** A partnership happens when you and another person join forces in order to operate the business together. Both parties are equally responsible for the success or failure of the business. Be careful about partnerships—if your partner buys or leases equipment for the company and the business goes under, you may wind up paying the bill. Generally, I shy away from partnerships because I think the word "part" is included there for a reason.

• **Corporation:** A corporation is a legal entity that can encompass one owner or many. You incorporate through the state where you are primarily doing business. Once incorporated, you are generally liberated from personal liability; the corporation will bear any problems arising during the course of business. There are several types of corporations: limited liability (generally, a partnership of corporations who have joined forces for a limited term or project); S-corp, in which there are few shareholders and the business typically has one owner and few employees; and privately held corporation, in which several people own large shares of the corporation.

✎ BACK TO THE BOARDROOM ✎

Five Good Reasons for Doing a Business Plan

1. Direction
2. Focus
3. Inspiration
4. Experience
5. Growth

✎ IDEA CENTER ✎

A Mission Statement with Meaning

The corporate buzzword of the '90s was "mission." Everyone needed to have a clear mission statement—one that said who they were, what they did, and who they did it for.

The problem is, many of us wound up with statements that looked like they said something, but didn't really say anything meaningful about ourselves or our companies.

Specifically, many mission statements left out the customer. For example, one mission statement I recently saw said, "We make the best product at a competitive price. There is no reason to go anywhere else." Well, that tells you what they think about their company, but not very much about what the customer's feelings are.

A better example would be something like this: "XYZ Company exists because of its customers. We strive to provide the best buying experience for all of our customers, and are committed to continual improvement for their sake."

What is your mission, and how does it benefit your customers?

✎ IDEA CENTER ✎

Plan Ahead for Success

If you want to build a new business, or make your current one more successful, we've listed tips for your "success plan" here:

- **Start with a solid business plan.** You should begin with a mission or vision statement, then align everything else in your business plan with that mission. Give yourself a clear picture of who your clients really are and how you plan to service them. Don't forget the basics of where and how you'll do business, now and in the future.

- **Develop an easy-to-understand marketing plan.** Include networking with other women business owners, as well as a strategy for making it easy for customers to do business with you. How can you get more customers to your door (or computer) in the easiest, fastest ways possible? (See Chapter 3 for more information about marketing plans.)

- **Invest in your image.** Too often, women start businesses with little regard to professional image. These same women wouldn't be caught dead in a polyester suit, but what they put out there in terms of their business materials is the paper equivalent. If you're going to scrimp, just don't scrimp on your business's image. Business cards, brochures, and even your Web site are often your customers' first contacts with your company and you. Hire a good artist to develop a professional, enticing logo for you and use it on all of your materials. My own logo is a purple star man with yellow bursts of light shooting out from his star points.

Is your resume a dinosaur? Can it swim with the sharks?

The artist, Cecilia Sveda of Minx Design, understood my business completely; she got it that my business was not just about resumes, it was also about empowerment and self-esteem. The card (and my Web site, which uses the same colors and logo) gets so much positive response that I'm proud to hand it out. You should be that proud of yours.

- **Understand what your office communicates.** If you are in a service business such as accounting, and you have files scattered all over your desk, what kind of image does that portray to new clients? Think about your surroundings; evaluate them as if you are a client walking in for the first time—and looking for reasons to NOT do business with you. Would you choose yourself as a service provider? Make your office as comfortable and inviting as you would like it to be if you were the customer, and make sure it matches your image.

- **Improve your customer service efforts—annually.** Each year should be better than the last if you want repeat customers. Offer more than you think the customer is expecting from you. Maybe it's as simple as mailing a birthday postcard—with a $5 off coupon for your products or services. Respond within 24 hours to any customer complaint. Remember: Nothing travels faster than bad word-of-mouth.

- **Get connected to the future.** If you're not on the Internet already, it should be part of your future plans. Imagine having a place where potential customers can check you out while you're both in pajamas—and miles apart! Having a Web site can effectively streamline your time, too, by eliminating unnecessary or time-consuming calls from folks who just want to know a little about you and your company. Send them to cyberspace first, and you could save yourself hours per day or week in repetitive calls.

- **Position yourself as an industry leader or expert in whatever you do.** If you know window blinds better than anyone else, offer to send articles to local newspapers, do a workshop for new homeowners, or conduct a seminar for interior designers. Speak at women's clubs about the joys of window blinds. Sing their high praises everywhere you go. Be creative in your promotional efforts. I know a woman who wears a T-shirt with her logo embroidered on it; everywhere she goes, at least one person asks for more information about her company.

- **Remember that you are the key to your success.** If you don't take care of yourself well and allow yourself to get caught up in the stress of running your business, who will take over the wheel when you need a break? Be sure to include things like long weekends, vacations, and at least one block of time each week for no one else but you. Success is a journey, not a destination, as they say, so plan for breaks along the way.

✄ IDEA CENTER ✍
The "Annual Report"

I mentioned my "annual report" earlier in this chapter, and promised to give you more details about it here.

First of all, you should know that I am not referring to the lavishly produced document that is so familiar in corporate circles. No, I don't mean you should produce one of these glamorous (not to mention pricey) documents in order to look at how your business is doing. It needn't be 48 pages of lush pictures and numbers on glossy paper.

Here's how I do it:

- Get a piece of paper from an 8½ × 11 legal pad.
- Draw two lines vertically down the paper, each leaving spaces of equal width.
- At the top of each of your three columns, write the following: "Things That Worked" (first column); "Things That Didn't Work" (second column); and "Things I'll Never Do Again" (third column).
- Fill in each column accordingly. List as many things as you can remember, but you might also refer back to your business plan for the year.
- On the back of this sheet, write "Game Plan for Next Year." This whole side of the paper is for brainstorming ideas for next year's business plan. Some of the ideas might be more appropriate in your marketing plan (see Chapter 3), so you can transfer them to your marketing files when you're done creating ideas.

The point of this annual report is to educate myself on a yearly basis about what was effective and what was not—but mainly, to do it in a way that is actually fun and nonthreatening. I don't spend a lot of time beating myself up over the things that didn't work; I laugh them off, learn from them, and move on to the next stage of my business's life with an eye toward the future.

If you spend too much time evaluating and obsessing over what didn't work, you're not being a visionary anymore, you're being a historian. As Helen Keller once said, "When one door closes, another opens, but we often spend so much time focusing on the one that's closed that we never see the one that is open before us." Don't spend too much time focusing on the past. Concentrate your efforts on the future of growing your business.

As you can see, the business plan evaluation you should do each year does not need to be elaborate to be effective and memorable to you. Once you have employees (if that's part of your plan, of course), you can have an "annual review" party and enlist their help in filling in the columns.

Understand that in addition to this simple annual report, you will need to run your numbers and make sure you are still profitable from year to year. (For more details on the profit-and-loss statement and budgeting, see Chapter 5: Money Matters.)

⬚ IDEA CENTER ⬚

10 Common Business Plan Mistakes

1. **Not enough detail.** Many business plans fail to include enough information for a banker to base a loan decision on.
2. **Too much detail.** No one wants to read a hundred-page dissertation on why your company is deserving of a loan. Keep it short and to the point.
3. **Facts are not backed up well enough.** Do your research, and cite your references. Include photocopies of articles that support your business concept.
4. **Numbers don't match up.** If you aren't sure of your financial projections, ask for an accountant's help. If you overlook this important component of your business plan, a bank will overlook your request for a loan. It's that simple.

5. **Lack of focus or direction.** Make sure that your business plan doesn't ramble. Follow a sample from any good book on business plans, or use a software program such as Biz-Plan. Have someone else proofread your plan for flow and consistency.

6. **Incorrect assumptions.** Base your projections and predictions of your business's success on documented similar successes. Look for others who have succeeded in your chosen field, and emulate them in your plan. Don't try to convince a bank that you know everything about your field, but at least offer ideas based on solid experiences or research.

7. **Not keeping the document current.** Remember the secret of this chapter? Your business plan is a living, breathing document that can and should change as your business evolves. A stale document isn't going to help you move into the future.

8. **Unclear objective.** What do you want to achieve with your business plan? Is it simply for your own internal management, or are you asking a bank for money? Decide which it is, then be sure to state your objective in the first paragraph of the plan. You'd be surprised how many women forget this critical component.

9. **Failure to include a contingency plan.** Do you have an exit plan? What steps have you taken to show that you've thought out all of the possibilities—including the ones you'd rather not think about right now? Demonstrate that you have a safety net—a plan that will help you get out of your business alive, should the need arise later on.

10. **Not interesting, compelling reading.** If you are not a writer, it will be hard to make the business plan sound interesting and viable. If your plan is just for internal purposes, it's not necessary to hire a writer; however, if it's a plan aimed at securing seed or growth funds, you'd be wise to hire a good writer or editor to review your business plan. Presentation counts in the business world!

⊿ IDEA CENTER ⊾

Knowing When to Move

Your files are constantly ending up on the kitchen table . . . and the work seems to follow you into your bedroom. Is it time to move to an office space outside of your home?

If you're carrying your work all over the house with you, it probably wouldn't hurt to make a clean break. Are you one of these types who can't stop working, even past 10 o'clock at night? Are you often at the center of family arguments over when to work and when not to? Or, is it just that you feel overwhelmed by customers who constantly invade your private living space with their own demands?

If you answered yes to any of these questions, it would probably be a good idea to start looking for office space, preferably close to your house but definitely not in it.

A new office, outside of your home, could do wonders in helping you to make the separation between work and home life (which we're sure your family will greatly appreciate). Too many entrepreneurs get caught up in their businesses to the extent that the work piles up and grows in the living room and other places in the home—even though there is a designated office space in the basement or studio.

Ultimately, the need to move is determined by two major things: first, have you outgrown your current space, and second, can this growth support a regular rent payment?

If you can substantiate the reason for moving, and can find a suitable space that allows for even more growth at an affordable price, you can build your empire in a classy space that could make you more productive—and consequently more profitable—than your cushy little space at home.

From the *Adams Businesses You Can Start Almanac*, by Katina Z. Jones (Adams Media Corp., 1996).

ᴂ BACK TO THE BOARDROOM ᴘ

Don't Be Afraid to Make Wrong Decisions

If you have the least bit of a perfectionist streak, sooner or later you will wind up in a state of frustration as a business owner, because there is a learning curve involved in virtually every step of the business-building process.

Everything you do today, good or bad, will pave the way for better tomorrows. You will learn so much by making mistakes, it will almost become difficult to call them mistakes at all. Because there is so much of you involved in your business, you will benefit from the growth experiences you encounter on your path to success.

It is much better to be open to mistakes, and adept at turning them around into positive solutions. That is what successful owners do all the time. You think they don't make mistakes? Wrong—they are simply better at turning their mistakes into opportunities.

ᴂ IDEA CENTER ᴘ

"Must-Have" Checklist for New Businesses

Here are some of the more critical items you'll need for your new business:

- Computer system with a printer, fax/modem, and special software packages pertaining to your business
- Phone system with voice mail capability, or answering machine.
- File cabinets with an organized filing system
- Comfortable, ergonomically designed chair (often a last thought, but incredibly important to your productivity)
- Desk with plenty of arm space (for working on projects without bumping into your computer)
- Bookshelf to hold your numerous resources
- Office supplies: stapler/staples, paper clips, pens/pencils, tape, corrective fluid, date stamp, etc.

- Storage shelves or cabinet (usually to house supplies)
- Garbage bins (don't forget a bin for recyclable paper)
- Background music (if that's important to you or your customers)
- Most important: good lighting (One tiny desk lamp just won't do, and your staff will work as productively as you do if you invest in proper, clear lighting.)

From the *Adams Businesses You Can Start Almanac*, by Katina Z. Jones (Adams Media Corp., 1996).

◢ IDEA CENTER ◣

Home Alone: How to Feel "Connected" When You're Home-Based

You work anywhere from 30 to 60 hours per week in your cozy little home office, where you curl up with a cup of coffee and enjoy the solitude of working alone. No office politics, no petty disagreements, no feeling of corporate pressure.

But too much solitude can be a bad thing. When the sound of silence gets to you, where can you go for some human interaction?

Here are a few places to start:

- Join a home-based business forum through the Internet.
- Join a professional organization made up of business professionals like yourself (check with your Chamber of Commerce for listings of such groups).
- Toastmasters International—this organization offers you the chance to improve your speaking/presentation skills as well as meet with several others in your community (and from all walks of life).
- Volunteer at your local hospital, community organization, or even professional associations.
- Work one day per week at your local library (pack up the laptop!).
- Take yourself to lunch.

- Spend at least one half-day per week networking at a function or event.
- Form a "buddy" system with another home-based worker, sharing trials and tribulations.
- Form a success team with a dozen or so other home-based business professionals, where you meet once a week to discuss your business problems and offer one another some solutions.
- Stop feeling alone—there are literally thousands of self-employed, home-based workers in the United States today!

The Balancing Act:
Juggling Your Many Hats

Katina Z. Jones

------ Secret 3 ------
You can learn to balance work
and family life in creative ways.

Whether men like to admit it or not, women are experts at the balancing act. After all, we've had more experience at it–perhaps an unfair advantage, but true nonetheless.

Every day, many of us wake up next to a partner who simply springs out of bed, not worrying a bit about which children can and can't go to school or day care today. The problem remains, unfortunately, in many American households as something the working woman must resolve.

I am a lucky woman because I am married to a man who believes in the equality of both partners in the home. In his previous marriage, he was a stay-at-home dad for five years. He handles the laundry, helps with the kids, is supportive of my business and holds his own full-time job. He is a true partner in every sense of the word, and no, he can't be cloned (I get asked that all the time!).

As American working women, we have for years juggled our own lives around the lives of everyone else in our family units, partly because of a society that demands it, and partly out of a deep-seated belief that no one else can do anything as well as we can. Ha!

Where did we get the idea that no one else can step in and do things to help us achieve some balance in our lives? Maybe it was the Superwoman syndrome of the 1980s, when we all wore little bow ties with our navy blue suits and ran ourselves ragged from home to work and back again. In the '80s, we were told we could want it all and have it all—but we wound up tired, burnt out, and perhaps even disheartened. "Is this really all there is?" became the battle cry heard across the country.

Our economic structures have been designed not to keep us from wanting more, but from actually getting more. Many of us started our businesses for that very reason. We said to ourselves, "Why do I keep working at this company where I'm only making enough to cover childcare costs?" Who needs that, when we can work fewer hours than we did for someone else's company and make more money that we can actually keep?

Yes, women are taught at a young age to help out in many different directions. As children, we were asked to care for younger siblings or relatives, help out Grandma or Mommy in the kitchen, help keep our rooms clean, be a good student and a nice person in general. All of this, of course, on any given day.

I am only 35 years old, but I can remember that my brother was responsible for far less than I was, simply because I was "the girl." Even in the 1970s, when the women's liberation movement was going fairly strong, there was a terrible inequity in how household and daily management duties were divided.

Many of us who now own our own businesses grew up under these same circumstances. Some of us even witnessed our mothers trying to do it all, and perhaps they failed or struggled. But because of what we saw and what we knew was expected of us, we often don't see the need or value in getting help.

It's no wonder, then, that we find it so hard to give up anything, to delegate some of our multiple tasks to others for the greater good of achieving balance and perhaps peace in our lives.

The good news is, we are getting better at understanding the need for balance and the benefits of hiring the right people to do the pieces we don't necessarily like doing.

I know plenty of women business owners who have proudly given up housework in favor of using their higher skills—in running their business, in raising their families, in living their lives. They hire nannies to work inside their homes, even if they are running home-based businesses. They have a cleaning crew come to their house once a week to freshen up their home environment. Some purchase the culinary services of a good deli or carry-out service in order to make sure a great meal awaits them at the end of their work day.

What if this is still hard for you to do? What if you are still stuck in the mindset that you should be the Superwoman who cooks, cleans, cares for others in the family, and runs a successful business? Well, does looking at it on paper help you to see something? The fact is, no matter how wonderful you may be, you cannot give 100 percent to both your business and your family life at the same time. They must take turns being first in order for it all to work.

You can, and must, find better ways of doing everything. And the thing is, the more women I talk with about this topic, the more ideas I find. Nearly every woman business owner faced with a juggling act has told me the same thing: "I've tried a lot of things, and what I've learned is that, above all else, you must be flexible. You must be able to change your solutions as your problems and opportunities grow and change."

But for now, we are still caught in the same difficult situations that we faced as a group entering the work force so many years ago. Who will watch our kids while we're at work? Who will help care for our aging parents? Who will clean our home while we're off being the president of our own companies? How can we make everything work without going absolutely crazy?

Is It a Business—or Extended Family?

What's interesting is that, on the whole, women entrepreneurs are more understanding of what others in their work environment experience.

Maybe it's because they've been there, done that, and no one else allowed them to find alternative solutions that could have helped make a sticky work/home conflict easier. These women feel an obligation to help others who find themselves in a family bind.

Whatever the reasons, women entrepreneurs can see such solutions in a much clearer light than their male counterparts. According to studies from the National Foundation for Women Business Owners (NFWBO), women owners are much more likely to offer extra benefits to their employees in the form of job-sharing scenarios and flex time. They are much more tolerant of certain types of workers taking their work home in instances where day care or other types of care are not working out. If a child is sick, for instance, a woman business owner would be far more likely to allow the employee to take the day off and make it up by either working at home or making up the time later.

Such understanding makes a woman business owner's employees much more thankful.

But what's interesting about the NFWBO study is that it is limited to women business owners. It does not include executive females in corporate environments. According to another study published in the Academy of Management Journal, women who managed to crash the glass ceiling in major corporations either still did not have the authority necessary to implement such changes in corporate culture or lacked interest in doing so.

I have worked with and for many women in my career, both business owners and female bosses within a corporation. Only one of the female entrepreneurs was a joy to work for; she understood the plight of the women caught in the balancing act. She gave us flex time and allowed us to work on some projects at home. She was understanding and helpful, offering suggestions and sharing funny stories about how she was treated when she worked for a large corporation "in the big-boy league."

The other woman owner was a controlling person who made the mistake of issuing edicts to her employees that they be as passionate about her business as she was—with the understanding that all of the glory (and most of the money) was to be for herself and her family (whom she also employed). She was harsh and demanding, with high standards she expected everyone to adhere to. She liked to think she was open, creative, and wise, but she destroyed the trust within the company by keeping scrupulous track of everyone's time and blind-siding them with ruthless indignation whenever she thought she had a problem with an employee.

You may make a lot of mistakes as a woman business owner, but please try not to make this one—it damages the morale of the people working with you to build your dream. Remember to treat your employees the way that you always wanted to be treated in the past.

Recognize that there are still women who believe that since they had to scratch and claw their way to the top, they have no sympathy for others. I used to say jokingly, "When I am queen, none of this will happen in my kingdom." Don't let it happen in yours. Be the kind of business owner you always wanted to work for—and with.

When I had an employee at my business (she has since retired and I now do more work via the Internet, eliminating the need for assistance), we had a very close relationship that worked because we both had a stake in it. She wanted a pleasant, open working environment, and I wanted a happy employee who would convey that happiness to my clients. In the resume-writing business, this is very important because many of the customers seeking such services are in unhappy situations themselves. Since I knew the resume business was really about self-esteem, it was important to have a cheery voice answering the phone.

But Paula and I, who hadn't met each other until she had responded to my help-wanted ad, grew to be much more like friends, and then even perhaps a little like family. She got to see lots of my daughter Lilly, and on one occasion even sewed up a little Snow White dress Lilly had ripped by accident. We saw each other through the ups and downs of both the business and our lives. When my second marriage collapsed in the middle of a critical point in our busi-ness, Paula was there for me and helped me through just by listening and being a friend. She cheered me on to the next stage of both my business and personal life.

We women owners do share more of ourselves with our employees than most corporate executives do. After all, we are still in the trenches as business owners, working right alongside our employees much of the time. They are the partners in our successes, and the sounding boards of our future. I couldn't wait to tell Paula every new idea I had to increase business; she would evaluate my ideas and encourage me almost like a mother.

Our employees, or extended family as we are likely to see it, can also be our most reliable allies in times of challenge or failure. They can continue the flow of business, and even when we are too tired to keep going, give us another good reason to get up in the morning and go after new business.

They are very important members of our success team.

Here are some ways you can keep your team members motivated and satisfied. Surprisingly, none costs a lot of money:

- Offer five "floating" days off per year, to be used by the employee for childcare emergencies, special family events, or just a healthy break when needed.
- Give gift certificates on their birthdays or major holidays.
- Offer extra time off as long as work is made up either at home or in the office during extra hours.
- Recognize their individual achievements regularly and make sure you acknowledge their successes in front of other members of your team.
- Take your employees to lunch every once in a while. You can write it off on your taxes as long as you are talking business.
- Think of the nice things you wish a previous boss would have done for you. Keep a running list of them, and do them for your employees. Make your business a great business to work for, and you will be rewarded tenfold!

The Family Plan: Incorporating Family into Your Business in Small Ways

When I first started my business in 1993, it was a home-based, shoestring operation that I literally ran from my kitchen table. I didn't even have a computer of my own yet.

It was easy at first, since I didn't really have the pressure of needing to secure immediate income. I took my time, developed my own marketing tools (business cards, brochures, and sample book), and ran classified ads in my local newspapers, looking for people who wanted a "dynamic nontraditional resume" to help them get their next job. I did a little bit of networking, but was able to work it in around my family's schedule; after all, I also had a one-year-old daughter to care for.

This one-year-old grew with my business. In many ways, I see them as twins. Both experienced so much in each year of their lives. Lilly took her first steps shortly after the business began to take its first steps. The business grew as she did, and there was joy in both experiences.

Soon after the first year or two of my business, my calendar began to fill up with more networking opportunities and client appointments. After I managed to get myself on a local morning television show, I got 89 phone calls and three months of solid, booked business. I was also under contract to write a book for entrepreneurs (the *Adams Businesses You Can Start Almanac*).

Lilly spent much of this time at her grandmother's house, not far from my office. I tried to work hours that were as normal as possible, but eventually decided that I was getting kind of wrapped up in what I now call "Mommy guilt." After thinking about these feelings for some time, I decided that it wasn't really about guilt. I just wanted to be with my baby as much as I wanted the thrill of running my own business.

So, I started blocking off Fridays for Lilly. We spent the whole day together, and got a great head start on the weekend, too. Mostly we went to the park, or shopping, but we would also go to lunch at our favorite Italian restaurant. That's about the time I started carrying a notebook around with me to jot down business ideas while I was having lunch with my daughter.

One time I started working on my new marketing plan for the next year. Lilly asked to participate, so I explained to her what I was doing and why it was important. What's amazing to me is that Lilly, who was by this time nearly five years old, got it. She understood that people needed to be shown that they need something before they'd buy it. From that time on, many of our lunches have been jointly referred to as "Mommy/daughter business lunches." Lilly still asks if we can work on my marketing plan, and offers to illustrate it in crayon. How many other women business owners can say that?

It's All in the Family: Special Tips for the Family-Owned Business

Remember the old "Saturday Night Live" sketch with the Greek restaurant and the "cheeburger, cheeburger" line? I can still see images of the John Belushi character hitting "Stavros" (played by Dan Ackroyd) over the head, and the two of them arguing with each other and just about every customer that came in.

What does this brief trip down television's memory lane have to do with the thousands of family-owned businesses in this country today? It reminds me of the family-owned restaurants I grew up with and frequented with my own family. There was always something going on, and you could often cut the tension with a knife. Somebody was always mad at someone else, and it only got worse when wives were added into the business. Suddenly, everyone had their own ideas about running the so-called family business—a volatile mix that made it difficult for nonrelated employees to function effectively because the messages were mixed.

As a child growing up with a few entrepreneurs in my family, I saw all the good—and bad—things that could result from involving relatives in the "family" business. On the positive side, it strengthens your family identity; you are no longer just "The Smiths," but the "The Smiths of the Grandview Diner." This has advantages in the community, and opens up more channels for networking with other family-owned businesses.

But the downside is that you can get so wrapped up in the family business that you forget the "family" in the business. After putting in 40- to 50-hour work weeks with your siblings and/or children, how inclined will you be to have that family picnic on the weekend? And how do you think your employees will feel knowing that their own chances of advancement may be limited due to the fact that they have a different last name? Not an easy predicament for any business owner to be in.

Weigh the advantages and disadvantages of owning a family business before you embark on building an empire. There are many challenges unique to this type of ownership, but there are many down sides, too.

There are plenty of places for you to learn more about family-owned businesses. Do an online search to find the most current information available. Look for a book or two on the subject. Then, make a serious, concentrated effort to evaluate each benefit and disadvantage together as a family, so that you can make the best decision for everyone involved.

Here are some general tips to help you and your family-owned business survive:

- Start with a list of common goals and dreams. What does each of you hope for and dream about with regard to the future of the business? Compare your lists, then try to compile one that includes everyone's input.

- Deal with issues of power as early as possible. The one thing that seems to really do a family business in is the power struggle. Remember what it did to the Ewing family on Dallas? Your situation may not be as dramatic, but then again, I've seen some real doozies. Talk as soon and as clearly as possible about exactly who has the right to make key decisions. If you can't agree on power issues before you get started, don't expect to be able to resolve them easily later on.

- Establish a chain of command. If one family member is better at marketing, that person should be put in charge of it. If another is best at accounting and bookkeeping, you've got that area covered, too. Just make sure everyone knows what they are doing, and what their boundaries are in terms of helping anyone else with their responsibilities. Some family members don't know when (or where) to stop.

- Develop a succession plan. Too often, we've seen family businesses go under because Dad depended on Junior to take over, and Junior never had any intention of following in the old footsteps. Women entrepreneurs tend to be a little more sensitive to this fact, since we tend to nurture our children into being what they want to when they grow up. Don't depend on your kids, or even your husband, to take over the reins unless they have already expressed the interest in doing so. Perhaps one of your "star" employees would like to take over the business should you decide to retire. Keep your options open.

- Watch for trouble signs. The biggest issues, say family business advisors, are things like sibling rivalry, compensation, and distribution of labor. If one child feels as though she's doing as much as another but being paid less, you've got a problem. Psychologically, you wind up with the "Mom-always-liked-you-best" syndrome—and no business needs that. Address rivalry issues before you start bringing family into the business.
- Include others in the mix. Don't limit your business to just family members. You need others (and their special gifts) to add variety, creativity, and vitality to your business.

Understand that all family businesses experience strain from time to time; this is as normal a part of your business life as it is of your family life. There are plenty of places you can go to for help with these kinds of problems. Seek the help of a management counselor/coach or attend a family business seminar (there are many offered across the country; call your local Small Business Administration for more information.)

The Two-Entrepreneur Family

If you and your husband or partner decide that you *both* want to be entrepreneurs, how do you run the businesses and balance your family life?

It's simple enough when you don't have children or anyone else you're caring for in the home. In that case, you just pick up and do your respective work each day, retiring to your home base for a candlelit dinner and a glass of wine.

Not necessarily so when you add more family members to the mix. When you have soccer, after-school activities, and daily trips to the day care center, it's hard for two entrepreneurs to do business in separate ways.

What is needed in those cases is good planning and communication. Schedule a weekly meeting on Sunday nights, before the work week starts and communication gets scrambled. Have copies of each other's schedules for the week, and discuss any changes as soon as they come up. Never leave anything to chance, or you will have some very unhappy surprises.

Just because everyone else might think you're crazy is no reason to give up the idea of being married—with businesses. Your businesses could find symbiotic or complementary ways of helping each other. For instance, what if you owned an interior decorating business, and your husband's business is involved in home building? You could wind up with some instant business, since people prefer doing business with people they already know.

There are other ways one of you can get involved and help in the other's business—and make it work.

Norma and I know many women whose husbands worked at regular jobs until they discovered that their wives' businesses were profitable enough for them to come on board. These are special people who dedicated themselves to helping their wives make their businesses work better and better.

Whether you decide to work together or apart in separate businesses, know that you will face challenges that many others will never see, let alone understand. The pressures may be quite intense, especially if the cash flow isn't there for one business—or worse yet, both businesses. You would do well to seek the help of a business counselor or professional coach who can help you both through the often turbulent waters of the entrepreneurial experience.

Critical to the success of the two-entrepreneur family are solid business plans and sufficient cash reserves. These two items can go a long way in preventing entrepreneurial—and marital—disaster.

Above all else, be honest and direct with one another. Don't hold back any information that could later come as a surprise to your partner—especially if it's about money. Many sociologists have said that money issues are a huge contributing factor to the demise of marriages—and entrepreneurial ones with secrets are at even higher risk.

Your Business or Your Life

When you first start a business, it's easy to get so consumed by it that you forget the others in your life. There is so much to think about and do, that at times it is overwhelming.

Soon, your family suffers from your absences—and starts accusing you of not being "present" for family dinners and activities. "You have that vacant look of someone who is thinking about her business all the time," you hear other family members say.

Even after your business gets going full-throttle, you can easily become swept up in its activity. For many of us, our small businesses are something like children. Larger companies are like extended family, full of people we are close to and want to care for much as we do our children. Everyone in the company, every "family member," contributes to the bottom line in some way.

But the bottom line is, there's more to your company than the bottom line. There's also more to you and your life than your business—no matter how successful or wonderful it is. I'm always amused by the saying that at the end of our lives, few of us will be likely to say we wish we'd spent more time in the office. That is so true.

Is there really a way to run a successful, flourishing business and still raise a family or have an outside life? Most of the women I meet at entrepreneurial conferences say that they love their businesses, but admit it is hard to keep up with the fast pace of the entrepreneurial track—especially when it is running neck-and-neck with the Mommy track.

Believe it or not, there are ways to achieve the balance that often seems to elude even the best of us. As a female entrepreneur, you just have to be more creative in how you go about achieving it.

Balance Is Your Responsibility to Yourself

Whether you work inside or outside of your home, whether you have kids or adults in the care equation, the bottom line is that you have to take responsibility for your own well-being.

No matter what your business and personal circumstances, the responsibility of creating balance in your life is ultimately yours.

I have worked as a personal success coach for many clients, and when I meet with other coaches to discuss our clients' needs and how we can best continue to meet them, we always have the same conversation about balance. Everyone wants it, few actually achieve it in ways that make everybody happy. Consider that when embarking on your plan. Allow room in your business plan for the things you cannot foresee at this moment but that might play a role in the future of your business. What if, for instance, you decide to have a child (or another child) halfway into your business plan? Will you allow yourself time to find help in caring for this child (or children)? Have you really considered every possible method of getting your work done while being good to yourself and your family?

Being good to yourself means pacing your business growth so that your business grows with your family rather than in spite of it.

So, be good to yourself. Take breaks whenever you can. Plan ahead for stressors that might affect your family. Don't let the stress get ahold of your better instincts. And, most of all, as the old deodorant commercial used to say, never let them see you sweat!

◿ BACK TO THE BOARDROOM ◺

The Many Roles You Play

I used to have a funny response to the question: "What's your title?" "I'm the president," I would say, "*and* the janitor." It always seemed to garnish a little laugh from the other side of the phone or desk. But it was the truth. I did move my company into the future, but I had some of my best ideas on the way to taking out the trash.

On any given day at your business, you are the president, the janitor, and everything in between. Sometimes you are the marketing department, sometimes the accounting department, and—more than you'd probably like—you are sometimes the collection department. But the fact remains—until you can grow your business large enough to delegate work (see Chapter 6: When Work Becomes Life, for more details and ideas on that topic).

Until that time, break your tasks into specific smaller pieces. For instance, you might try to do your accounting tasks at the end of the week (or even Saturday mornings), since most of your client calls may occur at the beginning of the week.

Here's how we brainstormed a "juggling hats" schedule for some of the women in the Boardroom Group:

- Monday: Client calls, marketing tasks such as cold-calling and direct mailings.
- Tuesday: Service clients in the morning; follow-up calls in the afternoon.
- Wednesday: Problem-solving day. Deal only with situations needing your immediate attention; in the afternoon, schedule time away from the office for what we call "planning for the future." This means that you will be brainstorming ideas that will help your company grow.
- Thursday: Client calls and potential new client meetings; service clients in the afternoon. (Note: I often use the afternoon and early evening to e-mail requests that I would like to see fulfilled by Monday.)
- Friday: If you have employees, this is a good day to recap the week's activities and plan ahead for the following week so that your weekend can be business-thought-free. I know lots of women owners who take the last half of this day to be with their children, particularly if the kids are still young. The important thing is to leave your office on Friday with a list of things to do for the next week—then not touch the list again until Monday. Not the easiest thing for some of us to do.

Your business may require that you work other days of the week, or hours other than those covered in this example. Tailor these tips to your business in whatever way you find works for you. The key to better balance is time management. Stay on top of your business and it won't get in the way of your life!

⊿ IDEA CENTER ⊾

Seven Warning Signs of Too Much Stress

1. **Forgetfulness.** You seem to be forgetting things more than usual; names, dates, and even appointments start slipping your mind.

2. **Irritability.** Do little things get to you more than they used to? Are you snapping at others? Is anyone telling you that you seem a little irritable? Does that make you more irritable?

3. **Lack of follow-through.** Suddenly, projects and creative ideas begin to fall through the cracks because you can't keep up with them.

4. **Clutter buildup.** Many professional organizers believe that clutter in your office or home is a sign of many decisions you have to make. If you have lots of clutter, you are not making decisions effectively. Lots of unpaid bills piling up? Perhaps you are afraid of not being able to pay your bills.

5. **Poor or impaired decision-making.** Do your decisions seem less effective, on the whole (and clutter aside)? If so, you may be under too much stress.

6. **Dropping out.** Have you been networking or continuing relationships effectively? Are you staying in more, afraid that if you are not there, work will not get done?

7. **Physical signs.** Has your blood pressure been high lately? When was the last time you went to the doctor for a routine checkup? Are you breathing normally, and can you find ways to relax yourself easily? If not, you need some TLC—and maybe even medication. Listen to your body—it will never lie to you about stress.

⋈ IDEA CENTER ⋈
Creative "Balance Breaks"

- A lunch away from the office, in a quiet setting such as a park
- A small road trip to another town
- Taking a walk with your child or dog at midday
- A luxury bubble bath at the end of the day
- Meditation at the beginning of the day
- Taking a five-minute "breathing break" at your desk
- Doing some work in a different place, such as the park, a restaurant, or library

- Volunteering time at your local hospice, food bank, or crisis shelter (this will give you better perspective as well)
- Being kind to yourself and others as you work for the common good

⊿ IDEA CENTER ⊯

Five Creative Ways to Get Work Done

1. **Give yourself incentives.** When you get your work done, reward yourself with a shopping trip, day spa visit, or anything else you consider special. It could be as simple as a hot fudge sundae.

2. **Find help.** If someone else can do a portion of your work, consider farming it out. Delegation is a great way for a few people to accomplish a lot. (See Chapter 6 for more on the topic of delegation.)

3. **Use technology to its best advantage.** I have Caller-ID, a pager, e-mail, and a regular phone/fax. Because of all of this technology, I can be very choosy about whom I want to talk to and when. Very few messages need to be dealt with immediately. If you feel too nervous about this, record a message on your voice mail that says something like: "I'm swamped with a special project today, but will check my messages periodically. If your call is urgent, page me at ——. Otherwise, know that I will be in touch with you soon." Be sure to follow up afterward. I love my e-mail most of all—if I could do all of my business online, that's where I'd be. E-mail allows the most flexibility for an entrepreneur.

4. **Teach.** It may seem like a difficult task to teach students or other women entrepreneurs something about your work, but I've found that teaching forces me to clarify what I'm doing and make it simpler to understand. Offer to lead a brief seminar on the topic that you are working on; we've both taught mini-seminars on many of the topics in this book. Richard Bach once said that we teach best what we most need to learn.

5. **Break the work into segments.** Smaller pieces are easier to digest—and finish. Carve your work into small pieces spread over a larger period of time, if you have that luxury. Don't wait until the last minute to do all of it—the stress will make it much harder on you and others around you.

⊿ IDEA CENTER ⊾

Care Options Worth Considering

If you have children under the age of eight:

- Day care center
- Care at a grandparent's (or other family member's) house
- Co-op with other parents in your neighborhood; you take one to two days per week each, taking turns caring for kids and working
- Enrollment in a Montessori school that has after-school care
- Stay at home and use a babysitter when you need to go out on appointments; this is easier for writers and other creative types (but I've seen it work for accountants, too)
- Hire a nanny or au pair to be in your home with your children, whether you work from home or not

If you have children over eight years old:

- Have them come to your office at the end of the school day; this gives them a chance (and a desk) to do their homework under your watchful eyes.
- Enlist these older siblings to help care for younger ones (if you have them); this usually works only if you are present in the home and not in an office situation.
- Hire an adult caregiver to be present in the home after school; this person can also be a relative.
- Sign the child up for a creative (and fun) after-school program, such as soccer, art, or theater classes.
- If you have a teenager, help him or her get a job after school.

If you have a parent living with you who needs care:

- Hire a care professional to look in on your parent daily.
- Check with your parent's insurance to see if a visiting nurse (or hospice worker, if there is a terminal illness involved) can come to your home on a regular basis.
- Use an adult day care center; most offer car service to and from the center as well.
- Consider the option of assisted living; be sure to include your parent in as much of the decision-making process as possible.
- If your parent is still healthy and able-bodied, enlist their help in parts of your business or home life; I know many entrepreneurs whose parents answer their phones (and do a great job of selling customers on the business's products or services!).

⊿ IDEA CENTER ⊾

How to Interview a Caregiver

Finding a person to care for your children (or maybe even an aging parent) is not something to be entered into lightly. After all, this is the person whom you will entrust with the care of those most important to you. So, after you place or respond to an advertisement in your local newspaper under the "Caregivers" heading, you'll need to be armed with the questions that can help you determine whether the candidate is indeed a good fit.

- What are your credentials for caregiving? What is your experience in the field?
- Did you ever have a challenging caregiving situation? How did you handle it?
- Do you like children (or older adults)? (Note: This sounds like a simple enough question, but you'd be surprised what you can tell from the answer. Enthusiasm counts.)
- Tell me about your worst experience as a caregiver, and what you feel you learned from it.

- How were your own experiences growing up? What positive things did you learn from your own family about caring for others?
- How willing are you to be flexible? (Because you own your own business, your schedule may fluctuate from time to time. You'll need someone who can put up with this, or at least help you to know the boundaries of what you can and can't expect from them.)
- Have you ever been terminated from a caregiving job and, if so, why?
- How would you handle an emergency situation?

◿ IDEA CENTER ◺
Juggling Family and Work*

Let's face it, raising a family and growing a business are each full-time jobs. So, how can you give 100 percent to each and still maintain your sanity?

First of all, set aside a special time each day or week that is designated "family time." During this time, you will accept no phone calls, set no appointments, and not even think about your business. You will probably not even want to stay near your office. Think about going out to dinner and sharing the three best things that happened to each family member during that week.

Or, if you feel you can incorporate your family into parts of your business, it might help them to better understand your needs and constraints. It's one thing for your spouse or children to see you completely stressed out; it's quite another for them to be in your office when that high-volume order comes in on short notice. Especially for children, it's a good idea to demonstrate your commitment to your work.

Smaller children, particularly females, need positive workplace role models—and who better to pave the way for them than Mom or Dad? Historically, children who are raised by entrepreneurs do tend to become entrepreneurs themselves.

What should you do in the event that a client or customer wants to meet during one of your special times? You can handle it one of two ways: First, you could rearrange your family time. But the better solution might be to simply say, "I am already meeting with a client at that time . . . is there another time that works for you?" Others will respect your attention to commitments, and you never have to offer any explanation regarding with whom you're meeting and why.

However you decide to work your children into your business, or your business into your family life, one thing is for sure: there will never be a time without challenges and disruptions.

You will need to develop the skill to work around any obstacle or challenge, and the best way to accomplish a good balance between work and home life is to learn to follow a time-management program. Scheduling your time is the best way to make sure that everything gets done. The rest is just recognizing that it is possible to have two loves: your business and your family.

From *Easy to Start, Fun to Run, and Highly Profitable Home Businesses*, by Katina Z. Jones (Adams Media Corp., 1998).

◢ BACK TO THE BOARDROOM ◣

Prioritizing Issues

In the Boardroom Groups for Women, we have many members who must juggle their many responsibilities as both business owners and parents.

What we discover as we begin to talk about these issues is that the women need help in figuring out how to prioritize better. It's not as much about being a good business owner or parent as it is about being a good priority-setter.

The question that comes up most frequently is how do you decide what is most important to do?

"What if I have a business meeting scheduled with a new client, and my child gets sick that day?" asks one owner.

"What if my child complains that I'm spending too much time working and not enough time at home?" asks another.

The questions take on a similar tone, and the answers are pretty much the same. You must first set your priorities—the rest will fall into place like dominoes after the initial decision of what is most important at this very minute.

If you are having cash flow problems and need to keep a meeting with a potential new client, you will find a relative or friend to care for your child for those few hours spent bringing in a new client. You must not label yourself a bad parent just because you were meeting a financial need for yourself and your family—after all, they benefit from your business doing well.

In the instance of a child thinking that you are spending too much time away, you will need to find ways of including the child in some pieces of the business, so that they can begin to see what takes so long. But you may also need to delegate some things to others, either inside or outside of your company, in order to have some special time with your child that is separate from the business.

Interestingly enough, many of our Boardroom Group members have found ways of dealing with the juggling act effectively by simply brainstorming with each other. Here are some of the tips that have come out of those sessions:

- Buy a planner that has room for both your personal and business schedule. Franklin Covey planners incorporate both family and business schedules to help you prioritize well.
- Schedule a "date" with your child (or children) on a regular day at a regular time. This consistency is important to the child, who will learn to look forward to those special days. You will also alleviate some of your own guilty feelings, however unfounded they may be.
- Keep a file that's called "Resources Needed for Growth." Here, you will place all of the clippings of ads, articles, and other materials about services, ideas, and so on that will help you move forward in your business—while keeping your family life running smoothly. Keep all business cards of cleaning companies, caregivers, and even pet sitters in this file for ready reference.

- Take a hard look at what is not getting done in your life, then ask others how they solved the same problem. For instance, if you are letting your housework go because you are so busy with your business and family, ask another business owner how they get their housework done. Some hire outside cleaning companies to do the work, while others simply delegate house- hold chores to others in the family. Interestingly enough, the ones who hire others usually tend to enlist the services of another woman-owned business. Such loyalty we have!
- Use your network of other business owners to its greatest advantage. In our state, several directories of women business owners are published and distributed each year. This way, when we need a particular service, we can readily look up another woman to do business with—and many times, barters can be established or long-term relationships built between the two businesses. Some owners discover a synergy that helps both businesses grow.

⚐ IDEA CENTER ⚑
Who You Gonna Call?

Here's a list of service-type businesses you might need to call when you need help performing your balancing act:

- Accountant
- Attorney
- Public relations specialist
- Graphic designer
- Babysitter
- Day care center
- Cleaning service
- Food delivery service
- Pet sitter
- Gardener/lawn care service
- Barter service (to negotiate a trade in products or services)

- Bookkeeper
- Calendar service (they call or e-mail you with dates you need to remember)
- Virtual assistant (a high-tech secretarial service that handles correspondence, e-mail, and details of your business without being an on-site employee)
- Child care referral service
- Pet taxi service (for trips to the vet or groomer)
- Professional organizer (to help get a handle on your paperwork, filing system, or home storage system)
- Insurance agent (to make sure you're covered effectively should you encounter disability, which will surely upset the balance you've worked so hard to create)
- Lead exchange/networking service (will save you time in getting some quality sales leads)
- Laundry service, preferably with pickup and delivery
- Management consultant who can help you continue to set better priorities
- Personal shopper (to shop when you don't have time to)
- Errand service; most handle everything from bill paying to grocery shopping
- Nanny service
- Computer tutor to teach you every innovative new way to use technology to stay ahead of the game

Putting the Word Out: Marketing Without Fear

Norma J. Rist

——— Secret 4 ———
Marketing your business can be fun—and painless.

An owner I'll call Ms. Shy arrived at my marketing workshop and, in her introduction, told the group: "I am *never* going to sell and nothing that I learn in this class will get me to do it."

The group was astonished. But I said, "No problem—I'll just teach you how to market so that your phone rings."

"Okay," she said, still with some hesitation. "But I'm not *ever* going to sell."

The word "sell" has a negative connotation to many women owners. Particularly for new business owners, it can be hard to understand the difference between selling and marketing for a particular product or service.

How Is Marketing Different from Selling?

Very simply defined, marketing is everything that helps prospects that are looking for you to find you.

A woman named Carol owns a benefit company; she's a licensed agent. She sent out a series of four postcards to small company owners who might want additional benefits for their employees at no cost to the company. Each card briefly stated one of four benefits available to help employees. This is marketing—it lets the owners know about a great service they might not have otherwise located. It doesn't necessarily ask for an immediate order, as it would if it were strictly a sales piece.

Marketing is even better explained as **everything that tells your target prospect about the distinct improvement your product or service could provide them.**

A computer consultant named Jane provides free 30-minute presentations on database management for owners who want to do direct-mail advertising. She teaches the process and the incredible benefits so clearly and accurately that many participants want to engage her to manage their mail program. This is great marketing—conveying the specific improvement the prospect is seeking in a way that is not a hard sell.

Selling—legitimate selling, that is—involves talking with a target prospect about the benefits of your product or service that fit her needs, then trying to nail down the business immediately.

When Carol sent out those postcards about benefits, one owner phoned her and asked several questions that Carol answered. He asked Carol to meet with him and further discuss whether her program fit with his employees' needs. This meeting led to a new client for Carol. Carol was selling in this stage—talking with a prospect about benefits that fit his needs and trying to secure his business.

Let's look at Jane again. Those presentations that Jane provides, explaining database management to small service firms' owners, will usually get someone interested in her consulting. An owner will come up after the talk and ask questions about his particular service business. Pretty soon, he wants Jane to visit his firm and review his project. Then he asks for a proposal. This is selling—Jane provides a proposal that shows the benefits and the project management skills that fit his needs.

There are hundreds of ways to market, ways to help prospects to see the benefits of the product or service you offer, through advertising, brochures, radio, networking, seminars, and more.

The great thing about marketing is that when you create a good marketing situation, the prospects that are looking for you can see the benefit immediately. I call this "shining a light" on the specific improvement that you can provide—almost like the dancer who is center stage with the spotlight on her, except that it is not you or your company that will be seen. Instead, it's the benefit that will improve their life that will be seen.

Think about the ads on TV that you may remember. A child is drinking orange juice and then is growing up healthy—he's shown on the playground smiling. A child is helped by an after-school tutoring program and then is raising her hand in the classroom, obviously happy and successful. These ads focus on the beneficial difference made by the product or the service that is being sold.

This is a good approach to follow when creating the marketing materials that will represent your product or service. Think about the outcome of your good work. What do your satisfied customers say about the result of working with you? These are the words and phrases to use in your introduction and also in your printed marketing pieces. This should be the primary focus of your marketing.

An attorney's client might say, "You protected me from making a possible mistake when you reviewed my subcontractor's agreement before I put it into place." The CPA's client might say, "You helped me analyze the best form of business, from a tax perspective, so that I could start my venture on the right foot." The mystery-shopping customer might say, "You helped me identify the customer service training that was needed; now my employees are great ambassadors of the company."

These benefits become the core of your marketing focus.

Your marketing can be really successful when you acquire this approach; what you provide, not what you do; the specific improvement you can make in their life, not how you do it.

This new focus helps you create the words that you use when you are telling someone what you do at a networking event or in a workshop you offer. The same focus in words and graphic form is carried out in all of your print media: cards, letterhead, brochure, flyer, magazine or newspaper ad—wherever you want yourself to be seen and heard.

One last word about that "turn off" we feel about selling. Try to think about the most professional sales representative you ever met. Was it a woman explaining the program for her cell phone company? Or a woman in a dress shop listening to the type of event you planned to attend in a cocktail dress? Perhaps you met a woman who owned a catering company or was a print broker, and she was so helpful that you would never consider calling her a saleswoman. This is professional, relationship-based selling—and it involves a lot of listening.

On the other hand, maybe you had a bad experience with a person who seemed to push a product on you, trying to obtain a sale without asking what your needs were. I had this happen once at a new car dealership when the salesperson showed me the net in the trunk to protect my groceries; at the time I was managing the Pepsi Cola franchise in town and someone else was doing my grocery shopping. I needed a full-size car and the color needed to be businesslike for entertaining clients. The dealer representative didn't ask any questions and wasn't listening to what I was saying. He simply assumed—and was wrong.

Remember the first example, the salesperson who is incredibly helpful, listens to your needs, and discusses whether her product or service is a good fit—this is the appropriate kind of selling, the professional who fills a need. You can stop worrying about the second example, the salesperson who pushes his product on any prospect he meets—this is not professional selling, and you won't be using any of those negative techniques. Most women are wonderful, natural salespeople simply because they listen.

Why You Need a Good Marketing Plan to Survive

A small business owner like you might start a new venture and find customers right away and wonder why other owners need to have a plan. It's possible that an individual is already known in a field, such as a CPA who leaves a firm and starts her own small firm, and prospects who knew her before are already familiar with the services that she can provide. If she is fortunate enough to already belong to some community organizations and has enough contacts that'll call her in sufficient numbers, she might be able to get started without a marketing plan. I think, however, that this is the lucky exception.

Most start-up owners need a marketing plan to build a business with the customers they really want to have—the customers who value their services, provide referrals, pay on time, and more. Even when an owner already has a good customer base, a change in her industry or a change in the particular service she wants to provide may require a good plan in order to develop a new customer base.

A good marketing plan provides an excellent track for you to run on. Consider where you want to go and how you are going to get there in order to construct the plan. This process is invaluable—I can't even imagine operating an existing business without a decent marketing plan.

Look at your existing customer base and decide which customers are the best—i.e., meet the criteria that are important to you—then figure out how to find more of that kind.

In a new business, the marketing plan will provide the steps to build a customer base in a reasonable amount of time. It helps you to determine the prospects most likely to buy from you and how to find them. You want to get up and running and profitable in the shortest time possible.

When an owner named Molly called and wanted to meet with me on a Saturday morning, I knew something was going to happen. She told me she had met with her employer on Friday and they agreed to separate; she had the opportunity to pay her employer for the privilege of taking her key customers with her. She needed to decide by Monday if she wanted to start her own business.

In a three-hour meeting, Molly made notes about everything that she needed to do to start her own company. She already knew how to market and how to sell—and she'd have a small customer base to give her a start.

Beyond the CPA and attorney to set up the form of business, taxation method, and the bookkeeping system, she needed a marketing plan. She needed to get up and running on her track as fast as possible in order to replace lost income from her prior position.

So, Molly created her plan and had the start of a new business in less than a month. She moved very quickly—partly because she had the contacts for all of the professional advice and the marketing materials that she needed, partly because she had a checklist for her start-up, and mostly because she knew the value of a marketing plan.

The Elements of a Good Marketing Plan

A marketing plan for a small business usually includes:

- a clear identification of the product or service you will provide
- the unique benefit that will differentiate you from others
- the marketplace that is available; and why they want this benefit
- the identity or position you will attain in this marketplace
- the criteria for customers that are important to you
- the prospects most likely to buy from you
- the plan to become known to prospects
- the method you choose to reach them
- the way you will secure them as customers

Identification involves developing a clear, concise statement of the benefit of your product or service that is understandable and repeatable. Owners often have more than one service or a variety of products that are sometimes related to each other, but in the eyes of the prospect, this can be confusing.

Susan, a writer, wanted to work with business clients to provide good technical writing. She also included in her brochure: marketing materials, press releases, books, magazine articles, ghost writing, and meeting preparation. When a prospect saw this long list it was confusing; was she really an expert at something or a Jill-of-all-trades, so to speak? It wasn't apparent to the reader that she was an outstanding writer.

The truth is, she is an excellent writer, but she was probably not as excellent at all of the services she included in her brochure. Although it was possible that she could deliver all of those services if she needed to, it was not possible to market all of them effectively. Susan decided that she wanted to narrow her services to good technical writing and proofreading. She could always accept other writing opportunities if a prospect called and asked, or if a current client needed those additional types of writing, but she would market to the business prospects who needed technical writing. She would develop an identity and become known as an outstanding technical writer.

Your **unique benefit**, the specific difference you can make in the life of your customer, is the primary way you'll differentiate yourself from others in your field. Looking at the result that you provide, the improvement that your satisfied customers tell you about, or the change that will likely occur with your service, will help you to articulate your unique benefit.

Donna Dawson, president of Garden Stencil 123, offers a great product for gardening wannabes. Novice gardeners buy her kit, purchase the plants listed on the back of the kit, go home and plant a wonderful window box. The kit includes fertilizer, and a stencil to place over the dirt with holes indicating the location of the plants. Plant the flowers, add a little more potting soil, water, and "wow"—you've created a beautiful window box. This is a unique benefit, a one-of-a-kind helping hand for a gardening wannabe like me.

A service provider may differentiate by offering a slightly different slant on a traditional service. Attorney Georgia Maistros wants to help small business owners stay out of trouble by reviewing all of their contracts before they are used. She talks with them about their future plans at each meeting in order to help prevent legal problems.

CPA Cheryl Lyon helps her small business clients with growth—planning for the accounting and bookkeeping needs as well as the cash requirements. She lets her small business clients know that this will be part of their meetings and phone talks, so the discussion is ongoing.

The **marketplace** refers to the type of customers you want to find. Do you plan to market to small business owners, large corporations, or only auto repair shops? Is your market retail dress shops, gift stores, or ice cream parlors? If you plan to sell to a business, how can you define your niche more narrowly—getting it down to the very business that will become your best customer?

If your target market is an individual, how would you define the individual by demographics—for example: female, discretionary money to spend, interested in entertaining and decorating her home for guests.

Put a face to your ideal client. Picture a great customer with a face, name, place you can find them, and details about what they want. That's your market.

The **identity or position** you will attain in that marketplace involves how you want to be known. How do you want others to think of you? How will your prospects see you in this marketplace?

Perhaps you have a new, gourmet all-natural "tastes-like-home-made" pie filling. The gourmet, natural, "tastes-like-homemade" is distinctive; that is the unique benefit. The identity in the market or the position in the marketplace is that it is sold only in upscale kitchen retail stores. You cannot find it in a supermarket.

Sometimes positioning involves location, sometimes quality or price. Sheila Moten, owner of Heavenly Pastries and Party Planning, wanted to start her catering business and become known in Northeast Ohio for her gourmet desserts and upscale party planning. She knew that it would take some time to become known and wanted to accept any catering opportunity that came along.

She provided some lavish lunch buffets for nonprofit events where the budget was very small—and the board members took notice. She baked gourmet cookies and included them in an event for high school girls—and the school sponsors wanted her for other adult events.

Sheila made little profit on these first events; she used them as a way to become known for her excellent food. Her Boardroom Group helped her to define her market as hostesses of small (under 50 people), catered parties, featuring gourmet food with outstanding presentation. Her ideal prospect is a hostess looking for a one-of-a-kind incredible theme party the guests would remember for years. Now Sheila markets to obtain this type of small upscale event; she refers the more traditional type of catering to other owners.

Establishing the **criteria for the type of customers** you want is essential in order to build the business of your dreams. Make a list of the criteria that would single out the very customer that would be best for you. You want them to pay a premium for better quality, to value the incredible service you provide; you may want them to provide referrals or to become long-term customers.

Other criteria may have to do with their location, how soon they pay, whether selling to them will lead to bigger contracts, or whether you really like doing business with them. Make a list of what's important to you and keep it in your marketing plan; you'll use it for the next step—finding the prospects most likely to buy from you. And, of course, you'll specifically look for prospects that meet these criteria.

Becky Morgan, president of Fulcrum ConsultingWorks, Inc., provides manufacturing consulting. After starting her consulting business, she realized that she wanted to work with experienced, well-functioning management teams in these manufacturing plants. These teams recognize her expertise and value the knowledge that she brings during a machinery upgrade or other process improvement. In addition, this team would be willing to accept responsibility to complete the change successfully. This is a part of the criteria she established for future business prospects.

The **prospects most likely to buy from you** are the ones that have been looking for you, understand what you have to offer, and are ready to purchase. Dream clients, right? But they do exist—and you can find them.

Think about the prospects who want your product or service. A customer profile for a business that sells to consumers might include age, sex, buying preferences, discretionary income, location, lifestyle, or a situation or trigger in their life.

For a business-to-business product or service, your desired customer profile might include size, product type, location, number of employees, SIC code, a trigger event, or other demographics.

Boardroom Group member Carolyn McCullick, owner of Country Harvest Ceramics, produces a wonderful, hand-painted tea-for-one teapot and gift box set. It's an exquisite gift. The prospects most likely to buy this gift are shopping in tea rooms and gift stores in quaint towns all over the country. This is her market: retail stores in quaint towns where people shop for one-of-a-kind gifts.

Sarah Sawaya, owner of Sassafras Design Services, produces wonderful marketing and advertising materials for small business owners. She had previous experience designing ads for a phone company.

Business owners who are ready to run an ad in their weekly paper or in the phone book are ideal prospects for her because they are most likely to buy. Sarah's Boardroom Group encouraged her to send a marketing letter to 100 business owners three months before the phone advertising is due, inviting the owners to contact her for a great new ad.

The prospects "most likely to buy" will be calling her; some who already have a satisfactory ad may call her to update their other marketing materials. It's a good idea that works.

The **plan to become known to your prospects** is the most exciting part of the marketing plan. It is fun to try different methods and see which ones work the best and how long it takes.

The very first thing that you might have done to become known when you started your business was to send a press release to all of your local newspapers or to a trade journal for your industry to announce the opening of your business.

Now you need to find more ways to stay in front of this marketplace, so that when a prospect is thinking about buying, they'll think of you before anyone else.

At the very least, this plan will help with credibility; when someone meets you they may say, "Oh, yes, I have heard of you." Or they say, "Yes, I have seen your ad in the weekly paper."

Offering seminars or workshops or being a speaker at an association meeting where you want to become known can help to establish you as an expert. Be certain the topic that is announced represents you the way you want to be known—and give the announcer an introduction written by you.

A writer from a local small business publication called me a several years ago and asked if I surfed the Web. I said yes (that was a stretch— most of the time I am too busy!), and asked why. She said she wanted to start a column on recommended Web sites and would I like to submit two or three sites and something about them.

I said I would be pleased to submit them by fax the next day. Did I submit the sites that I look at? Good grief, no. I spent two hours researching the very combination of three sites that would properly represent the way that I wanted to be known. My consulting involved helping small business owners with strategies for growth. I worked with women owners in Boardroom Groups, and men business owners individually as coaching clients. My speaking was primarily to professionals who wanted growth and profitability.

I selected *www.sbaonline.sba.gov*, (the Small Business Administration), *www.nfwbo.org* (National Foundation for Women Business Owners), and *www.smalloffice.com* (Home Office Computing). I checked them out and made sure that they had the image I wanted to portray, that they reflected the way I wanted to be known to my target market. It took me some time, but it was worth it; thousands of small business owners read the article.

In addition to public relations, you may do direct mailing, attend association meetings, or go to the organizations where you find people who do business in the market you want to reach.

Some professionals say to me, "I just need to be known in the general public. I am a divorce attorney and I need enough people to know me so that they call me if they or a member of their family needs my services." Attorneys and other professionals who need to become known by a wide number of people can often accomplish this by membership in service organizations and community events.

Being active in Rotary or Kiwanis, helping your city with the annual Fourth of July event, participating in a school or alumnae activity every year, or being active in your church or other place where you regularly see people will also help you become known and to receive referrals.

The **method you use to reach your prospects** may vary depending on what works for you. Who is the person that you need to reach in order to do business, the decision maker? We do business with people, not with organizations. Who do you need to reach and how can you make contact with them?

Shirley Matz, president of Matz Bookkeeping Services, Inc., is a very quiet person. Like many of you, she would not be comfortable making cold calls and setting up appointments to talk with prospects. She prefers to mail a letter and a brochure to owners who have been referred to her.

On the other hand, Pat Conry, owner of Conry Office Services, loves to talk with people and attends the Chamber of Commerce events to meet prospects. She even offers existing members of the Chamber a small, very reasonably priced service: with their letter, letterhead, and envelope in inventory at her office, she will prepare a welcome letter for all new members of the Chamber. The existing member has a great letter mailed timely to all new members. The new and existing members all see her accurate work and are inclined to use her services if they need more office support.

In the Boardroom Group, the owners brainstormed a good way for Kathy Hetrick, CPA and owner of Strategic Focus, to reach her prospects. Kathy provides activity-based costing (cost by job activity) and process improvement (eliminating bottlenecks) for forward-thinking management teams. The team looking for Kathy's process improvement services is usually aware that they are losing profit because their systems are not working correctly.

Her Boardroom Group suggested that she mail 30 good prospects (prospects identified in local publications as fast-growing) a 12-inch piece of clear plastic (drain) pipe. With a cap on each end, mailed conveniently in boxes designed for blueprint shipping, each drain pipe would contain small toy replicas of something significant going down the drain. One-inch plastic people represent turnover; play coins represent pennies falling through the cracks; play money represents dollars lost due to bottlenecks; and play wristwatches represent time lost. After four mailings, three weeks apart, the prospect would understand what Kathy is offering. Then she can make the follow-up phone call to talk about the solutions she can offer. This unique mailing was memorable and made it easier to secure appointments and new clients.

The **way you will secure customers** may depend on what is customary in your business situation. In any event, it will involve talking with your prospect about how your particular product or service will fit her needs. You may finalize the agreement with a completed order form, or a consulting contract. Perhaps you send a letter of agreement to confirm your conversation. Any sale, other than retail or professional services at an hourly rate, usually needs to have the details about the sale documented in some way.

The agreement to produce a Web site, for example, will be a detailed contract. The agreement to speak will include a confirmation letter with the details including fee. Computer resellers typically provide a quotation.

Remember, the only reason that you market is to achieve a sale. If this is difficult for you, listen to other owners use words to complete a sale.

Read books about professional selling; they often give suggested phrases that may work for you in your business, phrases like, "What do you think about this option?" "Do you think this would work in your business at this time?" or "Can you picture this piece of artwork in your home?"

Keep working on the concluding phrases that will help move your marketing to the sale you want to achieve.

Marketing Plans for a Service Business vs. a Product Business

The plan for a service business may be achieved by following the outline above. But if you have a very unique service, perhaps one that the market may not have heard about before, it'll be more difficult to start.

I remember 20 years ago when temporary firms did not really exist as they do today. Employers understood permanent placement agencies, but most hadn't worked with a temporary firm, and they were slow to try them.

If your business is a new industry, you may need to do some market research to find out if there really is a market for your new service. This market research will become part of your business plan.

If there ever was a case for marketing to the prospects most likely to buy from you, this is it. You cannot afford to invest a lot of money or time in a service that people do not understand. You will need to identify those people who will have the greatest need and are the closest to understanding the benefit you can offer.

In the case of the temporary firms long ago, the best place to start might have been with companies that had high turnover and where the employers were too busy to interview for replacements. Or perhaps a company that was moving out of town and needed qualified people for a short period of time. Fast-growing firms might need temporaries until they decide how they want the newer, larger organization chart to work.

Finding the prospects who need you the most will lead to the greatest number of sales, particularly if you have a cutting-edge service. An example of one such business is background checking. The personnel department of many firms used to call for references; now you may want many more details about someone's personal and work history, so you'll use an outside professional firm to handle this process efficiently and legally.

Similarly, a new product business will need market research if a market for the product does not already exist. Sometimes the research is to find out how large the market is and whether it will support your business.

We didn't need many mouse pads until enough people had a computer with a mouse.

The market for bread-making flour wasn't very large until enough people had bread-making machines.

There are good books available on market research if you are bringing something new to market, and they are well worth your investment (see Appendix for more).

At the very least, search on the Web and the national yellow pages to see if you can find a business just like yours. You'll learn something valuable from this process—maybe how many similar businesses exist, or how they are listed in the yellow pages.

There are other differences in the marketing plan for a service business versus a product business.

In a service business, you'll need to invest much more time developing the section on how you want to be known, the identity you want to achieve in the marketplace. It is not immediately apparent when someone meets you or sees your brochure how you want to be known. It'll take longer to establish your place in the market. Many people have to meet you, work with you, and talk about you to others in the community in order for you to become known. This requires a good plan, patience, and time.

Pricing will be more difficult in your service business. For example, depending on your market and location, you could establish the fee for creating a business plan at $2,500, $5,000, or even $10,000. It'll depend on how detailed the plan will be, on your knowledge of the industry they are entering, and on what the owner will pay.

On the other hand, if you've got a product business, more often you'll have some competitive products that limit the range of pricing you can set. In a product business, you'll have some direct costs for raw materials, labor, and machine time to give you a start on a calculation. That mouse pad has direct costs associated with each unit produced.

Include some of your indirect costs, such as insurance and telephone, too. Then, you can add a mark-up to cover your salary and profit. It's nearly always clearer what your pricing range may be in a product business.

The other significant difference in a marketing plan for a service company is that it must be prepared in greater detail if it is part of a business plan to take to the bank. Bankers still have more familiarity with product companies than with service companies. You will need to do a great job on your marketing plan so that the banker is very clear how you will reach your market, earn enough income and—most of all—be able to repay the loan.

It's an Image Business

I sat down to dinner at the National Association of Women Business Owners meeting in Cleveland and an owner who was new to me joined me at the table. Her name is Nina Messina and she owns The Graphic Edge Professional Design, Inc.

Nina creates images for business purposes. She is highly skilled at determining the nature of the image needed to properly portray a product or a service. But her expertise at graphic design is only one part of the equation; she also understands the business world and the appropriate colors, fonts, pictures, layouts, and types of materials best suited to a particular type of company for a specific use. She designs and produces logos, cards, letterhead, envelopes, fax forms, brochures, media kits, direct mail pieces, advertisements, book covers, video covers, note cards, business invitations, catalogs, industrial product sheets, and just anything else you could imagine to represent you in print.

In addition, Nina can take your image and move it to your Web site so that everything looks smooth and consistent in the real world and in cyberspace.

Choosing a logo to represent your business is only one tiny part of the process to develop an overall image for your firm. Image includes everything that anyone sees, reads, or hears about you and your company. All of the marketing materials, including your Web site, are a big part of the identity that you present to prospects, but let's look at other ways that people "see" you.

How you look in person is also a part of your image. We don't usually see a woman artist in a pinstriped suit, and I can't remember seeing a woman banker in a jumpsuit. Your dress contributes to your image, and so does your body language. It's very important that you are aware of how your personal image fits with your business image—it must be consistent or you will confuse everyone about who you are and they will not be clear about what business you are in or what products or services you offer.

What you say in person or in writing also must be aligned with your business appearance and image. When I met Nina Messina that evening at the owner's dinner meeting, I asked her about her business. She said, "I provide graphic design services for business clients." She was very reluctant to toot her own horn, but I kept asking questions until I found out that she knew the printing industry backwards and forwards. She knew how to get the printed results to meet the needs of her clients. Her 20 years in the industry and her education in art and advertising provided all of the artistry and knowledge to provide an incredible business service.

Nina doesn't have to market or advertise to find new clients; they find her by referral. Her appearance that evening was tailored and businesslike; she was warm and friendly. Her conversation was professional and knowledgeable. Everything about her was aligned. What she said, her image, and everything about her business fit together, made sense. I was perfectly clear about what she did, what she could do for me, and whom I might refer to her. This is perfect alignment! Imagine if you met an organization consultant and she was late for the appointment, forgot her briefcase, and looked disheveled. She would not be credible; we would not believe that she could teach organizational techniques!

Everything about your business image must be aligned. Does this mean that all owners need to spend thousands of dollars to have the materials to represent their business? Not always.

Here are some examples where quality is essential (and has a high price tag):

- Cynthia Carlin, owner of Carlin Communications, worked in marketing with a Fortune 500 firm in New York City for more than 20 years. Now her company provides marketing programs to drive growth plans for large firms. Her prospects are large, often sophisticated firms who need outstanding plans for growth. Cynthia's own marketing materials need to be high quality in order to represent properly the incredible service she can provide.

- Artist Elinor Korow is an excellent portrait painter. Her advertising in an upscale publication such as the symphony program requires an investment for the appropriate image as well as the cost for the insertion. Her brochure is beautiful and probably quite expensive; the quality properly represents her fine work.

Quality is always essential, but it doesn't always require the investment we saw in the above two examples. Danielle Evans is a personal trainer and owns a fitness studio called Impulse Training and Assessment, Inc. She provides training for individuals of all ages who are serious about fitness. Her studio sees high school athletes and seniors alike.

Did they need to see an expensive brochure to come to her? Most likely all they needed to do was read her newsletter. She produces a great fitness newsletter filled with valuable information for the health-conscious individual. The newsletter is totally aligned with her image and has good writing and strong design. The price tag was moderate compared to our other examples. The most important thing was that the quality was there.

Quality is not always expensive but it is always important.

The business world is complex and there are messages everywhere. I remember when I worked with the Pepsi Cola franchise in Akron, we tried to secure signs all over town with the Pepsi logo on them. We paid for many restaurant and small grocery store signs in order to have the additional Pepsi logo on them, too. The more times a person could see this logo, the more likely they might choose this beverage at the vending machine or in the grocery store.

Now, there are advertising messages everywhere you look: at the movie theater (before the film); on your videotape before the movie starts (remember *Top Gun*? Pepsi Cola was the first to put an ad in front of the film); billboards; grocery store carts; flyers in the bag with a purchase; and Internet hot links.

When the world is filled with messages everywhere you look, your message must be clear; it must tell what you do and the benefit you provide. When you create a consistent, high-quality image, it will be remembered when all of the others are forgotten.

Marketing on a Shoestring

There are so many ways you can spend money to market, it's easy to unwisely invest many of those dollars. Paul Hawkin, author of *Growing a Business*, says that you'll spend the money you have and you learn how to spend more wisely if your funds are limited.

So, if you have a very small marketing budget, you might as well buy into this concept and figure out how to make it work.

There are hundreds of ways to add customers and build a business—some are free and some require investment of your time instead of money.

If you know the places where your prospects often go, then build it into your plan to go there, too.

Cheryl Lyon, CPA and partner of Lyon & Lyon CPA, provides tax and consulting services for small business owners. She can find owners at National Association of Women Business Owners dinner meetings, the Chamber of Commerce breakfast meeting, and the Board of Trade lunch meeting. Each month, her calendar includes attendance at each and every meeting. She regularly meets owners who are interested in finding the "right" CPA—and during conversation find that she has a strength in consulting. They would not pick her name out of the phone book; working with a financial professional is really a personal one-to-one relationship. So, this informal introduction is just the right setting to find prospects who are looking for her services.

Another inexpensive marketing tool is a free, one-page tip sheet full of information that you generally provide for free as a part of your product or service. Donna Zabel, president of DreamMaker Destinations, provides great travel-planning services. She wanted to help prospects who were traveling by air and looking for the lowest fare to know the easiest way to search. So, she created a resource on her Web site. Now her prospects can search to their heart's content and appreciate the leads that she provided.

But guess what happened as a result of that free effort? People now call Donna when they need her travel knowledge to put together a special trip.

Here are some other examples: An owner of a carpet-cleaning business creates a tip sheet called "Secrets to Carpet Cleaning Your Mother Never Told You." A CPA provides a record retention schedule. A writer shares "10 Ways to Write a Better Business Letter." In every case, the tip sheet demonstrates knowledge—and people are more likely to keep the sheet than they might a simple brochure.

Publicity can help your business grow and, the best part is, it's free. What are you doing that is newsworthy? Do you donate a portion of your profits to a charity? Do you and your employees donate a day to helping a local nonprofit? What program would be aligned with your image and be a natural fit for your time or talent?

Let's say you have no money, but want to do an event that would give back to the community and at the same time draw positive attention to your business. A software training company might offer one free evening a month to seniors over 75 who want to learn e-mail. A dog grooming service could offer free service for dogs with fleas one Saturday a month.

A caterer can donate one day of food preparation for the school carnival.

The publicity for these donations may be appropriate in a press release to the local newspaper, a mention in the program booklet, or an announcement in an organization's newsletter. In every case, the publicity is positive—and the only cost was time involved.

A consultant can market by doing workshops, seminars, or training at meetings and conferences. Denise Tarka, president of Employment Edge, Inc., helps firms with the human side of acquisitions. Offering to speak about blending cultures following a merger, Denise helps owners learn the techniques to use following the purchase and also shares how to assess people prior to a merger. The owners considering a

merger or acquisition hear an expert explain how to include due dili-
gence for the human capital as well as the hard assets. Experts like
Denise are very much in demand for speaking; this is a great way to
obtain access to prospects. Be sure to collect participants' names for
follow-up purposes.

Ask for referrals; you may be surprised at the results. If you specifically ask someone to provide referrals to you, they will ask about the
kind of referrals you want, the benefit you provide, and how to distin-
guish you from others similar to you.

If you ask people who are in a position to provide referrals on a
regular basis, you may have a steady flow of new clients.

Carolyn Helmuth, LPCC, owner of New Beginnings, offers counseling for women in transition. They may be changing careers, considering a divorce, or improving their life. She has met with several physicians about the particular counseling she provides and receives
referrals from them on a regular basis.

Suzanne Lipps, owner of Smooth Transitions, provides help for
seniors who are making a move. She needed hundreds of people to
know about the service she provides in order to receive enough referrals. The "referral team" includes social workers, senior center managers, independent living center managers, and so on. These professionals come in contact with families who need her service, and they
often provide a referral.

Make a phone call to prospects. It always seems difficult to make a
call to someone you don't already know, but it can be very worthwhile.

When I started the Boardroom Group, I only knew a few women
owners. I had a directory with names of more owners, but I hadn't met
them yet and I'm a pretty shy person. So, I decided to call ten owners
and see if they were interested in meeting a group of other owners.

It was hard to plan what I would say—I tried several different
approaches to find the right words to talk long enough so that they
were interested in trying my introductory meeting. It wasn't hard
because they weren't interested in me, in fact they were all very positive. It was me—I was the one initially afraid to make the call. I didn't
know what they would say, but I made 200 calls to women owners that
month anyway.

I found that after I learned how to do it (and got past being hesitant to dial every single time), I loved talking to them. I found out what was important to them and many of them came to my meeting, joined a Boardroom Group, and are still clients today.

Calling the retail outlet that carries your product helps you get to know your customer and also the ultimate consumer of your goods. When Carolyn McCullick, owner of Country Harvest Ceramics, calls the retail owners who carry her teapots, she checks in to see how business is going, whether her stores need any more of her teapots, and to get to know the owners. These discussions help her to know about the owner's challenges and about the customers that they serve. This can lead to opportunities, new products in the line, or a change in packaging.

Some advertising is very inexpensive. Look in association newsletters and check out the cost of a classified ad. Some of these small publications are read from cover to cover (including the ads), and the price for an ad can be quite small.

Find a strategic alliance (see Chapter 8). Team up with another company that would benefit by training together, advertising together, sharing a booth at a trade conference, creating a newsletter that serves two or more companies, or sharing office expenses. Include both logos and both company names so that your identity is truly co-marketed. Think carefully about who would be a good fit so that by doing it together you appear to be well-connected, bigger than you are, more credible, or more capable.

Look in the library for all of the current issues of business magazines; peruse them for ideas about how to market for a start-up business, or how to market without money. You'll find great articles about other owners and how they grew their business on a shoestring. Listen to all of them.

Having Fun While Marketing Your Service or Product

One of the exercises we do in my target marketing workshop involves looking at all of the ways that you might market and then deciding what ways you prefer to market.

Make a list of all of the ways you could let your prospects know about your product or service, then circle the ones that you prefer at this time. Most owners enjoy the marketing process more if they actually like the method they are using.

When Kathy Baker started The Write Choice, a public relations company, she thought that she would hate the marketing part. In a few short months, she discovered that networking to find prospects was one of her favorite activities. Talking to small business owners about their businesses and finding out whether they had a need she could fill was very energizing for her. In fact, she enjoyed it almost more than writing.

Now she markets more than ever because she is the rainmaker for her small firm; other freelance writers do part of the writing for her.

Prospects want to sense that you love what you do; it adds to the credibility of your product or service. So it's important that you have fun with your marketing–your energy will attract those prospects that you seek.

The Power of Networking

Networking can bring you a wealth of good results. You just can't tell what networking will lead to. Have you ever met someone at a lunch and found out that you had something in common–and that your new acquaintance had some information or resource that you were unaware of until you started talking? You left the lunch thinking, "Good grief, if I had not gone to this event, I would have missed finding the very thing I was looking for!"

Networking is also one of the best ways to stay connected to a group of prospects. It'll help you build relationships with other owners– and they have lots of answers to challenges, some of which you have yet to face. It can help you stay current in an industry or to learn about a new industry in order to attract new business.

Think about the purposes for your networking; make a list of those purposes. Then look at all of the organizations and association meetings that are available in your city. The library can help. You can usually find any number of organizational meetings in the different sections of your local newspaper, so save seven days of papers and page through until you find all of the locations. This will help you to make list number two.

Now start with one networking objective: finding prospects. What type of organization meeting will provide prospects most likely to become your customer? Perhaps the National Accounting Association is a fit. I remember Donna Early, owner of Providence Personnel, being active in the accounting association. She was not an accountant—but accounting managers hire lots of employees, financial and others. Smart networking.

Another networking objective: finding vendors. Joan Smith owns Gallery 143. She provides framing services, prints, and wonderful gifts from a collection of artists. Joan might attend art shows, art festivals, and art exhibits to find more artists' work to add to her gallery.

Networking objective number three: finding referral sources. Pat Vance, attorney, helps many small business owners with incorporation and contracts. She may network by serving on a local nonprofit board with other professionals. Bankers and CPAs she meets on these boards may refer work to her.

Networking objective number four: meet successful owners. Talking with owners who have been in business longer, have larger firms, have accomplished a merger or an acquisition, or have experience in a new distribution method can offer a lot of advice.

National Association of Women Business Owners has chapters in most major cities and can readily provide a great networking opportunity. Others include:

- Chambers of Commerce
- Boards of Trade
- All associations in technical and professional fields; for instance, Business & Professional Women (BPW); American Marketing Association (AMA); and Sales and Marketing Executives (SME)
- Rotary, Kiwanis, and other service organizations
- Not-for-profit boards of trustees

- Local tips groups (specifically developed to provide leads to one another)
- Garden clubs
- Senior meetings
- Merger and acquisition groups

Find the Prospects Most Likely to Buy from You: Think of the Apple Tree

An experienced saleswoman once told me, "If you feel like you are swimming upstream, you probably are!" It is possible to get into the habit of trying so hard to win over a prospect, you invest all of your potential profit into securing them as a client.

Here's an easy way to equate the work of finding a new client with the work of picking apples from a tree:

- **Out-of-sight prospects** are the ones that don't understand your product or service, don't think that they need any and aren't interested in buying. You don't have enough time in your life to educate this group of prospects. Out-of-sight apples are the ones on the top of the tree hidden in the branches and you would need to pay for mechanical equipment, an operator, and a picker in order to pick those apples. Too expensive and too time consuming to make a profit.
- **Difficult-to-reach prospects** are the ones that understand your product or service, but don't think that they need any and aren't interested in buying. The time investment will eat up all of your profits if you get them to buy. Difficult-to-reach apples are the ones in the middle of the tree. You could get them with a 12-foot ladder if you paid someone to hold the bottom of the ladder and help you move it. The cost for the other person and the ladder will eat up your profit.
- **Can't-reach-with-your-feet-on-the-ground prospects** are the ones who understand your product or service, think they might be interested someday, but aren't ready now. The time to follow up with this prospect may not be worth the investment. Can't-

reach-with-your-feet-on-the-ground apples are the ones that require a stepladder; you can pick them yourself, but you need a stepladder, and have to keep moving it around yourself.

- **Can-reach-on-my-toes prospects** are the ones who understand your product or service and think that they're interested maybe this year, but not today. These are good prospects if you limit your time investment for follow-up. Can-reach-on-my-toes apples are the ones that you can secure when you reach as high as you possibly can. You can get enough apples, but you'll be tired afterward.

Now at this point you are thinking to yourself, she's going to tell me that the best prospects and apples are those that I can easily reach without any effort. Well—yes, and no.

The **best prospects** are the ones who understand your product or service, know that they are interested, and want to buy today. In fact, they have already been looking for you! The best apples are the ones that, when you stand under the tree and hold out your arms, fall into your outstretched hand.

You can decide how much time and money to invest in securing a new client. A human resource consultant, for example, may decide that a reasonable investment in a prospect includes four to six mailings, a personal phone call, a company visit, and two follow-up calls. This is her *maximum* time and money commitment for turning a good prospect into a client. After this point, the prospect's name goes on a list to receive two postcards each year, and the consultant moves on to another prospect who is more likely to purchase. The first time you experience this cycle, you start to realize that you have probably invested too much time or money and the prospect was not ready to be a client. But you'll learn to see it much faster when you find yourself in this situation the next time—and you'll start to see how time actually *is* money. Eventually, you'll reach a point where you can screen your prospects on the first visit and know with reasonable certainty that this prospect is ready to buy or not ready to buy—the apple that drops into your hand or the apple at the top of the tree.

Members of my Boardroom Groups have all heard this story. I get feedback every month from someone who says, "Guess what—remember that apple tree story? Well, I was trying to pick the apple at the top of the tree, trying to secure a client that was far too difficult. I quit spending my time there and looked for better prospects—the best prospect, the one most likely to buy—and I just got a great new client!"

Working with Creative Professionals

As your company grows and your marketing materials need to be updated, you'd be wise to seek out professionals who can provide the words and images that best represent you.

Everyone starts somewhere in order to get started. Even the professional with a high-quality image will narrow her focus and want to serve some niche markets.

Few owners want to grow their business exactly like it is. Some market segments may be changing, you may prefer to work more with certain types of clients, your industry may be changing. Any number of things can cause an owner to market in a narrower way that helps them grow the part of the business they really want to grow.

But you'll still need to find the right creative professionals to help you with new materials, new ads, new programs, or new promotions.

Some owners may already have an ad agency that's perfectly suited to create the new marketing materials.

Others may need to go looking for individual professionals to help with the new focus. There are a number of ways to find all of the talent needed for your next step. The phone book provides listings under ad agencies, communications, and marketing consultants.

If you see a business with a good look, a great promotion, or a program that you like, ask who created it for them. Attend events with other owners and ask them for referrals for the particular change you have in mind. Remember that there is some difference in the professional who creates incredible promotions for product or retail firms and the marketing consultant who may be much better with a service business.

After you have a good working list of professionals, call and talk with them about your needs. Ask them if they provide an introductory meeting to see work they created for other clients. There is a tremendous difference in the work that is created from one professional to another and from one firm to another. You need to see samples and talk with the creative team about how they work with their clients.

A start-up owner I met at the Ohio State Women Business Owners' Conference asked me how to start creating materials for her service business. She would be offering software consulting, including Y2K. Her materials needed to match the quality of the service she would provide.

She preferred to work with individual professionals like herself. I suggested that she first find a writer who understood good business writing and had experience with marketing materials. After she interviewed and found such a writer, liked her business style, and hired her, the writer recommended a graphic designer. Business writers work with a number of graphic designers and can usually recommend one or two who would be a good fit. This owner took the great new marketing words, interviewed, and soon hired the graphic designer to create the look of her new brochure.

Don't be afraid to look around long enough to find someone who's a great fit with the way you want to do business, a talented individual who will want to keep you as a client as you grow and your needs increase. Like other business professionals you need, it really boils down to a synergistic one-on-one relationship with the person with whom you want to do business.

Sales Goals: Are They Part of the Marketing Plan?

You bet they are! In some companies, the sales goals are established first—and the marketing plan is developed to support the sales goals. In other companies, the marketing plan includes analysis of the existing marketing segments, what increases are possible in each segment, what new segments may be added, and more. This provides the information to put together good sales goals.

At Akron Pepsi Cola, we set the top-level sales goals and overall volume increases, and the marketing part of the business plan supported those goals. The marketing plan was a specific plan by product, by size, and by flavor within each market segment that would enable us to achieve the sales goals. Here are some sample sales goals for a one-year period:

SHEILA MOTEN, PRESIDENT, HEAVENLY PASTRIES AND PARTY PLANNING:
1. Achieve or exceed the sales revenue budget for the year.
2. Increase wedding cake orders from 20 to 30 by December 31.
3. Acquire six new corporate customers who order elegant cookie baskets for their holiday gift list.
4. Cater six dinner parties contributing $500 profit each.

LINDA LITTLER, PARTNER, CAREY AND LITTLER STAFFING:
1. Achieve or exceed the sales revenue budget for the year.
2. Secure 12 new corporate clients by September 30.
3. Increase temporary staffing placements by 15 percent.
4. Increase permanent staffing placements by 20 percent.

No matter how you do it, the sales goals need to be established in writing. They need to be measurable, achievable, and time-restricted. If you have more than four goals in any given year, that's too many. You may have many steps in your action plan to help you achieve your goals, but four top-level goals is about the most any owner can focus on and actually achieve.

You'll find you'll make decisions daily to support the achievement of those goals. If you cannot remember them every day or if you have to look at a list, you will likely find it too difficult.

Setting your goals is a significant part of your plan. These goals tell you what's important, where you want to be and what you are striving to achieve. The marketing plan will help you make these goals a reality.

A woman owner once asked me a question about her goals. She had carefully created the annual sales goal and placed it in a prominent place where she could see it daily. After more than one year of trying, she had not achieved the goal. She wanted some ideas on how to be successful.

The first suggestion is to break the goal into parts. The outside parts may represent different types of markets or industries you serve, different types of customers you sell to, or some demographics of your customer base. Where will the revenue come from, on the outside? Make a list or create pie charts to look at those markets.

The second part of the analysis is to break into parts the products or services you may provide. This is the inside look. What kind of revenue will you bring in from which particular product or service? Make a list or create pie charts to look at the types of services or products.

Then decide what marketing programs will help you to achieve the goals you created. Knowing what particular product or service you plan to sell, and what specific customers you plan to sell to will help you create the plan for success.

The last suggestion is to break down the plan by quarter or by month. If you are a service provider, quarterly may seem more appropriate; if you are retail, monthly may work best.

This process also supports your budget. The sales goals and the marketing plan to achieve them will provide the basis for your sales revenue budget and the raw material or cost budget as well as your marketing budget.

This entire process creates a plan to follow to achieve your goals. It's a road map. Imagine if you got into the car and wanted to go somewhere in another state and didn't have a map to follow. You could follow your compass but there is no way of knowing the cost and time to actually arrive at your destination.

Without a sales goal and a marketing plan, you'd be missing the map and maybe even the compass. With your marketing plans in place you have the direction and the specific mile-markers to follow to arrive at your destination.

Is My Marketing Plan Working? How to Tell

Measuring results will help you to assess your marketing plan.

The first part of measuring results is to have a way to ask customers how they heard about you. It is interesting in my coaching business that when I receive referrals, people tell me in the first sentence on the phone exactly who told them to call. In many instances, it was more than one person.

If you have a retail store, such as Gallery 143 that Joan Smith owns, perhaps you could put a guest register (for your mailing list) and include a column for how you found the store. If your prospects come by phone, always find a suitable place in the conversation to ask them.

Once you know where your prospects are coming from, you know which part of your marketing plan is working. Find a good time to pull together the statistics, monthly or quarterly. Look at them and make adjustments to your plan. You may change your advertising if 10 ads have not yielded any new business. You may attend a different networking activity, if the association dinner you have been going to for a year is not providing any good leads.

Use your own common sense, too. Ruth Dean, owner of The Writing Toolbox, told me once that her largest client came from a networking activity *four years* after the initial contact. What is the lead-time you can reasonably expect from different marketing tactics? Think about all of that when you make a decision to stop some part of your marketing plan. Then, create a plan to begin something new to put in its place.

The marketing plan is a plan you mold, a process that can be changed as you find new and better ways to support your business growth. Talk to other owners in the same industry; get ideas and techniques from them. Try new things; give and receive honest feedback with other owners. They will be your best sounding board and source for new ideas.

I was asked one day, "What is the thing that makes the difference? What is it that you see in the owners who are wildly successful?"

The answer is simply, "The owners who keep putting one foot in front of the other, no matter what. They just keep trying until they succeed."

⊠ IDEA CENTER ⊠

How to Get Great PR

Here are some tips for getting great (and free) press:

• Understand the difference between advertising and public relations. Advertising is when you pay for exposure on local or national media (TV, newspapers, magazines, and Web sites). Usually, advertising depends on the quick, clever shot—i.e., a catchy slogan or song that defines who you are and who your target market is. PR is when you provide the media with useful information for its viewers or readers, positioning yourself as an expert on the topic. You are not paid for PR pieces, but you don't have to pay for it, either (unless you hire a professional PR agency to handle your work).

• Do your homework. Know exactly where and to whom you want to send articles and announcements. Nothing gets lost faster in the world of media than press kits addressed to the wrong people—and you could wind up losing a great opportunity if you haven't done the work of finding out whose name goes on the mailing list. Call ahead and ask, or visit the library for the latest media guides available. Sometimes, the newspaper, magazine, or TV show's Web site lists the appropriate people to send press information. Think from the audience's standpoint: would a piece about your company make sense in this particular medium?

• Develop a killer press kit. What's in it? A brief fact sheet about yourself and your company; a feature about some earth-shattering new detail you've uncovered and want to share with the world; a brief company history; and perhaps a professional photo of yourself. Newspapers, magazines, and Web sites do not have the time to photograph you, so include your photo. If you're not sure how to put a great press kit together, hire a professional or grab a book on the topic. There are many good ones (see Appendix for more).

• Follow up with the media. About a week or so after you've mailed the press kit, follow up with an e-mail or a brief phone call. Do not try to get an immediate commitment from a reporter—they hate this kind of approach. Instead, ask them if they need any additional information, or if they'd like to set up an interview with you. One phone call should be enough to do it—and don't continue calling them every day with new ideas. Editors hate to be hounded by people with their own agendas. Remember, editors have a responsibility to their readers to provide great information—they are not in the business of promoting you.

• Send a regular media tip sheet with story ideas to editors. Four or five ideas per sheet is a good example of what works. Given a few choices, editors can quickly decide if they're interested in any of the angles you've presented. These are particularly effective with radio people.

• Tell editors something they don't already know. Most of the reporters we know absolutely love to be educated—and we love educating them, since it gets us such great press. It can work the same for you, too.

⊿ IDEA CENTER ⊾

Becoming a Networking Giant

Want to move to the networking fast track? Here are some great tips on becoming a top networking professional:

- Develop as many contacts as you can. Add one new person each day, and you'll have met at least 20 new people per month.
- Tell people the one thing you feel you do best. Don't give them a rundown of everything you can possibly do. If confuses, and even annoys, some people when the conversation seems one-sided; be concise about what you do so that the other person may reciprocate.
- Become a host/leader, not a wallflower. Show initiative; introduce yourself. Don't throw your card at anybody until after you've established a verbal introduction.
- Cultivate your contacts. Don't try to use the situation to get immediate business; instead, ask to meet privately later on. Nobody likes to feel pressure in social situations.
- Extend your own expertise first whenever possible. Be available to those who call on you for help when they need it.
- Keep in touch. Mail or fax articles that might be of interest to your contacts—it shows you were listening when you met them, and that you remembered what they said.

From the *Adams Businesses You Can Start Almanac* by Katina Z. Jones (Adams Media Corp., 1996).

⚞ BACK TO THE BOARDROOM ⚟

How to Make Money While You Sleep

Here are some ways you can make even more money—even while you sleep:

- Hire additional help on a contract basis. By hiring additional help, an accountant, for example, you could take on more clients, thereby earning a profit from the work of others.
- Convert a service business to a product business. One creation could provide numerous sales. Examples: selling a booklet on how to get great PR, or a how-to tape on computer networking.
- Create a newsletter for a niche market. Each month, a writer might create a newsletter for a niche market—and sell the same newsletter to thousands of individuals or companies.
- Produce a video or audiotape. Someone with a great deal of experience in a given field could use their expertise to produce a video or audiotape educating others about what they do.
- Write a book or develop a guide. Use your knowledge to write a book. It's a great way to become perceived as an expert in your field.
- Organize a seminar that could be used by trainers in various markets. Seminars are a great way to reach a lot of people at the same time. You might do well to share what you know.
- Create a catalog. Most service industries have trade journals. However, there may not be a catalog of the supplies, information, or goods needed for those businesses. Someone involved in the industry is a likely candidate to create such a catalog.

As a sole owner who works seven days a week to make ends meet, you may find it difficult to allocate time for changing your business's direction. But once you do—once you are able to turn your service into a product that represents your expertise—you'll find that making money is so simple you can do it while you sleep!

—NORMA J. RIST

⊿ BACK TO THE BOARDROOM ⊾

Overcoming Fear of Rejection

Many Boardroom Group members shudder at the thought of having to call on potential customers. Some have even confided that marketing and sales functions make them physically ill!

Understanding the basis of this anxiety is key. What are you most afraid of, really? Ninety-nine percent of the Boardroom Group members expressing anxiety about selling admitted it was the fear of rejection that was really at the heart of the matter.

So, how do you overcome this deep (and rather negative) fear? Try these methods:

• Use visualization techniques. Try to picture the best possible thing that could happen, and hold that picture in your mind until after your sales call. Do not let a negative thought creep in!

• Use your schedule book to help. Some of the most successful women we know actually schedule a small amount of time each week to lament things that didn't go right—allowing them to focus on positive things the entire rest of the week.

• Develop (and use) a buddy system. Find another woman entrepreneur who is in a business similar to yours, and create a buddy system with her to help each other through the rough times. Schedule a weekly telephone chat or lunch just to talk about the rough spots.

• Keep your numbers up—and stay focused on them. If you know it takes an average of 100 calls to get 10 "yes" responses, stay focused on your goal, knowing that every "no" is one step closer to a "yes."

• Rely on written material if you feel under-confident as a sales pro. Use your marketing materials, or even your business plan, as background for your client meetings or phone calls. Many women business owners write up a script for cold calls, so that they can glance at their notes as they're speaking and not worry about forgetting something.

• Spend more time educating your circle of influence. Let these wonderful people, your advocates, speak for you as much as you can. Referrals are almost always rejection-free, since the leads are coming to you
in a prequalified manner. Capitalize on this method!

• Don't give away your personal power. Only you can decide to let
one rejection ruin your day. Why give anyone else that kind of power
over you? A "no" is only one "no."

• Learn to use rejection as an educational tool for your business.
When a prospect says "no," find out what their objection is. Consider
whether this objection is something you can use as a catalyst for
change in your business. Maybe the customer has a point—and you can
improve your business because of it.

4

Building Bridges That Reach Customers and Keep Them Coming Back

Katina Z. Jones

—— Secret 5 ——
The key to winning customers is to become more than
they perceive you to be. Add value wherever possible.

The other day I was listening to my husband, John, talk to one of his customers on the phone. It was a technical service call; he works for a company that specializes in computerized point-of-sale systems for restaurants. Typically, once a restaurant goes "live" with their equipment, there are problems. So, his pager goes off and he has to coach his customers through the rough spots.

What was so fascinating about this particular call was that my husband was so patient with the customer. The restaurant manager was hyperventilating with frustration; he wasn't very experienced with computers and this new way of entering sales tickets was like a new language for him. He was "techno-phobic."

John calmly told the manager to take a deep breath and relax. He said reassuringly, "We'll be able to fix this problem in a few minutes.

You're doing a great job of working through this." Then, he proceeded to coach the manager through his computer crisis. At the end of the conversation, John said, "You know, Larry, you're getting good at this." What a terrific way to empower the customer!

This is why my husband is so good at customer service: He understands that the customer wants to feel good about their new product or service. But he also knows (instinctively, I might add) that his customers need his patience, kind words, and constant reassurance. Simply put, they need to feel that they have bought his kindness and understanding, along with a $25,000 computer system that changes the way they do business. His customers always feel that level of commitment from him—and that's why, whenever they have a problem, they insist on talking to him. They feel connected.

As women business owners, we, too, have a need to connect with our customers in a positive, reassuring way. We want them to feel good about our products and services, so that they will provide us with referrals and, ultimately, with more business from them.

When we first start our businesses, we are often so optimistic that we tend to see the entire world as our oyster. Our customer base is so broad in our minds that there often doesn't seem to be anyone who *isn't* a customer.

Thankfully, our business plans—and experiences—force us to be a little more realistic.

Thinking back to when I first started my own business, I can say in all honesty that I made the same mistake of initially believing the world was my oyster. After all, everyone needs a resume—right?

Wrong. There are some folks at the blue-collar level who simply fill out applications; they don't need a good resume to get a job. At the opposite end of the scale, there are executives who get their next jobs from an executive recruiting firm or personal contact. In between are all the people who need resumes, at various levels of experience and income.

So, how did I figure out who my customers are and what they want? By the process of elimination. The people who just wanted the standard, run-of-the-mill resume, which I did not offer, would go to typing services and copy shops, or buy a template they could use themselves. These folks didn't want to invest in something different; all they needed was a piece of paper that said something about what they've done in their careers to date.

But the people who really cared about their careers, who were seeking the next level in their profession or wanting a change that defied logic—those were my real customers. Typically, these folks don't mind paying a premium for excellent products and services.

How do I service them? I take a genuine interest in who they are; I don't just sit there and take notes about what they've done career-wise or have them fill out a form. I listen to the story of their career, how they got to where they are, where they see themselves carving out a new future. I listen to their hopes and dreams. Then, I compose a document that reflects their vision and offers potential employers some insight into who they are as well as what they've done. It's a step above and beyond what the standard resume does.

After I've finished a resume for a client, I maintain an interest in how they are doing. I check back with them periodically, usually via e-mail. I ask them if they are happy in their new situation once they've gotten a new job, and they feel free to contact me again should they require an update for a promotion or a subsequent job. Much of my business has been the result of previous clients singing the high praises to potential new clients. I love it when I get a new client who tells me, "I was told by my friend not to bother calling anyone else." That tells me how well my customer service efforts are going.

Good customers like these—and a steady eye toward improving customer service on a continual basis—is what will keep your company alive and thriving.

But where do you start, especially if you've not had to work directly with people before? I suggest you use the bridge analogy, in which you visualize your customer service efforts as the bridge that keeps your customer coming back to you again and again.

Building the Bridge

Great customer service doesn't just happen as a result of your doing business. It is something that is most successful when planned into the process of doing business—ideally, at the business planning stage.

Back in the second chapter of this book, I mentioned that I found creative ways to incorporate my six-year-old daughter, Lilly, into my resume and writing business. One of the things we did together was create a marketing plan (fully illustrated in crayon, of course). Let me tell you how that marketing plan came about, and how it pertains to customer service.

We were sitting in a restaurant together with a blank place mat and a cup of crayons. While we were waiting for our lunch, Lilly asked me what a marketing plan was and why it was important. So, I explained that good marketing is how we get others to want to do business with us. It's telling or showing them that our product or service will be very good for them and get them something they want, too.

Lilly thought quietly for a moment, and then said rather excitedly, "Mommy, I know exactly what you need in your marketing plan. Your customers need a bridge." She then grabbed one green and one brown crayon, and proceeded to draw two islands and a bridge between them.

"See," she said, "Now your customers can get to you easily."

I called Norma that same day and told her what Lilly had done for me. "She gets it!" shouted Norma. "I teach this to women all the time, and none of them has seen it this clearly." So, we shared Lilly's insight at the next Boardroom Group meeting.

That's how I came to have one of the first fully illustrated marketing plans, but it's also what has given me deeper insight into my own customer service efforts. Now that I see customer service as the bridge that draws more customers to me, I have been much more successful in building strong relationships with my customers.

How does it happen? The same way you build a bridge: one plank at a time.

Great customer service is an art, not an accident. You can't expect customers to keep crossing your bridge if you don't put in the time needed for its upkeep. After all, if one plank breaks and is not replaced, where does that leave your customer? Perhaps stranded on the other side—and on your competitor's shore.

The one advantage small businesses like yours have over large conglomerates is the ability to provide great, personalized service. Our customers are willing to pay a premium for our services because they know that we truly care about them in a way that a large company simply cannot. They know our names, our phone numbers, and e-mail addresses, and sometimes we even become like family to them.

How does this level of intimacy come about? Through service, service, and more service! Fortunately, as women, we are well equipped to care for others and provide exceptional service. This is something we've done for nearly every person in our lives.

Men are finally beginning to come around to one central fact of business that we've probably known all along: People like to do business with others who are like them. They like to work with people whom they like, too. So began the start of the era of "relationship marketing" and "relationship selling."

The reality is, we've known for a long time that relationships are the way to go. We naturally acknowledge milestones in our clients' lives, such as the birth of children, customer birthdays, and weddings with at least a phone call or a card.

It is this kind of "staying in touch" with our clients that sets us apart from the large companies we often find ourselves competing against. Ignoring customer service principles can destroy your business before it really even gets started.

What Is Great Customer Service?

But great customer service isn't just staying in touch with your customers. It's constantly making sure that their every need is met.

At its best, customer service is a multifaceted, complex concept. It has many components:

- **Anticipating your customers' needs.** If you can think of some additional product or service of yours that the customer might need later, you can offer it now and plant the seed for more business.
- **Understanding your customers' wants.** Learning to think like a customer will help you understand what they want from you.
- **Exceeding your customers' expectations.** Going above and beyond what the customer expects from you is certain to make a positive impression. I often send notes to my clients when I hear they've been out on a job interview. It lets them know that I care

about them beyond the financial transaction. Value-added service is where it's at in today's marketplace.

- **Offering additional services that build relationships more than your bank account.** The best example of this that I've seen in action is the Concierge Program from Coldwell Banker Real Estate Corp. This program offers homebuyers more services beyond the initial sale; for instance, you can call your realtor after you've closed on the deal to get information about related services in your new neighborhood. If you want to know the name of a good contractor for putting in skylights, for example, you can call the Concierge Program hotline to find out. This is a company that cares about its customers even after the sale.

- **Dealing with problems efficiently—and effectively.** Don't let a problem fester with a customer just because you are afraid of confrontation. See the section on dealing with difficult customers ("Trouble in Paradise") for more tips on handling problems.

With all of the opportunities that exist in today's business marketplace, there is no reason why your company can't hold its own against larger, more established ones. The Internet is the great equalizer in the business playing field—but remember that it also opens up opportunities for your customers, too. Now that they have more choices than ever before, they can quickly find another business to work with if your customer service isn't up to par.

⚔ BACK TO THE BOARDROOM ⚔

Four Types of Customers Who Have Already Crossed Your Bridge— and How to Get More Business from Them

Want more business? You have four basic types of customers to choose from:

1. Current customers who may buy more of the same service or a different service

2. Current customers who may provide a referral
3. Past customers who may buy again after a reconnection
4. Past customers who may provide a referral

1. Current Customers

What does your current customer base buy from you and what additional services might they be interested in buying? If you look at your current customer base, you may find that some of them are purchasing your services and are very happy with what they're getting. If you make a list of everyone who purchased from you last year, it might look like a page of customers, each buying a small amount of service from you. What would make them purchase more of your fine services? What is the benefit they receive and how could you increase your sales to these same good customers?

Boardroom Group member Ruth Dean, president/owner of The Writing Toolbox, is a writer who provides exceptional services to a variety of clients. She can provide writing for books, pamphlets, newsletters, speeches, marketing materials, tapes, and more. Her clients are happy with her service. What could she look at to increase her business with those same good clients? Each of those clients is a small business or corporation who needs more written materials—each of them needs more writing services from Ruth.

Maybe some of the clients are busy completing some project and aren't ready to start a new one yet. Maybe others would like to do a new project and just have not taken time to call Ruth and set up an appointment to discuss it. Still others have actually envisioned a new project in the next six to twelve months and are looking forward to discussing it soon.

If Ruth would take a closer look at her client base, she might be able to identify those who would be most likely to embark on new projects. She could send them a note expressing her interest in working together on another project.

She could invite a client to lunch and talk about opportunities to work together on the next project. She could call to check in on how everything is going and express her interest in working on more projects.

Some clients may need a reason to start something new. Perhaps Ruth has a week next month that is partly open and she wants to let her client/prospect know that time is available for more work and that she'd be happy to schedule it. Maybe there is some reason that the client would want to order more services: a pamphlet to sell over the Internet, an article for a magazine that would bring good public relations, a semi-annual newsletter that would bring new clients to the business.

Talking about the benefits of the work that Ruth would provide might help the client/prospect to decide to start the next project.

The real benefit of Ruth deciding whom she wants to approach is that she can ignore the clients that were too hard to serve for the amount that they paid. She can approach the clients that will bring her the income that she is interested in achieving. She can provide the incredible service that she offers and be paid a premium for her good work.

2. Current Customers Who May Provide a Referral

Sometimes current customers will provide a great referral to potential clients on your "hot" list—and whom you could not easily reach in any other way.

Let's say you decide that your current clients might be willing to provide referrals for you: How would you get them to do that? You might send a letter to them telling them about a project that you recently completed and tell them that you are interested in doing more of this kind of work and would appreciate referrals. You might choose five clients who are more than satisfied with your work and tell them that you would appreciate referrals in certain areas of your business. Of course, you will choose the areas or services that will result in premium payment.

Often, clients are willing to provide referrals—and all you need to do is *ask* them. They do not usually start sending you clients unless they know you want them in the first place.

Dee Emmert, who was president of a small computer consulting company, asked Norma one day to join her for a cup of coffee at a local restaurant. She talked about her business and the kind of client that was important to the long-term growth of her organization. Then she said, "I would like to ask you to provide any referrals to me when you think that an organization might benefit from my services."

Norma told her that she would, and within four weeks made a referral to a local organization that needed a new computer system and wanted a consultant to organize the purchase of the hardware and the software. The business owner was one of several consultants considered—and was eventually offered the contract. It was only because she was crystal-clear about what kind of work she was looking for and had *asked* for the referral that Norma was able to provide her name to the organization so that she could compete for the work.

3. Past Customers Who May Buy Again after a Reconnection

Past customers may purchase from you again if you make a reconnection with them. It is amazing how many previous clients simply do not know that you are interested in doing business with them again.

You might think they don't need you or else they would call you—but, with the number of failed start-ups out there, how do they know that you are still in business? You might choose to send a letter to all of the past clients that you can locate and wish them a holiday greeting that includes a business card. This greeting can be done any time of the year—Fourth of July cards work well, simply because not too many others send that type of greeting.

Once again, don't just sit back and assume they'll call if they need you. I've heard it said by marketing experts that, if a business sent you a check any time in the last five years and you have not sent them any communication in the last six months, you are missing out on possible new business.

Karen Brubaker, owner of Indoor Air Repair, and a Boardroom Group member, advertises in a local women's newsletter that is distributed to 1,000 women in the community. The ad is in the classified section, costs $10 per month and simply says to call her for information about the air purifier that she distributes. Every month when the women read the newsletter they know Karen is still in business.

Find a way to let your past clients know that you are still alive and well, in business, and would like to do business with them again.

4. Past Customers Who May Provide a Referral

Past clients will provide referrals for you if they were happy with your services and if they know you want them to tell other people about the service that you provide.

Remember, when you did your introduction, you used the phrases that conveyed the benefits and also the idea behind the service that you provide. Create one good sentence and provide this in the letter or in the phone call you make to past clients when you ask for a referral. Make it very, very easy for them to refer you to the right prospects. This takes practice; in Norma's target marketing workshops we go around the room and every owner says, "A client I want is . . ."

This helps get everyone used to telling other people what kind of new business they want. Your past clients do not know exactly how to refer to you unless you give them the words to use, and unless you tell them that you want more business. For all they know, you're so busy you don't need more clients. Make it clear that you do.

Feeling the Customer's Pulse: What Do They Really Buy from You, and Why Do They Buy It?

Now that you know more about who your customers are, it is important to really understand what it is your clients are buying from you. What is it that makes them pick up the phone and call you instead of the dozen or so others who are in the same business? What is it that makes them sign on the dotted line? What is the very thing that brings you to the point of a successful sale?

Here's another secret about your customers: The product or the service that you are selling is not really the thing that they are buying. That is part of the problem when people introduce themselves by telling only what they do.

Prospects don't really care what it is that you do. They only care what you might *do for them*. And what you might do for them might not be the exact service that you say you offer. The truth is, the client will only see the benefit that you will provide, so you need to be able to clearly state the end benefit in your product or service, to say it in your introduction, and write it in your marketing materials.

The specific benefit behind many products and services is centered around an idea. Let's look at the idea being sold in the chart below:

PRODUCT/SERVICE	DESCRIPTION	IDEA BEHIND IT
Perfume	Scented water	Hope
Disneyland	Rides and characters	Safe family adventure
Coffee shop	Coffee and tables	Ambiance, relaxation
Tax preparation	Tax forms filed	Peace of mind
Homemade pies	Dessert	Family, homey feelings
Office space plans	Furniture arrangement	Higher productivity
Speech writer	Good speech	Confidence
Web design	Web site	Cutting-edge marketing
Miniblind cleaning	Clean blinds	Time saving
Temporary staffing	Employees	Flexible work schedules
Financial planning	Investments	Protection, safety
Artist	Painting	Happiness, reward
Resume service	Resume	Self-esteem

As you can see, marketing a benefit or a distinct improvement is often accomplished by focusing on an idea. It is the *idea* that the individual or the business is buying. What idea is behind the service or the product that you offer?

After you have identified the idea behind your service or product, look at the ways you can use that information. The first way is to be able to introduce yourself using the very phrases that will convey the idea behind your service. This will tell the person more than what you do, even more than what you could do for them. It will tell them why they would want your services. Better yet, it will tell them why someone else would want your services, and that someone else might be a friend or acquaintance of the person that you are meeting. It is so much easier for someone else to provide a reference for you or referral to you if you give them the right words to do it.

A Boardroom Group member named Kathryn Musholt offers career consulting with her company, KSM Careers & Consulting. There are several such consultants listed in the local phone book. Norma found that if she wanted to refer Kathryn to a friend who needed her services, she needed a better way to describe the reason they should call her instead of anyone else in the phone book.

What Kathryn does is career consulting; the benefit she provides is an easier way to find new work—but the *idea* behind her service is that people work with her to find work that they love. Her card had only her name, address, and phone number. Her brochure sounded like the standard, run-of-the-mill laundry list of benefits. For others to be able to refer her, they needed to be able to focus on the idea behind her service.

Finally, a way to provide a great referral became apparent. Kathryn attended a national conference of career consultants and was voted the most valuable consultant at the event. This event was hosted by the author of a famous career book.

Kathryn issued a press release about this award and finally Norma had the best way to refer her to others. She gave them a copy of the press release and said, "This consultant is outstanding; she helps you *find the work that you love.*" Provide a referral based on the idea behind the service, the thing that people *want* to buy, and good things start to happen.

You need to give people the words they can remember so that they will pass on your name and you will become known. These words of referral, when you and your marketing materials are not there, have to do the work for you. Find the idea behind your service and provide these phrases in your materials, press releases, and your introduction and you are more likely to receive the referrals for the services that you want to provide.

One of the best introductions I've ever heard was from Linda Truby, a travel agent and former Boardroom Group member, who says, " . . . and I tell people where to go" at the end of her introduction. It nearly always draws a laugh—and people remember it. Then, she finishes it with, "I also tell them what to do once they get there." Think about finding a way to be as memorable when you are putting together your "20-second commercial" introduction.

Your 20-Second Commercial

Here is an easy way to create that perfect, 20-second introduction that magically attracts the right customers. After you have thought through the services you offer and narrowed the list or created umbrella groups so prospects will understand what it is that you offer; after you have decided what the idea is that prospects want to buy from you, then you can create a very good introduction for yourself.

Instinctively, we want to tell someone *what* it is that we do. You can think of that as the "inside" definition. This would be trade titles such as the printer, the florist, the CPA, the attorney, the writer, the graphic designer, the consultant. The problem with the inside definition is that it doesn't give the listener any reason to call you. Everyone thinks they know what a printer or a florist does, and there's no compelling reason to start doing business with them if they are like everyone else in their field.

So the beginning of a good introduction is to eliminate the inside definition. Or sometimes keep it at the very end, so that the person listening will hear the benefits first and not stop listening after they hear the word that they understand.

The "outside" definition tells the listener the benefit that your service or product can provide—the specific beneficial difference that you can make in their life. This difference is very often described in terms of the idea behind the service, the reason that they really want to buy from you.

Here are some good examples of introductions that help you to listen to the benefit, described in terms of the idea behind the service:

- "Desktop Design creates brochures and newsletters to help companies reach potential new customers. We provide economical marketing materials for small business owners who want to grow."
- "My company gives you the edge in marketing your products, services, or organization through major events to impress your customers, your industry, or your community. My name is Mindy, and I am president of Windsor International Event Planning."
- "I am Jean Rogers, president of Rogers Glassworks. Our contemporary hand-blown glass is available in fine art galleries across the United States, in Japan and France. Our exquisite glassware will add beauty and style to your home or business."
- My own 20-second commercial goes like this: "I'm Katina Jones, president of Going Places Self-Promotions, Inc. I produce innovative resumes that give people more choices in their career futures."

Each of these introductions provides a focus on the idea behind the benefit. Remember, the listener only wants to know what's in it for him or her.

Creating your own introduction in this format will help you to convey the idea and improve the chances that you will find the clients that want to buy from you and will pay a premium for your services.

In the Boardroom Group we have discovered that an introduction is a work in progress. You may wind up changing your introduction many times over the course of running your business. It will reflect the improvement of your words and also of the focus and refocus of your business.

Be bold and experiment with your introduction. I can't tell you how many times someone has tried a new introduction, and someone in the room said, "I didn't know you did that!" Keep working on your introduction until it truly is communicating the value and the benefit that you provide.

Ask for feedback, and continue to refine your 20-second commercial until it's perfect. How will you know when that is? You'll know when the perfect customers begin magically appearing on a regular basis.

Trouble in Paradise: Working with Difficult Customers

When dealing with a difficult or unusual (to put it nicely) client, you must first listen carefully to find out what they really want.

You might ask, "So, what can we do to finalize this?" or "Is there something you feel is missing?" Try to get them to be as specific as possible; use a calm, reassuring tone for as long as you can.

The next step is to figure out how best to give them what they need. Sometimes, it's as simple as referring them to another person.

This was the case with a problem customer I once had. This young woman hired me to do her resume only after a two-hour session in which she had asked me just about every question you can imagine about my experience. This should have been tip-off number one. But then we set about the work of writing her resume, and when it came time for her to sign off on the proof, she refused to do so and kept insisting on making very minor changes. Back and forth we went with the resume proof, and by the sixth time I was getting antsy.

I brought the problem in to my Boardroom Group for help.

"What a demanding customer!" was the response from the group. Norma suggested that we look at the problem a bit more closely. "Maybe she just doesn't want to let go of the relationship," she offered.

I thought about this for a long time. Yes, that indeed made sense. I remembered that this particular customer had disclosed to me that she had "been burned" before by other professionals who had handled her parents' estate. She then alluded to the fact that she had been an only child, and that her parents hadn't been deceased for long. This woman was alone in the world! How stupid of me not to realize this earlier. Of course, she needed the relationship.

However, from a business standpoint, the time I was racking up on this project was starting to show that it was costing me money to continue to do business in this manner. While the sensitive side of me wanted to help, the business side of me kept saying, "time is money."

So, I pulled out my Rolodex and started working on a list of other women business owners I felt this customer could benefit from knowing. I printed it up for her and submitted it with her final proof. It worked! I felt her come alive with excitement about all of these people she could work with on other details of her life. She quickly signed off on the proof, we printed the final copies of her resume, and she went happily on her way to other women business owners who could be sensitive to her needs.

Understand that this was an unusual case, but it did almost get to the point where an adjustment was going to be the topic of discussion. She did try to suggest that a refund of sorts might be in order. Thankfully, it didn't go much further.

Don't take on more than you can handle, and if you don't feel comfortable working with a client any longer, look for a way to gracefully close the relationship. Maybe it's that you are "booked solid" for the next month, or maybe you take the honest approach and tell the client that you haven't felt comfortable and perhaps there's someone else who can better serve their needs.

In rare cases, or if you can afford it, offer a refund. One business owner we know offers a partial refund with a coupon discounting future services by 10 percent. This way, even though it didn't work out once, the opportunity exists for future business. Leaving things on positive, open terms is the best way to leave a good impression on a negative situation.

Keeping Customers Happy Without Breaking the Bank

Let's face it: We women generally provide far too many services for our customers. Keeping our client base happy is an important goal for most of us—but we may tend to go overboard. Yes, some women want to give every client 140 percent. The extra 40 percent, of course, comes out of our own profit or energy—not a happy scenario in the long run.

Here are some techniques to help you keep your customers happy and not reduce your value or your profit.

On the matter of pricing, particularly in services, it can be very helpful to have an artificial selling price. If you set the price higher than you believe that the market will pay, you can discount down to the amount that you believe is correct to get the work. For example, let's say you provide Web site design. You may price your Web sites at $4,000 for the design of an outstanding Web site including all the bells and whistles. The marketing of that site might be priced at an additional $4,000.

In order to offer a proposal to an organization that you want as a client or an influential person in your town who you are just dying to have on your client list, you propose to perform the design work for $2,500, a discount of $1,500. You might call this a "new client" discount. You might offer this price for a proposal that includes a $1,000 deposit to be paid within seven days. Whatever the reason, you are willing to provide the service for $2,500, but the client believes that the value is $4,000.

This has been a great way for many service providers to increase their prices slowly as they get used to the idea of charging more money for their services.

This lets them provide the services for the same old price, but to begin to look at the package as having much more value. (It probably does.) It is then possible to inch your prices up by decreasing the discount. Maybe you start the discount at a full 50% or $2,000; then $1,500; then $1,000; then $500. This is a great way to raise prices and earn more money while providing the same great value.

Another way to keep your customers happy is to find out what complimentary service will add to the value but cost you next to nothing to add to the package.

One Boardroom Group member had a consulting business and offered training classes in supervision. She had a client who needed individual training delivered at the business location. The proposal included all of the basic supervisory training, tailored to meet the needs of this client. However, one person in the client organization needed training in how to handle emotional situations.

This was not in the proposal, but the client wanted it included. It would have cost the owner a great deal to offer one-on-one training for this individual, two half days of time, equivalent to $750. Instead, she offered to enroll this person in the next group class she was teaching, the same material and more, at no charge. The client was very happy with this arrangement and Jean was able to offer it without any additional outlay of her time.

In order to keep your clients happy, you need to ask them what value was really essential to them in the work you have already provided. Was there any part of the service that they appreciated but didn't really require? What was the most important part of the service and met their needs exactly? This is not easy to do, and you need to find a way to ask that is comfortable for you. Usually if you ask, "What part of my service will future clients really value? What part should I be sure to highlight in my new marketing materials?" This will let you discuss the future instead of the past—often an easier conversation to have.

Listening to your prospect or your client will also help you understand what it is that they really value at the outset of the work. Do you have preconceived ideas about what they will expect? Are you listening to the service that they expect and what will satisfy the contract? Or do you think that they want everything that any client that you ever had in the past demanded? Decide what you will provide as a part of any contract or agreement and then stay with it. Don't keep adding services just to make sure that the client is overwhelmed with your business. You want them to be more than satisfied—what will do that?

Have you ever had a supplier that wanted to provide such good service that you knew it could not be making any profit on the arrangement? You don't really expect people to provide a service and lose money. Your clients don't expect you to lose money on a contract; in fact, they won't respect you if you do.

Keep thinking about the things that you can do to keep a client happy that do not cost you very much money or time. Sometimes, just as in gift-giving, an important part is the thought—the right small addition or the right attention to the clients' needs that helped them know how much you value them as a customer.

Measuring Your Customer Service Success

How do you know if you're an "all-star" at customer service?

The main way you'll know is when your business is moving along seamlessly from customer to customer, with few complaints and lots of great ideas about how to make your business better.

Here are some good indicators:

- Number of referrals you receive from past clients
- Formal survey (see Idea Center on Building a Customer Advisory Board) with lots of positive feedback
- Follow-up calls that generate positive response—I usually call or e-mail my clients within three months after they've gotten their finished resume package. I check in on them to find out who has responded to their resumes and whether they got any feedback (good or bad) about their resume's style and content.
- Healthy response to direct mail pieces offering additional products or services—if you receive more than a 1- or 2-percent response to your mailing, you are on the right track from the customer's standpoint

Paying attention to your customers' needs—anticipating them and exceeding them—is the key to great customer service. Revisit your customer service efforts often. Don't be afraid to ask your customers what you do well and what you could improve upon.

Most of all, don't let the bridge between your company and your customers collapse for any reason.

◿ IDEA CENTER ◹
Hi-Tech Customer Service

Great customer service isn't limited to in-person sales calls and business dealings. The Internet also requires that you pay attention to your customers' needs—only in a much faster, more personal fashion. Your customers need to feel individually recognized when doing business in the less personal world of cyberspace.

Two of the best online examples I can think of are Amazon.com and iVillage.com, which greet you by name each time you return to their site after registering or buying a product. I have to admit that I love it when the message at the top of my iVillage.com home page says, "Hi, kat666" (my e-mail address at iVillage.com). I know darn well that they do this for everyone, but this particular greeting has *my* name on it. Dale Carnegie was right—using a person's name is the best way to build a business relationship.

Here are some tips for great online customer service:

• Answer all e-mail inquiries promptly—and, if you can't, hire a virtual assistant (professional who acts as an online "secretary" for a monthly fee) or use an automatic responder. With auto-responders, you can be sure everyone who inquires about your products or services will receive answer immediately—which is when they tend to expect it. You can respond more personally later, but, again, don't let too much time pass. Nothing is more irritating from the customer's standpoint than sending off an e-mail request that seems to go off into oblivion.

• Include an FAQ (frequently asked questions) section on your Web site, if it's pertinent. Most of the time it is, since people tend to ask the same questions about businesses.

• Consider adding a section for testimonials on your Web site. I have a section on my site (*www.ohio.com/jobhunter/starachiever.com*)

where I use testimonial quotes from my clients. It's very effective in attracting new customers.

• Make it easy for others to do business with you. Automate as much of your business as possible. The reason companies like 1.800.FLOWERS do such phenomenal numbers in sales is because they have found ways to make it very simple for customers to buy from them. If you can accept credit cards online with a secure server, you will do lots of business while you sleep.

Online customer service is becoming so big that our country's top recruiting agencies are getting deluged with requests for more online customer service representatives. It's getting to be a hot field—and for good reason. You don't spend a whole lot of your money on a great Web site, then leave customer service to chance. In the competitive global marketplace, you must respond quickly or your customer will move on to the next business like yours. Remember, there's always someone else they can do business with—so, if you can't handle online customer service yourself, hire someone else to do it for you.

⊿ IDEA CENTER ⊾

Staying in Touch with Easy Relationship-Builders

Keep your relationship with your customers healthy and thriving in the following easy, inexpensive ways:

• **Send thank-you notes for new business—and returning clients.** Make sure every customer knows exactly how much they are appreciated. It needn't be fancy or expensive—just remember that your thoughts count as much as their business does. Short and sweet always works.

• **Use e-mail to check in on customers.** Whether you are sending a newsletter to your entire client list or individually reconnecting with customers, you need to use this easy, fast and economical method of staying in touch with your customers. Use any of the online greeting card services to e-mail a follow-up note or card. I follow up with many of my customers every few weeks to see if they've gotten a job yet—and many of my clients stay in touch with me via e-mail. I've had one who has moved across the country twice—and always e-mails to let me know where she is and how she is doing. Many of my out-of-town customers have become friends—and many have kept in touch for years when we have not even met or spoken to each other. That's customer loyalty.

• **Clip and send articles that would be of interest to your customers.** One realtor clips a real-estate writer's weekly column and sends it to her current customers as a way of keeping her name in front of them—while providing them with that "extra" touch.

• **Congratulate your customers on their triumphs.** When you see that one of your clients has won an award, or been recognized for a particular achievement, send a note congratulating them. Celebrate their successes as you would your own.

• **Use direct mail to your benefit.** Mail postcards that announce a new product or service—or offer a "preferred customer" discount. Your customers, like you, want to feel special, and using words like "preferred" and "valued" in front of "customer" will go a long way in making them feel valuable to you. My optician sends me a birthday postcard every year—and that is why I will never go anywhere else to buy eyeglasses. Little things really do mean a lot.

◿ IDEA CENTER ◺

Keys to Customer Service

• Listen—and ask key questions. When I talk to a resume client about their job situation, I actively listen and respond to their career problems. They tell me all about the company where they are currently employed, and then they tell me how intolerable their situation is getting. They are frustrated, often angry, so I just let them vent for the first five minutes or so. Then, I recap to them what I heard them say: "I can hear the frustration in your voice. We need to put together a good self-marketing piece that will help you attract the right company for you—a place where you'll get the respect and recognition you deserve. The bottom line is, you need to be happy." Do you see how I move them into a sale? Think of how you would like to be treated, and understand that the customer needs to be heard first.

• Be honest and forthright. Tell the customer in an open, forthcoming manner what they will and won't get from you. So often, small companies fail by over-promising just to get the business. If you can't do something for a prospect or customer, tell them—then whip out your Rolodex to give them an immediate referral. Your best position of strength is to be expert enough to know when to find another expert for your customers. Wouldn't you like that from the companies you deal with on a regular basis?

• Anticipate needs. Don't be reactive, be proactive. I sell cover letters as a separate service for my resume clients; often, when I send the client the final copies of the resume, I include a brief note asking them if they had considered a cover letter on matching stationery. Are they able to resist? Not often. People like doing business with others who think more about what they need than they do. In our busy society, anything you can do to make life easier for your clients will win you respect—and more clients.

◺ BACK TO THE BOARDROOM ◿

Making It Easy for Others to Do Business with You

Are your marketing processes standing in the way of bringing in more business? Do you have a cumbersome catalog that is too overwhelming?

Your barriers to business may be much simpler than that: It could be that your long-distance customers are starting to find it expensive to work with you.

Here are some ideas the Boardroom Group has generated in response to the question, "How can you make it easier for others to do business with you?"

- Put together a "starter" kit of small items related to your business, and offer them at a special introductory price. Include easy follow-up or ordering forms so that your customers have a quick way to get right back to you.
- Get an 800 number so that potential customers aren't turned off by the thought of incurring long-distance charges before they've even committed to doing business with you. These are much less expensive than you might think.
- Build a Web site that gives tips or ideas for free—and provides a place for inquiries from customers. Always try to give 24-hour turnaround in answering queries, and say so on your site. People surfing the Internet expect quick turnaround on everything; provide as much "instant" business as possible.
- Offer incentives (such as 10 percent off) for returning customers. When you ship the first order, it's your prime opportunity to get more business. You are fresh in the customer's mind, and at this point they usually still like you enough to want more.
- If you must use voice mail or an answering machine, update your message frequently and let people know when they can expect a return call. If you have a Web site, refer callers to it from your voice mail message so that they have another place to check you out while they're waiting for a return call.
- If it's easier for your customers to use credit cards, talk with a bank about becoming a merchant. Figure out a secure way for your customers to automate their buying on your Web site, using their credit card.
- Create a fax order form and install a separate fax line that's ready to accept orders 24 hours a day. Talk about making money while you sleep!

◿ B A C K   T O   T H E   B O A R D R O O M ◺

Giving Great Service—Without Giving It All Away

Women business owners tend to worry more than any other owners about their "likeability" factor. So often in Boardroom Groups we hear them say: "But if I don't do what the customer wants, they won't like me anymore."

One of the biggest business maturity indicators I've personally experienced was a result of a conversation with a fellow Boardroom Group member named Kathy Baker, president of The Write Choice, a public relations company. It went something like this:

Me: I'm really upset that this customer of mine isn't seeing the value of what I'm offering. I wish there was some way I could win him over.

Kathy: Why? You've tried three times to explain that your services are worth what you're asking for them and he hasn't gotten it. In fact, he seems to be more about giving you a hard time.

Me: Yeah, but I just don't like to lose a sale over someone who doesn't understand what I really do.

Kathy: Did you explain that to him?

Me: Yes.

Kathy: Well, then, my dear, you have to stop wanting him to like you. Isn't that what this is really about?

She had a point. I mean, I've always cared a great deal about the opinions of others—even those that really don't matter or make sense. As a young girl, I had a desperate need to be liked—and Kathy somehow picked up on that, probably because she recognized it from her own life.

I stopped "needing" the sale, but more important stopped needing to be liked by everyone. Not everyone is an appropriate customer for me, and in that one moment with Kathy I began to understand that.

I sent a postcard to the prospect, thanking him for calling me and noting that, when he was ready, I would be happy to help him.

He called me back almost one month later—presumably after shopping other resume services and coming up empty-handed. "I'm ready to talk business now," he said. "You'd be surprised how many other companies didn't show me the attention you did."

It doesn't always work out like this, but remember that you don't need every customer who comes your way—and the ones who don't seem ready today might be later. This is why it is so important to be courteous and respectful at all times: You never know when they'll come back to you.

⊿ IDEA CENTER ⊾
How to Get More Referrals

Here are some great sentences to get referrals. When someone says to you, "How is business?" Your answer should be: "It is absolutely great; I have finished one major project and I am looking for one additional client." Or, "It is absolutely great. I have room for one new client." Or, "It is great and I hope to find two new clients this quarter." Everyone wants to do business with a busy, successful owner. This is a way to tell them that you are successful and also looking for a new client.

By the way, if you get business by speaking in front of groups, you have a great opportunity. Send a letter to everyone that you know and tell them that you are available for speaking. Tell them the kind of groups that you want to be referred to and tell them that you plan in your schedule to speak to a group six times each month and you would appreciate having your name passed on to those who are looking for speakers. I received a letter like this once and I have never forgotten it.

Sometimes you hear a good speaker, but you don't know if they want more engagements. Is it an imposition? Do they speak regularly without being paid? Do they want to speak to more groups, and if so, what kind? The letter that you send will answer all of these questions and also will tell the reader that you plan to speak and that they will be helping you to complete your marketing plan by passing your name along. Try it!

⊿ IDEA CENTER ⊾
Building a Customer Advisory Board

What is a customer advisory board, and why should you have one?

A customer advisory board may be particularly effective when you are first starting your company, or at a later stage when you are considering a growth step (such as expanding your business or buying an adjunct one).

When you are still in the start-up stage, a group of a few customers you enlist for the purposes of feedback and input can be as informal as a written survey and as formal as a breakfast meeting at a local restaurant.

In a period of major growth later on in your business, the process can remain the same—you can still use a questionnaire or survey, or hold a more formal dinner.

But what information do you want from your customers? What will be most useful to you as you poise your business for greater success?

For starters, you'll want them to assess how you've been doing up until this point. Find out if you have been as effective as you thought in each of these areas:

- **Sales.** Are your sales materials enticing enough to attract more customers like the ones you already have? Can they be modified easily to attract new customers? Are you offering enough choices to your customers, and making it easy for them to buy from you?
- **Marketing.** Are you doing well at making the rounds of local networking opportunities? Have your customers been aware of you even when they do not physically see you for awhile?
- **Management.** Are projects being completed exactly as you might have stated in your contract, in a timely and efficient manner? Are your employees capable of handling almost everything you can? How smoothly is your business operating?
- **Customer service.** This is the most critical point for input from your current customers. What do they like best about working with you or your company? What do they like least, or feel you can most improve upon in the next six months? What ideas do they have that can make your business better? Do they have a "wish list" of things they'd like to see you offer in the future?

Getting input from your customers on a regular basis will help you to stay in touch with their needs—and to steadily improve your customer service efforts on a regular basis.

◿ IDEA CENTER ◣

How to Think Like a Customer

Want a little insight into what makes your customers tick? Think about what you appreciate when you are a customer. What do you really want?

- **Fast service.** We live in a fast-food society—one where we expect instant everything: from e-mail responses to the ability to use a credit card and order something that appears the next day.

- **Great service.** We want things now, but we also want everyone to be nice and accommodating to us. When a company goes over and above what was expected, that is great customer service. My vet sends birthday cards to my animals, along with reminders that they are due for shots. A nice touch, and more than I expect for the small amount of business I must represent to him.

- **Great price.** Now that we can purchase virtually everything from virtual storefronts, price competition has become fiercer than ever. As customers, we want the best price we can get—and if we can't get it at one place, we now have 3,000 others to choose from in the online market. If you're a patient person, you can always find a better price than the last one you were offered.

- **More options/choices.** One of the things Norma has found to be effective in Boardroom Groups is for the women to think of ways to package their services in order to offer more of a menu to their customers. We like choices and the ability to pick only the pieces of a service or product that we really want or need. Making customers buy more than they need with what I call the "do or die" package is not only bad business, it's offensive. Empower your customers with choices they can make on their own, after some education from you about the benefits and features of each unit or piece.

- **Customization.** Customers want to feel as though a product or service was created expressly for them. My resumes are a good example of that kind of service: each one is uniquely created for the customer based on their experiences and business philosophy. There are no templates, and my customers are discriminating enough to appreciate that because they know that I appreciate their individuality.

- **Personal attention.** Every customer wants to feel like they are your only customer. Is this true? Of course not, and they are smart enough to know that they are, in reality, one customer among many. However, if you are smart, you will find a way to make them feel like they are receiving your complete attention. When you meet with them or talk to them, do not put them on hold or accept interruptions of any kind (unless it's *really* an emergency). Focus on them completely; listen to their problems and turn them into positive solutions.

Money Matters: Finding a Financial System That Helps Your Dollars Make Sense

Norma J. Rist

--- Secret 6 ---

*Your money can tell you the story of how well
your business is doing. Finances aren't as hard as you think.*

At this point in your business, you probably have a tight business plan, terrific marketing materials, and more customers than you ever imagined. Your business is growing—along with the amount of things you must think about on a daily basis.

It's a little overwhelming, isn't it?

One of the details that most women business owners hate (and I mean hate) is keeping track of their finances. But I can tell you that your financial picture is one of the clearest indicators of success or failure—and it's important for you to see and understand this picture even if you aren't the "artist" who created it (and a qualified accountant is).

Learning about your business's financial health is an ongoing process—one that can't be absorbed overnight. After all, you need to learn how to understand (and accept) a bookkeeping process that can work for you—not an easy thing in and of itself. Add to that the learned skill of interpreting what your financial reports are telling you about the past, present, and future of your company, and you've got your work cut out for you.

Trying to learn all of this overnight would be like skipping the E-Z Sew Pattern and moving straight to a sophisticated Vogue Pattern—or skipping the introduction to French and moving into a third-year course. Most women business owners just can't absorb finances that quickly.

Should you be afraid? Not at all. In fact, the only thing you have to be afraid of is *not* having a clear picture of your company's financial health. In this instance, what you don't know can absolutely hurt you.

Starting Simply

When you have a small company, the financial knowledge you need to get started is fairly simple. You open a business bank account, process your transactions, and look over your monthly statement.

But looking beyond this beginning step, you might consider using computer software such as Quicken or QuickBooks to keep track of your regular bills, payments, income categories, and taxes. These programs are the most commonly used ones, and should be acceptable for submission to an accountant for quarterly review.

The best thing about these two programs is their ease of use. You can quickly develop a complete financial picture of how your company is doing—and develop a budget for future expenses—all by simply entering what comes in as income and what goes out to pay the bills. You don't need to think like an accountant to use these programs, and you can easily turn the disks over to your accountant for review.

Quicken and QuickBooks both provide a profit-and-loss statement—one of the best indicators of your company's wellness. The P&L, as it is called in larger corporations, tells you where you made and lost your money over a given period of time. You can do these as often as monthly, or perhaps quarterly, but the main thing is to generate these reports so that you can get a clear picture (in graph or pie-chart format, if you wish) of how you're doing.

Look at the revenue and expenses to see if the numbers make sense to you. Are you losing too much by giving too many things away—a problem common to many female entrepreneurs? Or are you making a lot of money on a product you haven't yet focused a marketing campaign behind?

So many of my Boardroom Group members have encountered some astonishing facts about their businesses simply by generating a P&L statement. One owner found that she had spent way too much money promoting a product that hadn't sold much quantity in two years. Another discovered that her main stream of income actually came from doing press releases instead of lengthy writing projects that seemed to be priced higher but took longer to complete.

As an owner of a business, you have the most insight into the accuracy of your financial reports. After all, if you're like most women owners, you were probably there for all of it: every transaction, every piece of return business.

So, you need to know how to evaluate the accuracy of financial reports such as the P&L in order to ensure that everything is being entered into the program correctly. Mistakes happen, but they can be costly should there be an audit of your record keeping later on.

Moving to the Next Level

Once your company grows and becomes more complex, you will be in a better position to hire someone else to do your bookkeeping—something that usually makes Boardroom Group members sigh with relief. Remember, many of us don't like handling the details as much as we enjoy making new business happen.

Dorie McCubbrey, Ph.D., president of Dr. Dorie, Inc., is a Boardroom Group member who started her business part-time while working at a university as manager of their Women in Engineering program. Her doctorate in bioengineering was a way to add the human side to her math and scientific skills.

Dr. Dorie, as she is now called by many, had created a new approach to weight loss issues. She wrote a book *(Dr. Dorie's Don't Diet Book)* and went out on a speaking and book promotional tour. Soon, she had enough interest in her work to warrant a jump to another dream: to have her own wellness center and retail shop.

Her approach to tracking her income and expenses was simple at first; it consisted of a business checking account and software to keep track of income and expenses.

But as her business grew, Dr. Dorie realized that it wasn't as easy to find the time to do this for herself—and that her records were becoming more labor intensive because she had employees and shared office space with several like-minded counselors and wellness professionals. She had more money coming in and going out—and desperately needed to create cash flow projections that would show her how best to manage this money.

So, Dr. Dorie went to her certified public accountant (CPA), who helped her prepare a budget and a cash-flow projection in order to make better decisions about the future and avoid the kinds of cash-flow problems that could have sent her business into a tailspin.

She started with her basic knowledge and added to that the knowledge of a financial professional who could help her develop the skills needed to move her company ahead.

Hiring Outside Help

I have met women who were quite skilled at what they did but were afraid of starting a business because it meant they would have to do bookkeeping. Imagine that—being so afraid of numbers that you'd pass up the opportunity of a lifetime to own your own business. It's something I could not have done—but, then, I had the almost unfair advantage of having been a controller in my previous job.

As I've said, most of our Boardroom Group members have hired outside bookkeeping services—and most of those are run by other women business owners in the Boardroom Group or another network of women business owners.

Jill Manda owns Manda's Plant Farm, a wonderful place to purchase flowers and plants each spring season. She doesn't use pesticides, and even the herbs and vegetable plants are nurtured in her own special soil mixture.

In her Boardroom Group, Jill talked about how she just loved how her business was growing but that she really disliked the paperwork associated with it. One by one, the group started sharing their mutual dislike of paperwork and record keeping, but then they started telling

Jill how wonderfully easy their businesses had become once they hired a bookkeeper to handle their record keeping.

Even if you only have that bookkeeper work on your records once a month, it can be a welcome relief to you as it enables you to focus your efforts on moving your company along. By hiring a bookkeeper and/or tax accountant to handle the numbers, you will instantly have more time to concentrate on marketing, selling, customer service—and planning for your company's future.

What will a professional bookkeeper do for you? Keep your records current, for one thing. But they essentially pay bills, issue invoices, balance bank statements, and even handle payroll. Best of all, they know how to prepare your tax information in an easy-to-access way for your tax accountant—a time- and money-saving function.

You can find an independent bookkeeper by running an ad in a local paper or by talking to other owners about who they might recommend. I also recommend contacting the closest chapter of the National Association of Women Business Owners (NAWBO) by visiting their Web site (*www.nawbo.org*) or calling national headquarters at 301-608-2590.

Partners in Profit: Working with CPAs

A CPA can help you with a number of your business issues, from choosing your business's form (sole proprietorship, corporation, partnership, or LLC) to offering projections that could save you money in the future.

Most of my Boardroom Group members find their CPAs through their own networking. Of course, we do have a few CPA members, so these women tend to get a lot of instant referral business from within the group.

No matter how and where you find your CPA, I always suggest you interview at least three before making a commitment. You should know something about their backgrounds and their approaches. Try to find one who matches your professional temperament, since you'll likely be spending lots of time with this person.

What should you ask in the interview? Here's a quick list for starters:

1. Are you an independent or associated/affiliated with other CPAs?
2. What did you do in your career to arrive at this point?

3. What does your current practice look like in terms of types of clients? Have you worked with others in my industry before?

4. In what areas of small business management do you assist? Can you help with more than tax returns (for instance, banking, loans, lines of credit)?

5. Do you help with financial reporting, explanations, and advice?

6. Would you come to my office or would I need to go to yours?

7. How do you charge? By the hour? By the project?

8. Will you train me on bookkeeping and reports I might want to do myself?

9. Do you personally provide all of my help, or do you have additional staff that I might be working with at times? What are their backgrounds?

10. Which financial reports will I receive from you, and how often?

11. Do you have an attorney you could recommend who works with small business owners? (If they are used to being part of a future-planning team with small business owners, they will know a few good attorneys.)

These questions will provide you with enough information to make your decision. It should be relatively easy for you to compare the answers you get from all three candidates, then make your decision based on who you think has your best interests in mind.

You can find someone who will help you prepare your business for bigger and better things. Finding a good CPA who cares about you and your business is definitely worth its weight in gold.

My Banker, My Friend

Banking relationships, too, are an important part of your business equation. Unless you have a "cash-cow" type of business (one where the money just keeps rolling in and you can finance your own growth), you'll probably find yourself at the bank asking for a small business loan.

It's interesting to note that most award-winning women entrepreneurs always include a thank-you to their bankers in their acceptance speeches. There's a reason for that: The banker may have made the difference in the business' ability to reach new heights by offering a loan.

But small business loans aren't just handed out on a silver platter to every entrepreneur who asks for one. You need to have your own finances in order (see related Idea Center) first—not to mention a complete business plan that documents why your business has potential for greatness and, more importantly, why you are a good risk for the bank to take in extending you a loan.

What else do you need in order to convince a banker of your worthiness? Without a doubt, it's a positive working relationship. If a banker has known you for a while and witnessed firsthand your company's growth from concept to profitable enterprise, you will stand a better chance of getting the funds you'll need to grow.

Many women business owners make the mistake of thinking that it's too soon to start cultivating a banking relationship when they've launched their businesses. I'm telling you that it's critical; how else can they see how your company's grown?

When you have a relationship with your banker, you can talk about your company's progress, your challenges, and your opportunities for the future. The banker can offer you tips on how to manage your business better, or how to use new products or services the bank is beginning to offer.

Communication is key: You need to talk to the right person (small business loan officer, in most cases) and give them the right pieces of information. Don't tell a bank teller all of your good news about your business; the loan officer is the one who needs to be kept abreast of your triumphs and successes.

Try to align yourself with a banker who has some experience with others in your own or similar industries; remember that you are best served by a banker who is knowledgeable about your industry and business.

If you haven't already established a great working relationship with your bank, take a look at the advertising in your local business newspaper. Are any of the banks advertising services especially geared toward small businesses like yours? Those are the ones you'll be after. Many banks sponsor small business expos and trade shows; it's worth it to attend these just to stay informed about which banks are most entrepreneur-friendly.

Once you've found a bank you'd like to do business with, start working with the loan officer you feel most comfortable with. Schedule regular visits to talk about your business's progress—or, at the very least, keep the loan officer on your newsletter mailing list. If an article is written about your company, clip it out and mail it to your banker. Make sure they start to develop a healthy clipping file of items related to the progress and positive growth of your business.

To further develop and nurture this relationship, you should work up a track record of borrowing and on-time repayment in smaller amounts that are easier to get. Ask your banker what else you can do to lay the groundwork for future financing, should you need it.

A "No" Is Just One "No"

It's been my experience that women will tend to hold back from taking the next step until they are absolutely sure that it's the right thing to do. We don't ever want to make a mistake, so we avoid moving forward into uncharted territory until it is absolutely necessary.

Being prepared to make the move will help you reduce any concern about making mistakes. Understanding the process for the next step and being prepared to move forward as soon as the time seems right will help.

Understanding how banks work and how to develop a relationship with the right banker will help you to be prepared at the right time and not wait longer than necessary.

Old notions or past experience stick to us like glue. Many women remember that there was a time in the not-too-distant past when we couldn't have credit in our own names. As a college student in the mid-1960s, I started to create a credit file by borrowing money on a used Volkswagen. Through the process of five or six cars in the same number of years, I had started a good credit rating.

The first house I bought was co-owned with my spouse; it had a mortgage of 80 percent and I suppose it's possible that the bank was applying credit to my personal credit record. Our second house, a much larger, more expensive house that we built, had a much larger mortgage. I remember calling the bank, then writing a letter to make sure they indeed gave me credit on my own credit record for the timely payments on this mortgage.

Times have changed and individuals now accumulate their own credit rating, men and women alike. Credit has changed, banks have changed, and bank products have changed.

Anything that has ever happened to you before may be different now. If you have ever applied for a loan and been turned down, you need to remember that this is only *one* instance—one singular situation at *one* institution. You may find that across town, they would welcome your business! Don't let an unsuccessful attempt at one bank keep you from trying others. One "no" can mean that you simply haven't found the one bank that will say "yes." You could be one step away from that "yes!"

You will be better prepared for your business future if you find and keep a good bank relationship. Be knowledgeable about the changes in the banking world. Go to the library and read all the articles you can locate in the business and financial magazines about financing and banking for small business owners. Remember that you may be inclined to postpone the needed financing longer than you should if you are not comfortable with the process. Stay involved and you will be ready at the right time.

Other People's Money: Alternatives to Bank Financing

There are many more alternatives to traditional bank financing than there used to be. Many small business owners will use credit cards as a quick source of funds when they don't have an adequate line of credit, and there's nothing wrong with that. It's easier now because so many credit card companies are actively soliciting small business customers. The only real downside, of course, is that the interest rate may be higher. The payments must also be made in a timely manner (no matter when your customers pay you).

Credit unions are available for many small business needs, and several leasing companies are actively seeking business from smaller owners. Look in the phone book and call enough places to find out what is available in your region.

Other funds have been established specifically to meet the needs of women. Some of them are through banking institutions and some are outside the traditional commercial banks.

Here are some of the opportunities out there:

• Wells Fargo Bank established a program for the National Association of Women Business Owners, a loan fund of $1 billion,

for women who have been in business two years or have equivalent experience. To find out more about phone applications
for funding up to $25,000, and one-page applications for over
$25,000, call 800-359-3557, ext. 120.

- Women, Inc. has created a program with The Money Store, a loan
  pool ($150 million) for members ($29/year) with a business plan
  and good credit. They also offer *Business Line,* an unsecured line
  of credit that's an excellent source of the cash your business
  needs. It offers a range of services tailored to the needs of the
  small business owner. For more information, call 800-930-3993.
- Women's Collateral Worldwide offers collateral of $5,000 to
  $25,000 for women business owners in several areas of the
  country ($500,000 at each location); call 215-564-2800.
- Inroads Capital Partners, Evanston, IL, has a $44 million fund
  for venture capital investments of $1 to $3 million for women-
  and minority-owned businesses; call 708-864-2000 or e-mail
  carrington@inroadsvc.com.
- Women's Worldwide Venture Fund plans to offer individual investments of $100,000 to $1 million in women-owned businesses. Forty
  million is available; call 215-564-2800 to find out if you qualify.
- Blue Chip Venture provides venture capital for fast-growth
  women- and minority-owned businesses from a fund of $60 mil-
  lion; call 513-723-2300.
- Women's Equity Fund provides venture capital and loans to
  women through local banks. The fund is $750,000; call
  303-443-2620.
- Ark Capital Management provides $1 million to $5 million
  to women and minorities. The total fund is $25 million; call
  312-541-0330.
- Isabella Capital LLC, Cincinnati, OH, can be reached by e-mail:
  peg@fundisabella.com. Once formed, this new company will
  focus primarily on women-owned or women-led businesses with a
  target fund of $25 million. The typical investment will range from
  $500,000 to $3 million, usually given in more than one round.
- Black Enterprise/Greenwich Street Corporate Growth Partners,
  New York, NY, is a $60-million fund with its focus on minority-

and/or women-owned or managed companies. The average investment is $5 million to $15 million. Call 212-816-1308.

- First USA VISA Credit Card is a special credit card for members of the National Association of Female Executives (NAFE); it offers no annual fee and a 3.9% introductory rate; call 800-347-7887.
- Capital Across America, Nashville, TN, is a $28-million fund, including funds from the Small Business Investment Company (SBIC) program, which partners with the SBA and venture funds in the private sector. Although its primary focus is on women-owned businesses, the fund will look at any established small company that fits its investment criteria. The average investment is $500,000 to $ 1.5 million; call 615-254-1856 or e-mail *capxam@aol.com*.
- Viridian Capital, San Francisco, has a $24-million fund including SBIC contributions. Its target base is companies that were founded or cofounded by women, are led by women, or sell products or services primarily aimed at women. The average investment ranges from $500,000 to $2 million; call 415-391-8950.
- Women's Growth Capital Fund, Washington, DC, is a $30-million fund, including funds from SBIC, The fund targets women-owned businesses or companies with at least one top female executive. The average investment is $500,000 to $2 million; call 202-342-1431 or e-mail *info@womensgrowthcapital.com*.

There are also many places to look for investors, if you are ready for that step:

- Angel Capital Electronic Network (Ace-net), U.S. Small Business Administration, 202-606-4000; *http://ace-net.sr.unh.edu*.
- Investors Circle is at 415-929-4910.
- National Venture Capital Association can be reached at 703-351-5269 or *www.nvca.org*.
- Private Capital Clearinghouse (Pri-Cap) is 617-239-8071 or *www.pricap.org*.
- Wit Capital is 212-253-4400 or *www.witcapital.com*.
- Resources on venture capital may be found at Venture Capital Resource Library *www.vfinance.com* or Venture Capital Market Place *www.v-capital.com.au*.

Other sources of cash include partners, vendors or suppliers, private investors, joint ventures, incubators, bridge loans from mezzanine financiers, or royalty financing. If any of those terms are unfamiliar to you, go to the closest main library and ask the research librarian at the business reference desk to help you find articles about these types of financing. It'll be easy once you understand the terminology, how they work, and where to go to find them.

Several Web locations may help you:

- The National Foundation of Women Business Owners has an excellent site with lots of connections; look at *www.NFWBO.org* to get a variety of good information about women owners as well as financing.
- Also check out *www.sbaonline.sba.gov/womeninbusiness* for up-to-date information about SBA-backed loans and how to access them. You will find that the Small Business Administration is committed to supporting women business owners and the site will tell you what they are doing to help.
- The Small Business Credit Café at *www.experian.com/business.html* will help you find information about your credit report, how to secure credit, and how to offer credit.

Cash-Flow Projection: See It, Then Be It

One of the first reports that you will ever need is a forecast of cash flow. A projection of the movement of cash into and out of your bank account will help you to know that there will always be enough money to stay in business, or predict a shortfall that you should know about ahead of time so that you can do something about it.

A new owner named Anita Johnson prepared a cash-flow projection for her first year of business. She was about to buy a small business, and needed to make sure that if she made the purchase she could make enough money to pay herself (since she would quit her existing job). She needed to be able pay herself on a month-to-month basis so she wouldn't be behind in her personal bills (does this sound familiar?).

She included all of the projected income (conservatively), the loan repayment, the expenses, and a small owner's salary. She looked at the 24-month cash projection schedule and saw that it would work if she just had $3,000 in the second month. If she had the $3,000 to get past month two, then every month after that was positive. She could pay the bills, pay herself, and still have a tiny profit left. It would've been impossible to buy the company if she didn't have the cash projection to know how much cash she'd need.

Here's a sample cash-flow projection format you can use. It resembles your checking account and moves from month to month. If you have a balance of $200 at the end of January, then that is your beginning balance at the beginning of February, just like it is in your checkbook.

This cash-flow projection will work if you prepare it for your company on a monthly basis, or if you prefer you can just use four quarters of the year instead of all twelve months. Either way, a projection will help you to be confident that you'll have enough cash for your planned business activities and projects. It will help you to be in the leadership role, deciding what you want to happen—and not just waiting to see what happens.

At the very least, if you use the total column and fill in the totals you expect for the year, you will not have determined your month-to-month cash requirements, but will have filled in your projected annual cash sales and your projected cash expenditures. That alone is a major step, since it sets up the written projection as a goal.

Following are two pages you can copy out of this book and use to create your cash-flow plan. Know that you'll change it often; this is completely normal. Just starting to use a cash-flow projection as a mini-budget will be very empowering. It will give you the confidence of knowing you have a path to follow.

I always suggest that whatever plan you developed last year, do a little more with it this year. If you build your plan each succeeding year with more details, more accurate numbers, more understanding of how to achieve the plan, you will get better and better at managing your business.

A Simple Cash Budget

When you are operating a very small business, you worry every day that your checkbook will have a positive balance. You watch the mail, hoping a payment will arrive in time to pay bills. Running your business out of a simple checking account might work for a while, but with growth you'll need more information.

It can be difficult to create a basic cash budget (unless your background is in accounting). However, once you have started a simple cash-flow form and copied the months across the top and the revenues and expenses down the side, you will be halfway there.

The best part is filling in the projected revenues. It's great fun to anticipate income in larger and larger amounts. The wonderful result of performing this task is that you will have set goals for yourself. You need to have a cash plan—expectations—a track to run on. Then, when someone asks you "How are you doing?" you can honestly say, "I'm substantially over my plan." Those are powerful words!

Now, on to the expenses. What do you expect to pay each month in order to achieve your revenue goals? Don't forget to budget to pay yourself a reasonable amount. If you decide how much you want to draw for yourself each month, it will help you stay focused on your marketing plan!

Remember: "Making a profit" is the phrase we use when we talk about the benefits of a successful company, but the truth is that you have to have enough cash flow each month in order to stay in business long enough to make a profit.

If you haven't already found a simple cash-flow form that you like, try this one. If you have procrastinated and want some support, arrange to work on your form when your accountant or CPA is with you at your next appointment.

How to Do a Cash Projection

1. Put horizontal and vertical column names on lined accounting paper or a computer spreadsheet.
2. Enter beginning checkbook balance in January or whatever month you are starting with.
3. "Ending Balance" at the end of each month is entered as "Beginning Cash Balance" for the next month.
4. "Total cash receipts" and "Subtotal" expenses can be totaled (January through December) for an estimated budget.

COMPANY _____ CASH PROJECTIONS

	JAN	FEB	MAR	APR	MAY	JUN	JUL	AUG	SEP	OCT	NOV	DEC	TOTAL
BEGINNING CASH BALANCE													
Cash Sales													
Collections from Credit Accounts													
Loan or Other Cash In													
TOTAL CASH RECEIPTS													
TOTAL CASH AVAILABLE													
CASH PAID OUT													
Gross Wages													
Payroll Expenses													
Outside Services													
Supplies & Postage													
Repairs/Maintenance													
Advertising													
Car, Delivery, and Travel													

(continued on next page)

COMPANY _____

CASH PROJECTIONS

	JAN	FEB	MAR	APR	MAY	JUN	JUL	AUG	SEP	OCT	NOV	DEC	TOTAL
CASH PAID OUT *(continued)*													
Rent													
Telephone													
Utilities													
Insurance													
Taxes (Real Estate)													
Entertainment													
Interest Payment													
Education													
Donations													
Miscellaneous													
SUBTOTAL													
Loan Principle Payment													
Owner's Draw													
TOTAL CASH PAID OUT													
ENDING BALANCE													

How Much Is Enough?

Susan Smith wanted to start a business of her own. She had a group of clients she serviced as part of a larger firm. Her agreement with her current employer included the opportunity to become independent by making payments to her employer for the business she would take with her. She wasn't sure she could make it on her own. Would she have enough cash flow to make it month to month?

She sat in my extra office with a calculator and some 14-column accounting paper. She filled in the columns, starting with horizontal and then vertical, just as the form appeared. We talked about the revenue she'd earn from existing clients and additional revenue from new clients, and how to put the numbers on the form. I suggested that she complete the expenses that seemed easy and then call me to help with the more difficult projections.

Susan worked with me to complete the cash-flow projections, including the payment to her previous employer and an owner's salary for herself. As the final numbers were calculated and the projection showed a small profit in the first year, she looked at me in total amazement! It *could* be done—it *was* possible—and it was the skeleton for a new business start-up. Creating a projected cash flow demonstrated the opportunity and documented the plan to follow.

Your Budget: Start Simply

If this is your first real budget, start with a simple one. You can use last year's tax return to begin. Make a copy of the Income Statement; write it on accounting paper or key it into a spreadsheet on your computer. With the outline of your own income accounts and the expense accounts you actually use, it'll be easier to fill in.

Each entry is determined by calculating your best estimate for that revenue or expense category. Most companies budget by month, then total the 12 months. A few owners will project the total for the year and then break it down by month. Either process or a mix of both will work.

Here is a simple budget—notice that it tells a story, month by month, until year-end.

A lot of owners ask me whether they should correct their budget after the year starts, because you know more as the year progresses. If

NJR COMPANY
2xxx BUDGET

	JAN	FEB	MAR	APR	MAY	JUN	JUL	AUG	SEP	OCT	NOV	DEC	TOTAL
Sales	22	21	23	25	29	32	31	33	32	29	21	24	224
Cost	10	9	11	11	13	15	14	15	14	12	9	11	144
Gross Profit	12	12	12	14	16	17	17	18	18	17	12	13	178
Ware. Exp.	2	3	3	2	3	3	3	3	3	4	2	2	33
Sales Exp.	4	4	7	5	7	7	10	12	16	7	7	4	90
G&A Exp.	2	4	3	5	6	5	5	4	5	1	2	3	45
PBT	4	1	-1	2	0	2	-1	-1	-6	5	1	4	10

the budget is an owner's tool, not used for bonus or other internal goals, then change it to suit yourself.

A forecast is another budget report that can help you. It includes actual months of business, (designated as A), and budgeted months for the remainder of the period (designated as B). I call this a forecast because it includes both actual and budgeted numbers.

There are entire books written about record keeping and taxes. *Minding Her Own Business: The Self-Employed Woman's Guide to Taxes and Recordkeeping* by Jan Zobel, is a good book for additional examples.

NJR COMPANY FORECAST

	A JAN	B FEB	B MAR	B APR	B MAY	B JUN	B JUL	B AUG	B SEP	B OCT	B NOV	B DEC	F TOTAL
Sales	23	21	23	25	29	32	31	33	32	29	21	24	323
Cost	12	9	11	11	13	15	14	15	14	12	9	11	146
Gross Profit	11	12	12	14	16	17	17	18	18	17	12	13	177
Ware. Exp.	2	3	3	2	3	3	3	3	3	4	2	2	33
Sales Exp.	5	4	7	5	7	7	10	12	16	7	7	4	91
G&A Exp.	2	4	3	5	6	5	5	4	5	1	2	3	45
PBT	2	1	-1	2	0	2	-1	-1	-6	5	1	4	8

A=Actual
B=Budget
F=Forecast

Knowing Where Your Money Goes: Internal Control

With growth, some additional reports will be needed to make sure that internal control is in place. This means that **cash-type assets** (cash, inventory, checks, accounts receivable, etc.) and **fixed-type assets** (equipment, computers, software, etc.) are secure and protected. No money will slip through the cracks, and no equipment or inventory will easily be stolen.

The easy way to remember what internal control really means is this definition: "The procedures, checks, and balances that you put into place to keep honest people honest."

One day a business owner I'll call Laura stopped me in the middle of a restaurant and said, "You will probably read this in the paper, so I might as well tell you that my employee stole thousands of dollars from me." She was a professional who had an administrative person—a trusted employee of many years—who quietly took money over a long period of time. She was devastated.

The best way owners can prevent honest people from stealing is by putting procedures in place that prevent them from easily taking money or inventory. For instance, you have some considerable exposure if the same employee deposits the checks and reconciles the bank account all the time.

Your CPA can help you determine good controls for your size business. Ask her what internal controls you should have in place to keep your people honest.

On Your Desk Tomorrow: Reports You Need to See Regularly

The financial reports we've reviewed are often produced monthly, but in some small companies they're only done quarterly. You will want to see these reports as often as they are produced, then review them with your accountant or CPA:

- Cash Flow Statement
- Income Statement—for month or quarter
- Income Statement—year to date
- Balance Sheet—at that point in time

Below are the management reports that may be needed by your company as you grow and want more information to make good decisions for the future:

- Budget for year, 12 months and total
- Profit/Loss for month and variance to budget (accountant compares the reports by account)
- Variance Report/Explanation (accountant and owner review variances)
- Forecast for Year, Actual plus Budget = Forecast
- Unit Sales by Product Type, Client Type, Service Type, or Deliver Type
- Gross Profit by Product Type, Sales Type

Other reports you may want on an as-needed basis:

- Customer Sales History
- Productivity
- Actual Expenses vs. Budget
- Sales Activity/Promotional Activity

Okay, so now you are keeping all of the records that the government wants, but when do you produce what you want—or need—to keep your business running well?

These reports you develop along the way. Sometimes, you can look at a financial statement that comes in an industry magazine and see what they track. Or, if you look up some financial reports at the library, for another company in your same industry, you will find out how they track important indicators.

Purchasing Techniques: Making Money from Buying

You generally know that if you are a large company you have some opportunities to save money by purchasing in quantity. What you may not know is that there are many buying opportunities available to small companies like yours. Here's the caveat: You have to be willing to look for them and to ask for them. But unless you are a natural negotiator who's always on the lookout for a good deal (i.e., you are the one that loves to negotiate with a car salesperson), you will need to cultivate a new attitude and force yourself to think differently. You'll need to be aware that there are deals out there to be had, and if you don't ask for them, all of your competitors will have the lower prices and you will be giving away some of your profits to your suppliers.

If you gave each and every supplier a few cents more for each item purchased, or a few dollars more for each service you buy, you'll have given away most of your profit. Smart buying can make the difference between generating a profit or having a loss. Keep this in mind as you look at every opportunity to purchase at a lower price.

Here's a way that you can review all of your suppliers and vendors to see if there are any saving opportunities. By the way, if you've never done this before, you'll probably find savings available in almost half of the suppliers and vendors you currently do business with.

Remember that price is only one component of wise purchasing. It's also important to review quality, delivery, payment terms, service, and other resources provided by the supplier. A complete review of purchasing practices will provide new opportunities for reducing costs and finding better quality, delivery, and more.

This review is best accomplished by deciding that you're going to review all purchases, not just office supplies or a product that you buy from a catalog and don't care who gets the order. If you look at all suppliers over the period of a year, you will find some interesting new facts and be pleased you took the time to make the review.

It's true that you'll maintain some supplier relationships based on outside reasons (your sister provides your printing, or she is a graphic designer), but you'll make that choice after having more knowledge about the decision. We all make a few buying decisions knowing that there is a better deal, but we choose to pay the additional amount for what we consider to be good reason.

The plan to look for opportunities is the same for old and new suppliers alike. The goal is to locate price reductions while keeping the same good quality and service.

There are two primary ways to do this review. The first is to arrange your suppliers by size; the supplier providing the greatest amount of an item or the largest dollars in the expense categories should be reviewed first.

The second way is to look at your year-end income statement and create a list of all the expense categories, then add the vendors you've used to create that volume of purchases in those expense categories.

For either kind of approach, you now can proceed the same way. You are going to look at the list of suppliers and eliminate those who are no longer used and who bid on every order on a quarterly or annual basis.

All suppliers are provided with the same information for specifications. All are asked to tell you if there are ways to reduce the cost of the product or service. *If you don't ask them, they won't tell you.* You should tell all of the existing suppliers that you are looking for ways to reduce costs and maintain the same quality and delivery.

This process is easier if you create a simple form about each supplier. Include any of the following that pertains to your business:

- Last bid for each item supplied by that firm
- Service provided, such as inventory, delivery, etc.
- Other relationships with that supplier
- Written and unwritten agreements with the supplier
- Quality
- Order to delivery time
- Expertise from supplier staff
- Quantity discounts available
- Annual volume for each item purchased
- Person who normally orders from this supplier
- Person who normally approves orders from this supplier
- Problems with this supplier

Add to this form the specifications about the item or the service purchased. The specification sheet will be given to old and potential new suppliers alike.

You can use the library or the Internet to find potential new suppliers. You will be amazed at the resources available to help you to find new vendors. Look in your trade journals for targeted products. Trade associations often publish buyer handbooks for their industries. Get out those catalogs you've received in the last year and take a look at new possibilities.

Remember that pricing can vary in different parts of the country by a significant amount. You may prefer to do business locally when you can, but if your raw material can be shipped from three states away and you can double your profit through that change, it may be worth it.

Tell any supplier bidding that there will be only one bid. It's not a good procedure to tell an acquaintance, or someone who asks, that you will tell them the lowest price so they can match it. Tell all bidders that there will be only one bid and when quality, delivery, etc., are the same, then price will be the deciding factor. This is absolutely the only way that you will get back the best bids!

Also look at savings in mailing, fax post-its or lead sheets, long distance telephone, electric, gas, and water audits.

Here's a good way to keep track of the savings you may generate; create a form to track the anticipated results:

SUPPLIER SAVINGS INFORMATION

Product/Service Purchased: _____ New Vendor: _____

Description: _____ Old Vendor: _____

Start Date: _____ End Date: _____

ITEM DESCRIPTION (NAME, SIZE, COLOR, ETC.)	UNIT OLD COST	UNIT NEW COST	UNIT SAVINGS	QUANTITY	NET SAVINGS

When a Boardroom Group member named Jan decided to review her costs using the method just described, she was amazed. She owned a small retail store and had to replace lights in the store frequently. She discovered that the person purchasing the lights had changed suppliers—and the new supplier was charging a higher amount. Further review found a new supplier, and based on her annual purchases, she would save $60,000. That's an amazing amount to save on lights.

When another Boardroom Group member named Sally performed the review, she decided to include her telephone bill. It was always hard to read and she wasn't sure that it was all really correct. The bills were printed on both sides of the page and seemed to charge odd amounts for hundreds of small things. So, she prepared a spreadsheet; it had the months across the top (she started with one invoice from 15 months ago as a base comparison in the first column) and added the three current months. Then, she had four months to post on the worksheet.

Down the left column, she started by posting the parts of the bill: basic service (by each trunk line installed), incoming and outgoing service, tax, paging charge, voice mail charge, 800 charge, long distance charge, etc. Then, she posted the amount of the charge for each of these services into the column under each correct month. She posted the one old month as a baseline and then the three current months.

Wow! She discovered that when she added a trunk line six months ago, they added a charge for *two* trunk lines—and she had been paying for two ever since. At the same time that the trunk line was added, an old 800 number that had been disconnected six months prior to the trunk line change began to charge to her account again. The savings from the adjustment for these errors was a whopping $792! This would have been part of Sally's profit going down the drain.

It is definitely worth the time and trouble to review your vendors to find those who will provide the same great quality, delivery, inventory, and more—at better prices!

⚑ IDEA CENTER ⚑

Are Your Own Finances in Order?

Whether you are just starting out or considering an expansion of your business, you should be tracking your personal financial liabilities regularly to make sure you keep your credit record clean enough to secure extra funds, if needed.

A credit bureau report can be obtained by applying to your local credit agency (typically a $5 minimum fee, unless you've recently been rejected for credit) or by paying a small fee to access your records via the Internet. There are plenty of good books that explain how to read your credit report; *The Wall Street Journal Guide to Understanding Personal Finance* is one of the best.

Once you've figured out how to read your credit "score," you can take your credit report to your banker to put together a time frame in which you might apply for additional funding for your business.

It's important that you keep tabs on your personal spending in order to avoid burdening yourself with too much debt. If you wind up using all of your profits to pay for your own personal debt, how can you stay in business?

Check your credit bureau report at least once per year. It's not uncommon for mistakes to appear on credit reports, so check it over carefully each time you obtain one.

⚑ IDEA CENTER ⚑

Collecting Your Due: How to Get Customers to Pay

What do you do when you run into the difficulty of getting one of your customers to pay up?

You could first try the human approach—simply call them and ask if everything's okay. Find out if they had any problems with your product or service. Then, if they tell you everything has been all right, ask when you can expect to receive payment. If the customer expresses to you that he or she is in a state of "financial negativity," ask how much they can afford to pay you now—and when you can expect to see the rest of the bill paid up.

If this approach doesn't get you anywhere, compose a letter detailing what is owed and when you expect to see it. It wouldn't hurt to "cc" the letter to your attorney, particularly if the bill is way overdue (three months or more).

Women have a more difficult time asking for money in the first place–but don't let your customers take advantage of any insecurity they may sense on your part.

We have a few women business owners in our local networking groups who specialize in debt collection, so working with these kinds of companies is an excellent option for us. Fortunately, it hasn't come to that yet–most of our customers eventually pay up.

If you don't know any debt collection services, check in your business phone directory to interview a few of them over the phone. Ask them how much of a percentage or commission they take on each collection, and what their success rate is in collecting on past-due accounts. Each debt collector should be able to give you enough information to determine whether you should enlist their services.

⋈ IDEA CENTER ⋈
The "Quick" Key to Cash Budgets

For those business owners who are "mathematically challenged," here is a quick breakdown of the items that should appear on your cash-flow projection statements. Basically, you need to look at what's coming in and what's going out on a regular basis.

"In" column:
- Cash sales
- Accounts receivables
- Funds from sales of assets or equipment
- Refunds (such as tax refunds)
- Collections (outstanding accounts)

"Out" column:
- Inventory/stock purchases
- Operating expenses
- Fixed-expense payments

- Credit payments on long-term debt
- Tax payments (most often quarterly)
- Shareholder/stock payments

Taking a look at these items and how they change over a period of a year can provide you with a profit-and-loss (P&L) statement that clearly shows you what your business is earning and spending.

You can use this information to build your following year's budget, by making educated assumptions based on what happened the previous year. For instance, if you had a bad winter quarter because your business is somewhat dependent upon good weather, you'll know to build sales up in the fall to cover your winter operating budget and make sure the bills get paid.

From *Easy to Start, Fun to Run, & Highly Profitable Home Businesses,* by Katina Z. Jones (Adams Media Corp., 1997).

⊿ IDEA CENTER ⊾

Lease vs. Buy Decisions

If your business requires a lot of equipment purchases, you would do well to look into a "lease-option-to-buy" program that allows you to pay as you go. Why is this scenario more desirable than an outright purchase? Two reasons.

First, a lease allows you the flexibility of using equipment without long-term commitment to it. If, for some reason, your business goes under, you can usually negotiate your way out of a lease—and you're not faced with the prospect of having to find a buyer for your used equipment.

Second, your cash flow isn't tied up in equipment expenses—freeing you up to invest your capital in other, more immediate return areas such as advertising.

Most leases run 36 to 60 months, but you can often negotiate your terms in addition to your rates. Since leasing is a very competitive field, your chances of finding a deal that is suitable to your needs are quite high.

From the *Adams Businesses You Can Start Almanac,* by Katina Z. Jones (Adams Media Corp., 1996).

IDEA CENTER

Is Accepting Credit Cards Worth It?

The ability to accept credit cards can greatly enhance the number of customers you gain each month—but is it really worth it to take plastic?

It can be, if you're doing a significant amount of business using this convenient transaction method. Particularly when you have an Internet-based business, there are many advantages to accepting credit cards (remember the piece in Chapter 4 on Building Bridges, about making it easier for people to do business with you?).

But if your volume is small—say, four or five sales per month—you might want to reconsider a decision to accept credit cards. Most credit card processing companies charge a monthly fee of about $15 to $17, in addition to taking a percentage that can be as large as 5 percent of each sale. You'll have to do the math yourself (or call your accountant) to figure out whether you can really make enough money off of each sale to justify the cost of the transaction. Some women business owners charge a 5 percent premium to customers using plastic—or they offer a 5 percent cash discount to those who pay cash.

BACK TO THE BOARDROOM

Getting a Bank Loan: The Pampered Pals Story

Alison Kirby, a Boardroom Group member and owner of Pampered Pals, wanted to sell her pet-sitting business and start a dog treat business.

Each meeting she would tell other members about her wonderful treats, the ones she had created for her own dog "customers." The dogs loved the natural, veterinarian-approved, people-could-eat-them-too treats, and Alison felt she was ready to move away from the seven-day work week that the pet-sitting business had required of her.

Finally, Norma and the group helped her to put together a real plan for starting her dog treat manufacturing company. The graphic artist from Alison's Boardroom Group created a new logo to go with the company's name, Pampered Pals. Another graphic artist from a different group had many years of experience in packaging design, and she started the process of developing a design that would be attractive in upscale health food stores, airport gift shops, and more. These were the places Alison had targeted on her marketing plan.

On a weekly basis, Alison met with Norma to create a new business plan—one that would demonstrate to a bank that the market was large enough and that she would have a unique position in the marketplace with her vacuum-sealed, soft and tasty dog treats.

Each month, the Boardroom Group heard Alison report on her progress. She had found a person who was interested in buying the pet-sitting business, and she had a great start on her new business plan. She had worked through the marketing research (much of it available from a pet food association) and kept isolating the information that pertained directly to treats.

The market was very large, and it appeared that she could indeed capture a segment of it. Working on the numbers was most difficult; many estimates had to be calculated and explained in a way that a commercial loan officer would understand.

Visits to several banks were insightful, but no loan officer appeared interested. Then, Alison identified a loan officer who thought an SBA-backed loan might work.

Alison sold her pet-sitting business and hired a professional writer to complete an interesting, concise business plan. She got the loan—and suddenly had ten balls in the air at the same time: bank, SBA, accountant, selling a business, designing packaging, finding a manufacturing location and equipment, and learning about bar coding. All of this to get her simple treats out into an untapped market!

She is now beginning to manufacture the treats and secure retail outlets, all according to her business plan. She is also updating her business plan to secure an investor—and has plans to sell her treats internationally. Recently, she even began offering six-month supplies of her treats on the successful Internet auction site, eBay (*www.ebay.com*).

The key to getting financing is to have an airtight plan for your success.

When Work Becomes Life: Creative Delegating and What to Do When There's Not Enough of You to Go Around

Norma J. Rist

—— Secret 7 ——
Your business doesn't require as much of you as you think.

You're overworked—crazed, to be more exact. Lately, you find yourself dreaming of the ideal employee, someone whom you could depend on at any moment to do the things that need to be done. Or, more specifically, the things you really hate to do.

So, it's time to think about delegating—you know, hiring an employee. You are overworked and underpaid and are beginning to wonder why you even started this business in the first place. The next thing that you will probably do is put off hiring because you are far too busy to interview, let alone train someone. How could you possibly make the right choice if you're too busy doing all of the work yourself?

The fact is, we often try to do too much. There have been lots of books written on that topic alone, so we won't get on that bandwagon right now. But think about all of the things you do every day to run your business and your life–how many could actually be done by someone else (remember Chapter 2's "The Juggling Act?")? How many things have you already delegated or "let go of"?

I always tell women business owners that, in order to move to the next stage of growth in their businesses, they will have to let go of something. Maybe it means the laundry gets done by a teenager–or your husband or partner. Maybe it means you hire someone else to clean your house, or buy prepackaged foods in order to have a great dinner waiting for you after a long day of work.

Whatever you decide to give up in your personal life in order to spend huge amounts of time on doing your work and planning for your future, you will need to eventually do the same thing for your business in order to succeed. If you're up to your neck in marketing your business, finding a good person to pick up the slack in the office while you're out can be a godsend–and it can lead to even more business for you, since you'll have the ability to go out and get the work without the worry of whether the work's getting accomplished back at the office.

Not convinced yet that you need help? It's not surprising. Women will try to continue to add to their duties long after they should have delegated some work to someone else. Part of our culture involves the belief that we *should* do many things for other people. In our families, we will try to do many things for the good of the members of the family. Sometimes we will do this long after we should have delegated some responsibility to other members, because we'd rather "get it done right." As if no one else could handle the same responsibilities!

I remember a workshop led by a psychologist many years ago. The workshop leader was teaching us some insight into our tendency to do things for others. The example was a working mom who had a six-year-old son who didn't really like to go to school, but enjoyed gym class very much. So taking his gym shoes on the right day was very important, to say the least.

But this young boy simply could not remember to take his gym shoes to school. The mom was torn between always remembering to take the gym shoes for him, and letting him forget his shoes and potentially hating school. Her inclination was to always protect him, shelter him, and take the shoes because it was so important that he learn to like going to school. What she learned was that she had a bigger oblig-ation to him—the obligation to help him learn to be responsible for the things that are important to him. Only after she learned to let him be responsible did he begin to like going to school. He learned which days were gym class, learned to remember his own shoes, and felt confident of his own ability to be ready to take his favorite class.

But more important than even that, Mom learned to delegate responsibility in order to let him mature. She actually did him a huge favor, but freed herself of some responsibility in the meantime.

So what happens to us when we start our businesses? We believe that we should be able to do everything. We start out wearing all the hats and don't have a plan for when we are going to take them off and hand some of them to someone else.

To compound the problem, we sometimes undercharge for our prod-ucts and services and then our bank account tells us that there is not enough money to pay ourselves adequately, let alone pay someone else. We get the wrong signals when we don't use our pricing indicators correctly.

So, we may think we can't afford an employee, when hiring someone else may actually bring in more money in the long run because it frees us up to do even more business.

How Do You Know When You Need to Hire?

So how do you think through the need to hire? The first step is to look at your ability to bring in new business. Have you conquered the steps to successful marketing and are you capable of bringing in more busi-ness than you can handle?

If so, then the process of hiring an employee is next on your agenda, because you can market for more work, bring in additional rev-enues, and provide the cash flow to pay an employee. You just need the time to market and the time to service more clients. Hiring the right employee to do work for you will free your time so that you can indeed increase your marketing and increase your client base or increase your sales so that you provide the cash flow to pay your employee.

Kathy Baker, owner of The Write Choice, is a writer, and she learned over the first 24 months in business that she loved to market; originally having been afraid of it, she learned the steps and loved the process. Soon, after she got the hang of it, she started to become far too busy for one person. However, the thought of hiring someone was never in her plan. She pictured that she would be an independent professional and would wear all of the hats and once she learned to market successfully, she would live happily ever after. Instead she became too busy and had not yet achieved the financial level she desired in order to pay herself at a certain "goal" level. She felt as though she was spinning her wheels.

Kathy had been in a Boardroom Group with 10 other business owners and knew that there were many ways to provide herself with help. She knew that the work she disliked most was bookkeeping, so she looked for an independent bookkeeper to do that work for her on a subcontracting basis. She found a woman who owned a bookkeeping service and became a client. Now she has freed up many hours each week and can use those hours to market and service more clients.

Using a subcontractor for peripheral services might work for a while, but with more marketing and more work you might get right back to the same old place: "I need help fast. I feel like I just ran the Boston Marathon and I can't go a step further!" Now you know you are finally ready to hire an employee.

By the way, the corporate example of reaching this stage is when you are so overworked that you are willing to share your desk, your computer, and your secretary—anything, if you could just have some help.

Acknowledging the Need

So you made up your mind last night at eleven as you finally finished working. You are going to find exactly the right person to help you in your business.

What's next? Often, the next mistake we make is to make a list of the things that we want someone to do and decide to find a person to do those things. But doesn't that sound reasonable at first?

It is important to realize that employees come with education, training, background experience, situations, and attitudes. If you put together a list of duties and it is a combination of helping you with creative work; answering the phone and helping all of the callers; attending workshops and bringing back information that would be helpful to the company; mailing your newsletter and also preparing nine reports each week, you might be in trouble, since the competencies required for that complete group of duties may not be easy to find. Often, we think we need that one person who can just do a little bit of everything.

Let's look at two basic kinds of employees in a small company:

- One employee works on his or her own, as an **independent**. This person learns the job particulars, understands the standards of performance, and already has the training and background to complete the work.
- A second employee is primarily a **support person**. This employee has been trained with skills such as computer, phone, mail, fax, copiers, transcription, customer service, etc. The second employee is trained to be the main support system for his or her boss. This employee will be very happy to take care of your every need, but will not work well independent of you.

In your interest to find the employee to do that list of things that you do not want to do, it is very easy to forget that the employees who perform work usually fall into one of the above two categories described. If they are in the first example, they may not think clearly how to be a support person for you. If they are in the second type described, they may not work independently enough to free enough of your time for you to benefit from the situation.

One Boardroom Group member wanted to hire a full-time employee to do all of the work that didn't fit into her schedule. This included bookkeeping as well as helping her to get all of her work done each day. This combination of duties was going to be difficult to place because bookkeepers primarily work independent of other people. They focus on accuracy, balancing, and orderliness. They like neat, clean systems and perfect paper flow.

Helping to get this owner's work done meant making some phone calls, solving customer service issues, making people happy, and handling several verbal communications with a number of different individuals each day. This type of work is hardly a good fit with the traditional competencies of a good bookkeeper. It might be possible to find a person who actually is proficient at both of these types of work, but it will take longer since there will not be as many available.

You will need to be clear about what competencies you are looking for and how you will interview to find the person with all of the abilities and skills you need to rely on.

The Perfect Employee Profile

On to the next challenge. Finding the right prospects will be essential in order to find the right candidates. You can make this process easier if you have written the "perfect employee profile." This profile will include all of the skills and abilities that you require—but also those things on your "dream list." One way to start is to separate your thoughts into four categories: education and training, background experience, situation, and attitude. Think about these skills, abilities, and situations in terms of those that you require and those that you want. The work page that follows will help you put those needs on a chart.

- **Education and Training.** Remember that you may need to provide some of the unique training yourself; it is harder to find exactly the person who is ready to start to work on day one with all of the training you require. Finding the right *trainable* employee can sometimes be the answer.
- **Experience.** Try to consider the type of work done and not the specific job title that they held; job titles can be misleading. What about the person who always worked in a big company where the copier was handled by the MIS department? Will they be willing to try to fix yours if necessary? What about the number of hats this employee will wear? Have they worn a lot of hats in another situation? Experience is more than just the job skills. Think about the other types of experience that will be needed for your job situation.
- **Situation.** Sometimes you need a person who can stay after work when you need them, or a person who can drive to a workshop ahead of you in order to set up. What if you need a person who

has a computer in their home to make last-minute changes on your speech? All of these considerations involve the situation of the person. If they are not free to stay late because they pick up a child each day at five, they might not fit the situation that you have to offer. However, if they are willing to pick up their child and finish your project at home later, it may still be an option.

- **Attitude.** This is not a good attitude/bad attitude question. We suggest that you consider attitudes toward a whole host of things. For instance, what is the candidate's attitude toward learning new things and someday advancing themselves? What is their attitude toward working in small companies as opposed to large firms—are they expecting the perks that only large firms can provide, or will they view the opportunity to work in a small, friendly environment as a benefit? You should also have some sense about their attitude toward management styles and other viewpoints. Do they see themselves as a means for you to improve your business, or do you sense a hidden agenda (such as the possibility of building their own competitive business later)? Decide what attitudes you are hoping to find, then measure your prospects against this list.

THE PERFECT EMPLOYEE PROFILE

AREA	REQUIRED	DESIRED
Education/Training		
Experience		
Situation		
Attitude		

How to Write a Job Description That Works

Now that you have completed the first draft of your Perfect Employee Profile, you are ready to prepare a job description. This job description will be needed before you proceed to the interviewing process; it will help you to be precise when you are describing the job to the interviewee.

When a new job is being created, it generally has a major goal and also a list of job duties. Sometimes you know the goal first, and sometimes the best description of the major goal is easier to write after the job duties have been listed and refined. Don't worry about the order in which you complete this process; just so you end up with a job description that you like and that will work.

Let's start with a list of the job duties first. Make a list of everything that might be included in this job. Let's say it is a job of administrative assistant. Put everything on the list from answering the phone to watering the flowers to talking with a major client when no one else is in the office. The list may be very long like the one below:

JOB DESCRIPTION: ADMINISTRATIVE ASSISTANT

- Answer phones
- Return calls for owner to provide answers and schedule appointments
- Prepare all correspondence
- Handle outgoing mail
- Open and process incoming mail
- Record checks and prepare bank deposits
- Order office supplies
- Arrange dinner meetings for the owner's association once each month
- Prepare newsletter information for the printer
- Process the bulk mailing
- Handle the coordination of marketing programs
- Enter information into client database
- Prepare client reports from client database
- Enter information into prospect database
- Prepare prospect reports from prospect database

- Send out program materials for interested prospects
- Answer questions about the programs from phone inquiries
- Handle mail order requests, fax forms, fill orders, and send invoices
- Do library and Internet research
- Make copies and handle filing

This list of duties is now complete and the information needs to be put into the form of a job description. The next step is to create areas of responsibility by grouping the duties into areas that fit together. We will call these areas of responsibility "job result areas" and we will give a name to each area. The next step is to divide the list into the three, four, or five job result areas. You can do that by simply deciding what job duties fit together. It might look like the list below:

JOB DESCRIPTION: ADMINISTRATIVE ASSISTANT

Communication
- Answer phones
- Return calls for owner to provide answers and schedule appointments
- Arrange dinner meetings for the owner's association once each month
- Answer questions about the programs from phone inquiries

Written Stuff
- Prepare all correspondence
- Handle outgoing mail
- Open and process incoming mail
- Record checks and prepare bank deposits
- Order office supplies
- Send out program materials for interested prospects
- Handle mail order requests, fax forms, fill orders, send invoices
- Make copies and handle filing

Projects
- Process the bulk mailing
- Handle the coordination of marketing programs
- Do library and Internet research as assigned

Computer Maintenance

- Enter information into client database
- Prepare client reports from client database
- Enter information into prospect database
- Prepare prospect reports from prospect database

Any other work as assigned.

Now you've arranged the duties into "job result areas." This will be important when it is time for a performance evaluation; it is hard to evaluate someone on a list of 40 or 50 independent job duties, but easy to use the grouping of duties into job result areas to evaluate performance so that you can focus on areas for improvement or change.

As you continue to create this job description, remember too that words need to be included in the description that set standards of performance. Your new employee will need to be trained very quickly in the standards that you expect.

One Boardroom Group member had a new employee, a receptionist, and she wanted to be certain that the new employee was trained very well right from the beginning. She talked with the receptionist about the list of job duties that were carefully placed in the notebook on the desk. She tried to impress upon the new employee the need to provide excellent customer service by always answering the phone in less than two rings. She was setting a standard to help the new employee to learn how important the function of customer service was in the company. This was a good start for the receptionist's training.

It is even more important to remember that there is an end result to every action or every job duty. If you can think about the end result that you are looking for, it will help you to set the job standards that will really work in the long run. In the case of the receptionist, the real standard of performance is that every caller should receive the answer or be connected to the right person every time and in an efficient manner. If the receptionist is so focused on answering every call in less than two rings, she may transfer the existing caller without listening well enough to make the proper transfer, because she can hear the next call ringing.

This may result in answering every call in less than two rings, but the person calling will not receive all of the attention that they deserve.

Here's a worksheet format that will help you to create a job description that utilizes job result areas:

STANDARDS OF PERFORMANCE

Position Name: Administrative Assistant

Basic Purpose: To provide administrative support for the owner of the company including written, phone, and computer communications; to keep current all required records; and to help develop good relationships with prospects and clients.

Job Result Area #1:

Handle all phone inquiries, return phone calls, and event arrangements.
  This job result area will have been satisfactorily completed when:

1. All incoming questions and requests are handled with total focus toward outstanding customer service.
2. Timely return calls are made on behalf of the owner to provide answers and schedule appointments in a friendly, professional manner.
3. All event planning, including the owner's monthly association meeting, is handled in an organized, efficient, and pleasant manner.

Job Result Area #2:

Process all written communications, incoming and outgoing.
  This job result area will have been satisfactorily completed when:

1. Accurate and professional correspondence is prepared daily and processed in an efficient and cost-effective manner.
2. Incoming mail is opened, sorted, and prepared for the owner to review.
3. Incoming checks are prepared for timely deposit.

---

4. Purchase orders for office supplies and other services are prepared accurately and in a timely fashion, and bids are secured when needed.
5. An inventory of program materials is maintained and mailed as required within 24 hours of the request.
6. Mail orders including invoicing are processed within 24 hours of the request.

Job Result Area #3:
Handle projects as requested in an efficient and accurate process.

1. Process bulk mailing each month according to postal regulations.
2. Coordinate the suppliers required for each marketing program in order to ensure optimum success.
3. Handle library and Internet research as assigned.
4. Successfully complete any other work as assigned.

Job Result Area #4:
Maintain all required computer files on an accurate and timely basis.

1. Enter all updates to client database to keep current daily.
2. Prepare accurate and timely client database reports.
3. Enter all updates to prospect database to keep current weekly.
4. Prepare accurate and timely prospect database reports.

This job description will help you to perform the next steps—to find candidates, to screen them for qualified applicants, and to interview the applicants to find the person you really want to employ.

Finding Candidates

If you have never written an ad for the newspaper classified section, ask a friend who has this experience to help you. It will not help to run an ad and then receive 100 applications from unqualified people. If you are able to develop a good ad, it will screen the applicants so that you receive a good number of actual candidates. Try to include in the ad the training, skills, or situation that you require in addition to what's on your "dream list."

In addition, you may have places in your city where you can call to find a good candidate, or your own array of resources, such as a friend who owns a personnel firm. Or maybe it's a training program that helps to place people into good jobs, such as the Senior Workers Action Program (SWAP) in Ohio, an employment agency for older folks who have skill, talent, and dedication. Look deep into your Rolodex to find what you need. Ask other women business owners how they have found qualified employees.

You can also find excellent candidates using the great resources on the Internet. Post your job openings on high-profile career Web sites such as Monster.com, CareerMosaic.com, or CareerCity.com, where you can even be specific about your geographic location. This will limit the number of resumes you receive from candidates outside of a 50-mile radius of your location.

Most local newspapers also offer job boards on their Web sites, and this would also be an excellent place for you to post ads. Even if the newspaper's site uses a larger career site (such as CareerPath) as a partner, you can tailor your ad so that it only reaches the local market.

If you are looking for a virtual assistant or a home-based worker, an excellent place to post an online classified is HomeJobs.com, which home-based workers scour for jobs daily.

The applicants can be prescreened by comparing the applications forms or the resumes to your Perfect Employee Profile. In this way, you can eliminate the applicants who do not meet the standards that you have said that you require. You'd be surprised (and maybe even appalled) to know that a high percentage of resumes received for a particular job opening do not even remotely correlate with the job's requirements!

The remainder of the candidates can be screened a second time by a phone interview. One of the job result areas for this position was a friendly and professional phone ability. It is easier to screen for this capability when you do it over the phone, *before* you have met in person.

Remember that there are questions that you are not legally permitted to ask; if you are not clear about what questions are illegal to ask, consult your attorney for guidance. Generally, questions relating to sexual orientation, race, health, and family planning are considered to be intrusive and discriminating in an illegal manner. Seek advice from an attorney with a client base in employment law.

Getting Ready for the Interview

Your interview will be most successful if you are prepared with the questions to ask and you have a quiet time away from phone calls and interruptions.

There are two primary reasons to have the questions prepared ahead of time:

- You want to ask each candidate the same questions in order to provide a good comparison.
- You want to ask the questions first and talk about the job second, so that the candidate doesn't tell you the answers they think that you want to hear.

One Boardroom Group member liked to interview because she really enjoyed talking with people and getting to know them. She had a habit of asking a few questions to start the interview and then she would enjoy the conversation so much she would start talking about the company and about the position. She would tell them about the duties and what she was looking for in a candidate and what were the most important characteristics of the right person. At this point she would remember to get back to her list of questions and begin to ask for more information from the candidate.

Guess what! The candidate would repeat back almost exactly what this business owner was looking for. The owner had given the candidate the *exact* words to use. Now it would be difficult to find out what they really would like to do, because the applicant was just absolutely sure that this was the one and only job they really wanted. They wanted a job offer and then they would decide whether to accept it.

The Boardroom Group had encouraged this owner to use her question sheet first and tell about the job second. She had plenty of time at the second half of the interview to sell the applicant on the advantages of working for her company.

Twenty Questions to Ask Before Explaining a Job

1. Tell me about each of your previous jobs and the duties that you performed.
2. Tell me about the education and training that you have had that will be relevant to this position.
3. Tell me about any education and training that you have had that may not be relevant to this position.
4. What training would you be interested in having in the future?
5. What classes or education would you be interested in pursuing in the future?
6. In each of your jobs, tell me the part of the job you enjoyed the most and the part that you enjoyed the least.
7. What opportunities did you have in your previous jobs to do something beyond the scope of the job description?
8. What work did you do in your previous jobs that really was a part of someone else's job description?
9. What promotions have you achieved?
10. What promotions would you be interested in achieving in the next few years?
11. Did you ever have to work with someone difficult? How did you handle it?
12. Do you like to learn new things?

13. Do you like to learn to do your job very well and maintain it but not have to learn too many new things?
14. What kind of variety do you like in your job? Phone, paperwork, problem solving, customer service, reports, projects, etc.
15. Do like to work independently or in a team or supportive role?
16. Are you open to giving and receiving new ideas, and do you feel qualified to present them yourself?
17. What is your one shining accomplishment to date?
18. In terms of problem-solving, do you ask for help first, or present solutions and offer choices?
19. If you had to narrow your skills down to one thing you feel you do best, what is that one thing?
20. What is ultimately your dream job? What kind of environment do you feel best suited to?

Do You Really Have a Match?

It is interesting that women who own small businesses wait so long to start the hiring process—then rush off in too big of a hurry to get that fabulous person who is going to change their lives. It is almost as though the business owner cannot wait another second to hire some help and anyone who can do at least some of the work will be a great start.

We also tend to see the good parts of an applicant and don't as often see the drawbacks to hiring a certain person. Often, we seem willing to give people who are not entirely qualified a chance to prove themselves—and that's not always in the best interests of that person, let alone your business.

Women will tend to see the first two candidates, believe that they have found just the right person, hire him or her, and then discover that it wasn't the right person at all. What happened? The woman business owner was wishing that this person that she liked so well during the interview would in fact be the right fit—or turn into the right fit.

One suggestion that can help you during the process is to decide your time frame for this hire. Look at your calendar and

decide how many weeks you can afford. Do all of the interviewing–
no fewer than four comparisons of all rather equally qualified candidates–at least three days before you need to make the offer of
employment. After the four comparisons are complete, set them
aside for 48 hours and then pick them up again and review them.
This will help to make the choice more focused on job skills and
abilities and will remove some of the attraction to a personality that
you enjoyed or a person with some similar background to yours that
provided great conversation. Have lunch with them, but don't hire
them unless they're truly qualified.

Look for the person who has all the skills and ability required who
will also fit into your company the best. Then, you have the best opportunity for a match. Matching candidates to a job and a company is a
skill involving a little bit of luck. Remember, even after you have developed the skill, you cannot know everything and you will make a few
mistakes. On the whole, though, you should do a better job!

High-Maintenance Employees

Some employees are more difficult to deal with than others. They seem
to have more needs. Their lives seem to be more difficult and they
bring those problems to work. They don't work with their teammates
well and seem to require more attention from you.

How can you handle these employees? First of all, if you want to
keep them on your staff, they will definitely require more of your time.
Assess on a regular basis whether it is worth your effort. Each time
you make the decision to keep an employee, decide where and when
you will provide the extra time. It is an allocation of your management
resources and time that will not be available to your customers or
your other staff.

Decide on a focus. Do you want to help the employee to improve? Or
do you just want to keep the workplace on an even keel? If you want to
help them improve, part of your time will be spent talking with them
about changes. The changes in their behavior will be an important part
of their performance evaluation. You need to be clear about the behavior
they exhibit that has an impact on their work, since that is your *only*

interest. (You may be interested personally in helping them to improve as a person—but that is really outside of the scope of the workplace.)

You will want to focus on the behavior that will improve their performance: "Jane, working on this particular report requires concentration for accuracy; it might best be done early in the morning before the part-time employees come into the office and are distracting." Or, "Jane, I know that you enjoy talking with the part-time employees in the afternoon, but the result is that you do not get as much work done in the afternoon."

If you want to keep the office on an even keel, try to help the employee separate the office business from the personal business and keep the personal business to break time and lunch time. This helps them to keep their mind on professional work during working hours. You might say, "Jane, we all like hearing stories about a new restaurant in town, but if the discussion is held during break instead of during the workday, everyone can enjoy talking and it won't interrupt the office work." Or you might need to be very direct and say, "Jane, you have so many great stories, but everyone stops working to listen and then we can't meet our deadline; please save the stories for lunch and break time."

Sometimes it's helpful to attach the comment to an external source or a change coming from the outside. For example: "Jane, we seem to be having many more visitors in the office than we used to; we need to keep the personal conversations for lunch when visitors can't hear."

Another way to attach it to a change is to simply say that you really have a lot to do and a short time in which to do it. "Can we talk later about this?" is a good way to put Jane on redirect.

Sometimes this kind of intervention can be a great help to someone. You set the standard to the level you desire and teach them how to live up to it. It will actually help them sometimes to refrain from their emotional behavior or casual behavior during work hours. They will get more work accomplished and be proud of the results. Employees want to be valued. Help them to find a way to accomplish this, and you'll feel a sense of accomplishment, too.

If you are having a difficult time with an employee who regularly exhibits emotional behavior, you do not have to live with it. You can have a talk with them and discuss the behavior and what they plan to change in order to avoid that behavior. This helps to avoid finger-pointing and reasons why it happens. It will help to focus on the change that will bring about a different behavior. Of course, you will need to be calm and steady yourself during these talks. It's not easy.

Involving the Staff—When and Why

Many women operating small companies would like to create a state of democracy in their businesses.

This is an intriguing goal—but it's also a challenge. We tend to want to hear from everyone and let everyone have their say. Let's look at the situations that require some planning in order for this approach to be successful.

There are many decisions each day that need to be made quickly, efficiently, and in coordination with suppliers, subcontractors, and clients. An owner knows that there is limited time to satisfy everyone's need for answers and makes many decisions during the course of the day on the spot. There is no time for a consensus on these issues.

A different type of involvement can come during meetings with the employees. There are several types of meetings and being clear about which one you are having can help you to be successful with the outcome. If you are having a meeting to provide information to the group, and to answer their questions about that information, you will be doing the talking. If you are having a meeting to brainstorm about solutions to a problem, you will want everyone to participate and provide their ideas. You may even want to come to a consensus, or to choose one of their ideas. It is, however, up to you to make the decision about which answer or idea is the best for the company.

If you are having the meeting to obtain information from the group, you will be asking the questions and they will provide the details or answers. This kind of meeting is to gather information and you might want to make notes about the ideas so that they all see you are genuinely interested in the answers and will take them into consideration when you make a decision or a change.

Penny, a printer and Boardroom Group member, was always afraid to have a meeting with her employees. She was afraid that no matter what kind of meeting she had planned that the employees would use the time to express their anger at whatever was not working at the time. She did not think that the meeting would turn out okay because the employees would only want to use the time for "bitch sessions" and not for the good of the company.

This is all the more reason to have a plan for the meeting. Announce the plan, have an agenda that you review at the beginning of the meeting, and tell the group that you will be following the agenda. If they have any other questions or topics you will write them on the blank poster on the wall and if there is time you will add them to the end of the agenda. If not, they will become part of the agenda of the next meeting. (This will give you bonus time to work on the answers.)

It will help you if you decide ahead of time from which area of the operation of the company you would like to have input. Which area of the operation is clearly an owner responsibility? To keep your owner-ship from being at risk you must be clear about which types of deci-sions could affect the viability of the company and which decisions could be made several different ways for the company to still succeed. If you can write these answers on two columns on a lined pad, you will have made great strides in understanding which is which.

Handling Performance Evaluations

It is time to evaluate the performance of your two employees. One is full time and one is part time; it doesn't matter, both employees need to have an evaluation. Employees need to have feedback. Never mind that you tell them all the time that they are doing a good job. For an employee, nothing is a greater reward than to receive in writing an evaluation that says he or she is doing an outstanding job, above the target expected. Examples demonstrating how the supervisor knew that you were doing an outstanding job are even better. Therefore, a form that provides room for the examples is a better evaluation form than one that doesn't.

If you have ever been evaluated using a form from 20 or more years ago, you probably remember it. It never worked quite right. It said: "How do you rank this employee on volume of work? Poor, Average, or Good?" It further said: "How do you rank this employee on accuracy of work? Poor, Average, or Good?" If this is the form you have in your files today, I urge you to throw it away.

I'll show you a form that really works to evaluate an employee's performance. Here's what it does:

- Shows the areas of the job where the employee is on target
- Enables you both to decide together how to improve any areas of work that are below target
- Allows you to review together any areas of training still needed
- Lets the employee have a place to write their comments

The most important part of this employee performance evaluation is that it provides an easy format to follow to have lots of conversation. It is the conversation between the two people that is the most valuable. This form requires input from the supervisor in order to evaluate with examples about each job result area. This is why it's the best communication tool.

The other important part of this form is that it comes directly from the job description. The job result areas move directly to the performance evaluation form. Now the employee can be evaluated specifically on job result areas—just the way it should be.

Get your job description and copy the title, purpose of the position, and job result areas to the appropriate part of the form. You will then be ready to complete the form. This will all be done prior to the evaluation itself, and it will make your life so much easier.

Following is a sample evaluation form that I have recommended to many owners. You may copy it and use it for your business.

Get Prepared

To prepare for the evaluation, make an appointment with the employee. They need to know that you will be conducting their evaluation and the approximate time that they will need to be meeting with you. If they need to bring anything to the meeting, let them know. If you expect them to bring any questions about their job, let them know what to think about and be prepared to talk about.

You need to have the completed form ready for the evaluation and to have two copies: the original for you and a copy for the employee to look at. The place needs to be a confidential location without interruptions.

EVALUATION PERFORMANCE

Name _____

Area of Responsibility:

_____

_____

_____

_____

Evaluation:

_____

_____

_____

_____

_____

_____

Rating: _____

Area of Responsibility:

_____

_____

_____

_____

Evaluation:

_____

_____

_____

_____

_____

_____

Rating: _____

EVALUATION PERFORMANCE *(continued)*

Overall Purpose of Position or Responsibility:

_____

_____

_____

Overall Evaluation of Performance:

_____

_____

_____

Overall Rating: _____

Training Completed and Planned (Internal and External):

_____

_____

_____

Major Needs for Job Changes, Promotions, etc.:

_____

_____

_____

Supervisor's Signature: _____ Date: _____

Employee Comments:

_____

_____

_____

_____

This evaluation of performance has been discussed with me, and I have received a copy.

Employee's Signature: _____ Date: _____

So, where do you start? First, welcome them. Tell them how pleased you are to have this time to talk about their job and their role with the company. Tell them that you have arranged to be free for as long as needed so that you can talk about any topics that they wish. For some employees, this is the only time each year they feel it is an appropriate time to ask questions or to share their own opinions. So, this is a very important appointment for them. Treat the entire meeting with a great deal of respect. Think about every part of it from the employee's point of view as well as your own.

Next, review with them the form that you will be using. They will be very curious about their rating, so you'll need to review the top page with the rating explanations first. It won't help them to know that they received an "on target" for one job result area if they don't know what "on target" means. Explain that the "on target" rating is the rating that is expected in everyone's job. If every person in the company received an "on target" in every job result area, the company would be in very good shape. It takes six to 12 months to learn a new job well enough to be "on target."

There are two higher rating areas:

- "Above target" can be achieved through very hard work and only after some longer period of time of employment.
- The "significantly above target" would only be achieved by an employee who had been with the company long enough and had worked diligently to achieve this rating in one area of their work. Most employees would not achieve this level. But the level is there to reward the absolutely outstanding employee.

There are two lower rating areas:

- "Below target" means the employee needs to understand and learn some additional skills in order to achieve the "on target" status. The supervisor needs to work with the employee to understand exactly what will be required in order to move up to the acceptable "on target" evaluations in that area.

- "Significantly below target" in an important job result area means that the employee's job is in jeopardy. The employee fails to meet the minimum standards of the job and without improvement will not be able to stay. This performance classification for one job result area should *never* be a surprise. There should have been several meetings about this situation already. The employee should be working diligently in conjunction with the supervisor in order to improve in this area and to keep his or her job.

A woman business owner named Becky got ready to provide her first employee evaluation with the new form. She had completed all of the parts. She had worked diligently to provide two or more solid, specific examples in each of the job result areas so that the employee would understand exactly what she was doing well and what she needed to improve on.

Well, Becky got ready to start talking and forgot to explain what the standards of performance meant. This is a matter of interpretation and it is important that it is communicated consistently to each employee. You will see why in just a minute.

The first job result area was in the area of phone communications. The employee received an "on target" and several examples of her good work. She was devastated. She immediately began to look unhappy. How could this have happened to her? Only "on target"–and she had worked so hard!

Becky asked her what was wrong and she said, "Well the way I see it, I could have received SAT (significantly above target) and that would have been like an A. Or I could have received AT (above target) and that would have been like a B. But you gave me OT (on target) and that is only a C."

You've got to *first* share with the employee the standards of performance and what they mean. Your employees have to understand the meaning that you decide upon and your explanations must be consistent from one employee to another.

Providing carefully planned evaluations is an important part of the management process. Employees deserve to know where they stand. They deserve to know what they are doing well and why and what they need to improve on and why. This will help to build the strong team you need in order to be a viable, valuable company—and to free yourself up for future greatness, remember?

Working with your employees and talking with them in an employer/employee relationship is an important part of the workplace culture. If you do not act like an employer and provide good, objective evaluations, the employees will soon learn (or believe) that it is more important to be liked by the boss than it is to do a good job.

What About Raises?

Every employee wants to know how raises will be handled. If it wasn't discussed at hiring time, they soon will be wondering. In a small company, it's really difficult to have a set policy about raises because you may not know whether you're going to have a profitable enough year.

In a larger company, it's good to have an established time of the year to look at employee wages and decide if raises are needed for "cost of living" or for merit purposes.

Whatever the situation, your employees will be happier if they know how you're planning to deal with raises. You could set a time, maybe six months following the evaluation process, within which a raise might be possible. Employees are rarely paid exactly right all the time; some are overpaid and some underpaid. A review or raise period is your only opportunity to fix the inequities due to incorrect starting wages or employee growth and development.

Look at employees who are underpaid: Should they receive a small increase to reduce the inequity? How many raises would be given? What is the annual cost to the company to provide these merit increases? Can the company afford to make the raises? If so, the meeting to tell an employee about the increase are as important as the increase itself.

Set up private meetings. Think through the issue of what you will say if other employees who are not receiving an increase confront you about why they did not receive their fair share. Some employees believe that all raises should be made by seniority, not by merit. Be prepared to explain the merit system and how employees can learn new skills in order to become more valuable to the company.

Handing out raises can be a very happy time, but be careful to explain what the raise really means. I know personally that a 3 percent raise I had given an employee was more valuable (since it was the only one given) than an 8 percent raise at another time when the employee was expecting 15 percent. Explain what the raise means in terms of the situation. If you can't compensate an employee as you really want to, be honest and tell them. They will appreciate that you want to give them more and that you will do so when it is possible.

Remind your employees that salary information is confidential. If they have any questions, they can come to you, but they should not discuss salary with other employees. I've found that this will at least limit the number of people they will talk with.

What to Do When You've Made a Mistake

I've heard it a hundred times: "I have tried everything that I know to teach the new employee her job and it just isn't working. No matter what I do, she cannot perform the job to the standards that are needed by the company."

The first thing you should be sure about is whether the employee is in on this little secret. It should never be a surprise that the employee is not performing at the standards expected. The employee should have been in several meetings with you to talk about it. The first meetings can be informal, but later they would be formal meetings to talk about the performance problem and what can be changed in order to achieve the correct results. Remember—it is always about what *can be changed* in order to improve performance. We are not pointing fingers at the past. Obviously if things stay the same, the results will be the same.

The first meeting will be to clearly state the problem and to discuss solutions to the problem. The employee needs to suggest the solution that they think would work. It will be of little help for you to tell the employee how to fix the problem; you did that before and they didn't change. They need to suggest a solution and if you think that it would not work, write it down anyway and ask for some more ideas.

When they come to the very idea that you agree might work, suggest that this sounds like a very good solution, and would they like to try it? After their commitment, schedule a follow-up meeting to see if the problem was fixed. If it was, thank the employee for their help in solving the problem. If the solution didn't work, go through the process again. If you are meeting for the second time or the third time and the problem has not been solved, it is possible that this employee is not going to be able to solve the problem. It is entirely possible that this employee was not a good match for the job in the first place.

Every state has laws for different sizes of companies regarding the firing of an employee. In this case, let's say we have checked the employment law with our attorney and are planning to fire the employee.

In Boardroom Groups, I suggest some standards for firing. The goal is to make an employee happier when they leave the office after being fired than they were when they came into the office. How do we do that?

First, we are at this point sure that the employee is not the right match for the job—and we have some idea about the good skills and abilities this employee *does* have and could bring to a different job.

We then arrange for a talk with the employee at a good location and a good time. I know that I am going to fire the employee but *no one* else does. The time might be 10 A.M. and we go to a conference room that has no windows. I might expect the meeting to take about two hours and the person will be leaving during lunch hour when no one is at their desk. Another arrangement might be a 3 P.M. meeting.

Next, we prepare to stay with this employee for as long as necessary until they are happy with the change because they truly see that it is the right thing to do for them.

In my many years as a manager, I've discovered that when you have tried to help an employee for weeks or months, then tell them you have to make a change and that perhaps they need (deserve?) to be in a different position with a different company, you really get their attention. At that moment in time, you can provide career counseling, ideas about the kind of job where they can excel, when no one ever could have provided those ideas before and held their attention.

During the one to three hours I suggest business owners spend in a firing process, we tell them to talk about everything that the employee could do in a different job (one that you do not have available) and could excel. Every employee deserves to excel and to be valued.

This kind of approach to releasing an employee who has not performed does more good than you can imagine. It helps the employee find the right kind of job next time and it also says to your existing employees that you value everyone enough to even spend three hours with the person that you are firing because you care about them, because you want them to be a good fit in a position that they love where they will be valued by their employer.

Employees want to stay and to perform for supervisors and owners who really care about them. It can help to build a stronger team of dedicated employees when you do everything that you can to help them succeed, even when it is outside of the company.

Back to the Drawing Board

Once you've helped an employee leave your company successfully, you can then begin to start your search process again. Only this time, you'll be much wiser, much more apt to look for what you really need and not with the hope of turning someone you like into something they may not be. So, fine-tune your job description if necessary, and get going on writing your classified ad or calling recruiters to find the ideal person to join your team—your family of workers that are helping to propel you toward future success.

◿ IDEA CENTER ◺

How to Read a Resume for Results

When you have a stack of resumes piled up on your desk, all of them looking exactly the same, how can you tell which candidates are the straw and which are the gold?

Start with reading them for a sense of whether the person behind the resume has a background in the specific area you're looking to fill.

If you need a strong salesperson, look for numbers. By what percentages did this person boost sales in a particular territory? How did they measure their success? Did they consistently win awards and recognition for their efforts?

Other things I suggest you look for:

- Does this person seem to know how to promote him- or herself? Katina once hired an office administrator because she understood the nature of Katina's business (self-promotion)— she had placed an ad of her own and it caught Katina's eye. Despite a stack of resumes from qualified candidates, this woman turned out to be a winner because she understood what was at the core of the business.

- Are there lots of time gaps—and how are they explained? If a woman took time off to raise a family, but is now ready to return to work, how does she explain it in the cover letter or resume? If there are huge gaps of unaccounted-for time, call and ask the candidate or move on to the next one.

- If the resume is a functional format (one with a list of skills in one place and a list of jobs in another, without correlation), we suggest you either ask for a new resume in a reverse-chronological format or simply pass. Often, functional formats seek to hide things—and if you can't get straight information about a candidate at this stage, it may never happen. For all you know, all of the great accomplishments happened at an earlier job—and the candidate's been a real slouch since then.

- Does the cover letter seem to focus on your needs—or is it all about what the candidate wants? This might be a telling sign in terms of management-style compatibility. Do you want an employee who is dedicated to your success—or who constantly asks for raises and bonuses?

- Is the resume descriptive in terms of what the candidate actually did at each company, or does it merely skim the surface?

- Are references freely provided? This could make your preinterview process and screening much easier.

⊠ Idea Center ⊠

Writing a Help-Wanted Ad

Desperately seeking the ideal employee? Want only top-notch candidates? Write yourself a well-targeted classified ad, and you'll narrow down your search considerably.

What do you put into your classified ad? Naturally, you'll use the information you compiled for your job description. List the job results areas by category, and be as specific as your ad will allow.

One other important consideration: If you have a small company and the inability to deal with many phone calls, use a post office box or specify that you will not accept phone inquiries regarding this position.

You are the only one who can manage the hiring process, so take the time to design it in a way that makes you feel most comfortable.

Be careful not to get taken in by a glitzy resume. Take the time to ask yourself questions such as, "How do I expect this employee to earn what they're worth? What kind of return on my investment will I see within the first six months?" If you can see that an office administrator will save you 16 hours per week, and those are 16 hours that can bring in more business at $45 to $65 per hour, you'll recoup your investment.

⊠ Back to the Boardroom ⊠

Value the Person as Well as the Performance

I believe that you need to value the person as well as the performance.
Here's an example of what I mean:

• Situation 1: A supervisor seems to focus on the person instead of the performance. When the employee walks into the room, the supervisor says, "How have you been? How was your weekend? Whatever happened to your problem with your washing machine?" The employee answers the personal questions and then asks a question about the day's schedule. The supervisor provides a brief, cursory answer and then goes back to work. No focus on the work performance at all. No congratulations about the productivity the week before. What is really important here?

• Situation 2: The supervisor seems to focus on the performance instead of the person. When the employee walks into the room, the supervisor says, "How did you finish up last week? Did the productivity reach the goal that we set? Will everyone do his or her share? Did anything get in your way of duplicating the work this week?" No focus on the employee at all. No hello, how was your weekend? Might as well be a robot for all management cares. What is really important now?

It is important for the supervisor to have a balanced approach to performance and to the person. If you do not focus on performance, the employee will think the key is whether the supervisor likes him or her. And then they will spend all of their time making sure that the supervisor likes them (and doesn't like anyone else).

If you do not focus on the person, the employee will know that you do not value them—only the work. They aren't needed; someone else could do the job. Even if you don't intend it, this may be what the employee believes (and acts on).

Here is an example of balance. On a Monday you may inquire whether the employee had a good weekend and whether her son has returned to school after an illness. Then, after a moment, ask if they would like to meet at 10 A.M. to review the week's deadlines.

Management Issues: Why You May Be a Better Manager Than You Think

Norma J. Rist

------ Secret 8 ------

You are already a better manager than you think.

What is true management of your business? How do you know when your management of the business is successful?

Women measure success differently than men. For a male business owner, success might be defined strictly based on financial results. Most men have a bottom-line mentality.

Women, on the other hand, will cite a number of ways to measure their success. They value relationships as well as the numbers. The significant change that they are looking for is control over their future, lifestyle choices, the opportunity to take their own risks and reap their own rewards. Owning and managing their own business is a means to this end.

In the target marketing classes that I teach for women, I always ask, "Who wants to be wealthy?" About one woman in 10 will tell me that she wants to be wealthy; the rest tell me they want financial security.

When you look at everything that you might want out of your business—to be a boss, develop business knowledge, meet interesting people, have more credibility, build a better mousetrap, provide jobs for people, donate to a social cause, or provide a new service—you might, like lots of other women, find that you have a long list of "wants."

Boardroom Group women take my list of 30 possible wants and rate each one from 1 through 10, with 10 being very important, 5 moderately important, and 1 not very important. When they finish, they are amazed at the number of tens. They want *a lot!* One thing that is a universal desire is that they want to follow their own values. This could be another whole book by itself.

Measuring success, then, is more difficult for women; they have expectations at many levels. We'll try to cover a number of these in this chapter, but keep in mind that every owner decides which measure of success is more important than another.

Managing Your Business

Your business is made up of a lot of assets: name, good reputation, location, working capital, raw materials, finished goods, supplies, equipment, human talent, systems and procedures, and all of the customers you have served. These resources are limited and must be protected with good management or oversight provided by the owners and the managers.

As a controller for one of a group of Pepsi Cola franchises, when the corporation introduced a better job description, I saw clearly that each controller was responsible for the assets of the company. There it was—in writing! I began to see what it actually meant. I always knew that I was responsible for tracking and reporting inventory and loss, if any. Now, I realized that I was *also* responsible for the system to control the inventory so that there would never be a loss above standard. This clarity encouraged better management.

Building standards into the job description is a way to make sure that the assets of the company are protected and that managers will share responsibility with the owners, or shareholders, to protect those assets.

If you're a woman who's owned and operated a business for more than a year, you may have already learned many skills and techniques needed to manage or to properly utilize all of the available assets of the company. You may be looking for new techniques or additional, more complex skills. These could involve:

- Finding the talent, materials, and resources needed by the company;
- Hiring the people, purchasing the supplies or equipment needed;
- Supervising the use of the talent and/or materials so that they bring the most value to the company;
- Training other employees to understand proper management of talent or resources;
- Always looking for better ways to utilize the resources and assets; and
- Planning for the talent or resources needs of the company in the future.

Managing Assets

Your company already has lots of assets in place, and these are items you may use on a daily basis. Hard assets include all of the furniture and equipment purchased for use in the operation of your business. Desks, calculators, computers, cell phones, pagers, fax machines, and copiers are small (yet critical) hard assets; it would be almost impossible to do business without them. Selection of these technical support devices has become more difficult with competing companies demonstrating that their product is the best. Finding the right fit for these helpful pieces of equipment and finding it at the right time becomes more important—we depend upon them for efficiency and good customer service.

Larger companies need buildings, a fleet of trucks and manufacturing machinery; these are large hard assets or things that are expensive to purchase and expensive to replace. The hard assets must be selected carefully, purchased wisely, and protected so they can be used by the company through their expected lifespan. These are also the items the bank looks at as collateral in the event that you need to borrow money, since they could potentially sell the items to recoup their investment should you be unable to pay the loan.

In addition to the hard assets, consider the small supply items that are used in your day-to-day business: paper, ink cartridges/toner, pens, letterhead, envelopes, cards, marketing materials, postage, etc. The cost of these supply items may seem small, but squandering them is like throwing money down the drain. Someone in the company, either you or a person you've chosen to act as an operations manager, need to be aware of the cost and the use of these supplies and manage them well. That person should know when, where, and how to purchase the items you need to keep you in business every day.

Inventory is another category of assets that needs to be managed. An inventory of raw materials (flowers for a florist, as an example) needs to be purchased and managed wisely or all of the profit built into the price will be lost as flowers are damaged or lost.

Picture each item of inventory as a number of dollar bills—the rose might be $1 and the orchid might be $4. If roses fall on the floor or if an orchid is damaged because of the storage container, you lose as many dollars as the flowers are worth.

As your company grows, you'll need management reports to show you that all of the raw materials were used in producing a saleable product. You'll keep track of the number ordered for inventory, the number needed for sales, and the difference between the two, adjusted by inventory change. If you don't already have reports like this in place, ask your CPA to show you some sample management reports for controlling inventory.

Management reports are critical for the information that they provide; they are also important because they focus on a situation. Just the focus itself can make a difference. Bertha Jenkins, president of Liniform Services, Inc., a well-run 75-year-old laundry told me one day that they were buying too many hangers for the uniforms. Employees didn't seem to keep them picked up from the customers and in the plant so they would be available for reuse. She put in place a very small payment for the return of this supply and the results were amazing. It was not necessarily the value of the returned hangers that brought about the results, but rather the focus on the situation.

Managing Resources

Relationships between the company and outside suppliers and professionals need to be managed, too. Researching your suppliers, building a good relationships with them, and knowing their business so that you can have meaningful discussions with them about the future will help to protect your business during challenging times. Suppliers have lots of knowledge in the industry and may know about an expert at a time you need one, or they may know about trends that are important to your future.

Any professional services you enlist—a business attorney, employment law attorney, management consultant, or training consultant—need to be carefully selected and then managed. In this case you are making sure that the needed expertise is appropriately provided, timely, and that fees are as agreed.

Managing Employees

Most women owners think about managing employees as the primary responsibility in business management, and it is indeed a key part.

Identifying a job position, writing a job description, finding applicants, screening applicants, selecting good prospects, hiring the best candidate, and training/supervising/evaluating an employee are all important parts of the management process. Employees are a key ingredient of an organization—they help form the entity itself, and often represent the company in the owner's absence. Sometimes, they are the first connection your customers have with your company. But managing your employees is just one part of your overall management.

No Room for Mistakes

A small company cannot afford a large mistake in the purchase or use of any assets. Imagine hiring a person who worked at 50 percent of the requirements of the job. Who would do the other 50 percent? There isn't room for slow work, there isn't room for inventory loss, and there isn't room for supplies going down the drain. A small company makes a small profit and any loss will come right out of the bottom line, perhaps making the difference between a profitable company and an unprofitable one.

> Managing a business is the same thing as managing the assets, resources, and talent needed for a company to run. They are inseparable.

Styles of Management

The truth is, there are almost as many styles of management as there are styles of people. But there are a few basic styles of management that we can look at for the purpose of understanding how women choose the style they use to manage their company.

The management textbook used in Business Organization 101 in the 1950s and 1960s showed only one style of organization and one style of management to fit that organization. Most people who worked for companies between 1950 and 1960 have encountered this particular organizational structure: the triangle with the boss at the top and the employees below. If the company got bigger, then the triangle got bigger, but the boss always stayed at the top. This organizational structure and management structure has prevailed for many years.

This factory-type organization was created in the military and has been used very similarly to the way the military uses it. In the military, the higher-ranking person tells people what to do and they are required to do it without asking questions.

In a military model, then, all of the boxes on the organization chart have names of jobs on them, not names of people. This is because it doesn't matter who fills the job, as long as it is a trained person. This structure was adopted by manufacturing companies and later by most companies in corporate America.

The problem is, women do not always adapt to this organization style or management style. According to the National Foundation for Women Business Owners, frustrations with the corporate environment have provided significant motivation for women to become entrepreneurs. If we look back into history, we can see more clearly why the military model doesn't always work for women.

History of Women's Role in Organizations

In this country, the role of women in an organization started on the farm. Farm organizations were built around the family—and all members of the family, from the father to the mother to the children—played a key role in the success of the farm.

The woman was an equal partner in this organization and the contribution that she made was every bit as important as the contribution of the man. Nobody pulled rank, since everyone's services were needed in different areas.

My maternal grandparent's cousin and her husband were farmers in Jamestown, New York. Bessie and George made their living raising dairy cows. Much like his neighbors, George was outside tending to chores at 4 A.M., while Bessie was in the kitchen cooking at the same time. The water was in the pump room next to the kitchen/pantry. A huge wood-burning stove was in the central room and provided all the heat for the house. Breakfast included three kinds of meat, two potatoes, cereal, fresh milk, and homemade biscuits and was served at 8 A.M. As soon as this meal was eaten, Bessie started working on a similar lunch. The day included cooking, washing, cleaning, and mending; it required 14-hour days, seven days a week. This role was a partnership; her tasks were integral to the success of the farm.

Other partnerships existed in the general store or other small independent businesses. Any product or service that was needed could be provided by a man and woman working together to make a living. (My grandmother Susanna Lockhart came to the United States as a young woman from Ireland, married, and operated a general store all of her life.) The families helped each other, as a team, to provide for the needs of the community in addition to the needs of their own families.

Then came the day that men left farms to work in the factory, and the women—for the first time—were dependent upon men for survival. They stayed home and raised children, but were no longer a partner in the business of earning a livelihood.

When men left the factory to go to war, women had an opportunity and a responsibility to work in the factory. They supported the war effort and also earned a living for their family—only intending to be there until their husbands returned from the war.

Their role at the factory was quite different than that of their husbands. They simply wanted to get the job done, and they did it the same way that they did it on the farm or in the general store, by working together and pooling their resources in any way necessary. They were not trying to get promoted or to change the organization, since they were looking at their jobs as a temporary situation. This experience contributed to a cultural difference between working women and working men. The women continued to see the workplace more like the farm or the store. They built relationships and got the job done.

Men had a different experience. When they came back from the war and returned to the growing factories, the organization took on more aspects of the military. Larger numbers of employees, more layers of management and a method of control from the top—the boss—down to the employees.

The experience women had in the factories told them something, though. They knew that they could do the work; they didn't have to stay home and rely on someone else to provide for their livelihood. When some of these women re-entered the work force, in order to help with family finances, they entered an organization that was different from the team approach that they had formed earlier. Before, when there was a problem in the factory, everyone standing close enough would look at the situation and make suggestions until one made enough sense to try.

Before, when the workers had a larger order to complete and not enough time, the women would figure out who could help with the other women's children so there would be enough production hours. Now they found that the orders came from the top and you did as you were told or you were fired. The military model was essential on the battlefield but women were uncomfortable with it in the workplace. Men were telling them what to do and their opinion was no longer valued.

My mother, Neva Tompsett, was smart enough to have gone to college, but her father said no, only his son could go to college. She was hard-working enough that she could probably have gone through law school; instead, she was sent to secretarial school and even though she was not in the factory, the same situation applied to her in the office. Men told the secretaries what to do and the women's opinion was not sought or valued. Much later in life as a secretary/bookkeeper in a small law practice, her ability was obvious to the attorneys.

Many women became uncomfortable with this environment; that's why so many women today prefer to work in an independent setting, as their own boss, or in a very small, friendly company, instead of the military model.

Women's Management Style

Women tend to prefer a management style that resembles the family model. They want to make sure that all members of the team are satisfied with their jobs and that they enjoy their role with the team. This team approach is a holistic, more nurturing approach to management. It values each individual as a member of the team and encourages development. This style promotes good will and supports a positive business environment.

The downside to this style of management is apparent with growth. A woman will often start a small company and have one to 10 employees all reporting to her. As she adds new employees, each day becomes increasingly difficult, because growth in this model is challenging.

The business owner will not even entertain the idea of doubling in size because she is already tired of "taking care of" so many people. The nurturing model, then, only works for the very small company. When growth is needed in order to continue achieving goals or to become profitable, the model needs to be changed.

The team approach is a good substitute for the family model. In a team approach, the owner stops being the supervisor for one to 10 employees and instead creates work teams.

For example, if there are 15 professional employees, they form three work teams of five each. The work for each of these three teams can be assigned as follows:

1. Someone on the team provides coordination (as opposed to supervision). The coordinator keeps track of the responsibilities and accomplishments of the groups and this information is reported to the owner or president.
2. When the team needs help, the coordinator arranges for the owner or other appropriate staff employees, say the bookkeeper, to help them with a particular need.

This team approach can be very comfortable for you if you do not want to create an old-fashioned hierarchy. Becky Dorner, president of Becky Dorner & Associates, a nutrition consulting company, was growing at a fairly steady pace. Her nursing home contracts were increasing and at the same time she had a growing catalog of products for the nursing home industry.

She was beginning to speak nationally more frequently and had an increased travel schedule. Becky was looking for a way to restructure her organization so that she did not have to provide direct supervision to 20-plus employees. She introduced to her staff the model we just outlined and they put it in place in a matter of weeks. It was a good fit with her professional staff.

Make no mistake about it though, the old military model is easier and quicker! It is the quickest thing in the world to just tell someone to do something—in effect, command it to be done, and fire them if they do not perform.

All of the other models of management require more knowledge, more training, more delegating, and more monitoring of employees and their accomplishments. It is harder to work with every individual and to help them to become all that they want to be, to grow to the heights that they want to achieve.

Be prepared for more work if you want the more holistic types of business organization and you want to do it well. You will need every bit of management skill and a determined effort to make this style work for you and for your company. Successful results will be a significant achievement.

Creating a Workplace That Matches the Vision

What does the management vision look like and how do you create a workplace to fit that vision? If you're like most women business owners, you'll want to provide a workplace that is supportive and has room for people's other lives. Since women have significant demands on them in their other lives (as mother, spouse, or caregiver for parents), a woman business owner often wants to provide a workplace setting that cares about these other roles. It is a "family-friendly" environment that has some give and take built in, perhaps flex-time, perhaps just the opportunity to take time away from work without any penalty when an emergency occurs.

When my son, Brian, was born in 1972, there were no laws requiring pregnancy leave. I had saved my one week of vacation for two years in a row in order to have two weeks together at maternity time for a C-section. I recall being tired for a year; certainly, I needed more time off in order to return at full strength, but at that time your job would be in jeopardy if you didn't work like the men did. Much later, I realized that management provided six weeks of recovery for a hernia operation—we indeed had some catching up to do for pregnancy benefits!

The National Foundation of Women Business Owners reports that "women-owned firms are more likely than all businesses to offer flextime, tuition reimbursement and, at a much smaller size, profit sharing, as employee benefits. Among firms with 10 or more employees that don't have a retirement plan, women business owners are discussing the issue of retirement more than men business owners, and a greater share of these women intend to implement a retirement plan soon."

Delegating, Female Style

Another cold, hard fact about women business owners is that they tend to keep too much work for themselves. For them, delegating is challenging, and unless it is learned in a formal training environment, you might be inclined to go about it in a hit-or-miss fashion. Why? Because if you delegate some work to someone else and they fail to do it well, it could be a reflection on you.

This inclination seems to stem from a cultural belief that women have to be perfect; we cannot fail in any way. When I thought about this trait that is common to many women and asked why, it seemed to come from our need to "be there" for other people; perhaps this is part of the value system we have. Men are valued for what they do; women are valued for what they do for others, and cannot do things for others unless they are "there for them." This carries over into our business—trying to be all things to all people—not delegating for fear someone else won't do it as well.

I called a woman named Gail and asked if we could meet. She was busy for many weeks, so I asked for a date about six weeks in the future. Gail asked me to call her back in four weeks; she didn't want to make an appointment and then find that one of her clients, employees, suppliers, or family members needed her at that time.

To have an appointment *and* be needed elsewhere causes a woman some anxious moments. Women see a conflicting appointment as just that—a conflict. Many find it difficult to call and change an appointment, because in their minds the other party will be upset about the change. Most women need to learn that it is fairly easy to say, "I had a change in my schedule. Could we move our appointment to next week?" and that there are fewer ramifications.

The need to be perfect, to alleviate conflicts, gets in the way of delegating. But it is only by delegating that you can free up enough of your own time to maximize your highest-level skills.

Let's look at the delegating process. If you are preparing to delegate some task to an employee or subcontractor, create a sample dialogue to help you prepare for the meeting. Here is a checklist to help you get started:

- Review the responsibility that you are delegating.
- Talk about the details of this new work and your expectations.
- Ask for suggestions, feedback, or questions.
- Make sure that you listen and that they know that you listened.
- Ask for an indication that they are committed to this work.
- Offer your help if they should need it.
- Tell them that you are confident they will be successful.

If you treat delegating as an important part of the business development, you'll get better results from those that you delegate to. Mary Beth Harper, owner of Harper & Co. Communications, has a number of contracts for speeches, press releases, and other marketing/communication materials for local organizations. She uses writers and graphic designers as subcontractors to produce work; it must be timely, accurate, and meet or exceed the needs of the client. Her personal communication to the members of her virtual team must be clear and concise. She learned to delegate in a large corporation and uses her skills daily to be certain that Harper & Co. produces exceptional communications and thus the intended results.

Terri Maurer, president of Maurer Design Group (and president of the American Society of Interior Designers), utilizes numerous subcontractors in order to create wonderful work space for her commercial design clients. Her knowledge of design is one-half of the key to success. The careful delegation and tracking of results is essential in order to bring in a contract on time, on bid, and "wow" the client.

Kay DeBolt, owner of The Corporate Gopher, provides a great delivery service for small businesses in Akron and the surrounding area. She has learned to wear every hat in the business, from finding the customers to making the deliveries and mailing the invoices.

Kay is busy six to seven days a week, an average of 10 hours a day. She has reached the point in her business where she needs to hire other people to make the deliveries. It could seem easy: find a person with a car, tell them where to pick up and deliver the item. But there is so much more to the process.

Kay needs to delegate the duties well enough that the employee understands every part of her exceptional delivery process. Her employee doesn't just represent Corporate Gopher; he or she also represents the customer. The delivery person needs to be taught about possible delays and how to still be on time. The delivery needs to be made to the correct person and include good wishes from Kay's customer, the shipper.

All of this training will be essential in order to have someone else making deliveries for Kay and her small business customers. She will be challenged to find the right person, provide good training, and delegate new types of work and details on a daily basis.

Think about the work you process each day and whether any part of it can or should be delegated. This will be an important part of the growth of the organization; it will move you to the next stage—one where you are overseeing the processes of the business, not performing every single function of it.

Make a list of all of the things that you do. Put them into two groups: first, group the duties that you believe you must keep; second, group the duties that someone else could do if you delegated them properly. Doing the first group of duties, using your highest-level skills in your business for a greater proportion of each day, week, and month, will help you to grow a larger and more prosperous company.

Pam Williams, owner of Pam's Posies, has a staff of great floral arrangers on her team. Pam kept most of the management responsibilities on her own plate for a long time. One very busy season she delegated several ongoing management type duties to three members of her staff.

They not only performed well, they loved the new challenge. Pam came into the Boardroom Group that month and was so energized. She could spend more time working on plans for the future of her business because others were handling more of the day-to-day operations.

Organizational Charts

Here are some sample organizational charts you may find useful in the growth of your business.

The chart above shows an owner and three employees who report to the owner. This organization can function as a team or as an owner controlling most decisions by telling everyone what to do. Most women tend to use the team model, but even though they may draw the charts like the one above, they actually are using a model like the one below:

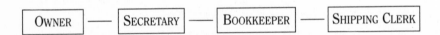

This model shows an inclination to treat everyone the same, a democratic organization where everyone's opinion is just as valuable as the others, including the owner. This model can be good, but if it is carried to the extreme it can be unwieldy. In that case the owner may be unable to make good decisions that benefit the company, because the others do not understand or do not agree.

When the owner needs to hire three more people to work in the shipping department and she was using a model like the first one, here is what the expanded chart looks like:

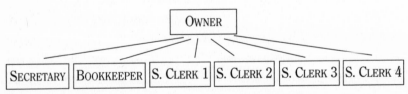

A woman owner will sometimes use a chart like this and still treat each person as a part of the team. This can get to be burdensome, and you can see why. With the owner at the top and everyone reporting to the owner, no one else is making decisions and the owner is taking care of everyone every day.

Now, let's look at an example of an organizational chart that indicates the typical triangle and one supervisor for the shipping department. The shipping supervisor handles some of the day-to-day transactions and this helps the owner to spend more time planning for the future. This model works and it can be very employee-supportive.

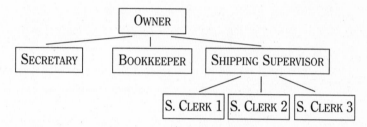

Some women avoid this model because they aren't out to build an empire. In fact, they probably just left some kind of an empire and don't want to own a company that resembles an organization that was cold, unfriendly, or lacking in support. Often, they think that these characteristics naturally go along with that pyramid organization chart.

A pyramid-type organization chart can be used to create an efficient and well-run business; below is a good model for a small growing company:

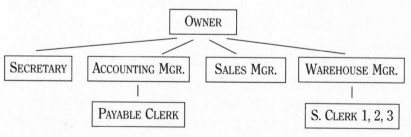

The employees listed below the owner are functional experts in accounting, sales, and operations. The employees in those departments report to the functional experts. This model works well because the functional experts can provide knowledge to the owner that the owner would not otherwise have time to learn. For instance, if you have a sales background, you might not need the sales manager as early as you would need the accounting and warehouse managers.

The great thing about the model is that each of the functional experts brings new knowledge to you and to the business every day. They read different business information, they belong to different associations and they think about how to improve that part of your business. You then have more time to plan for the future.

It is a tremendous step forward when you have good, trustworthy employees to handle the everyday stuff, while you set your sights on your goals, dreams, and visions. Having creative time to think about your business direction will enable you to draw the map that will get you there more quickly and easily.

Below is one final model of a team environment; one that is often more friendly for women owners who do not like the triangle version:

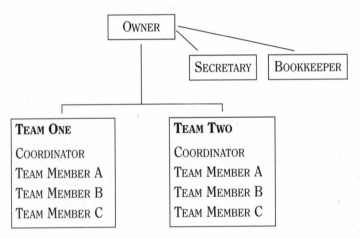

This model provides the owner with two teams and the coordinator for each team keeps records on the progress of the group including management reports for the owner. If the team needs help from the owner, or from the bookkeeper, they request the help. The owner monitors results based on the goals and standards in the management reports that were established at the time the teams were formed.

Picture this model in a service delivery company such as Web design. Pam Pierce, owner of Empowering You!, creates award-winning

Web site designs. Using a model such as the one above, each team would be responsible for a certain number of new clients and she could grow to any size by adding new teams.

Technology Supports Small Organizations

Many women—and you may be like them—prefer to limit their growth. They just want a small, friendly company that provides a good product or service and creates financial security. The future is embracing these smaller organizations that are able to respond to change very quickly. These business units understand customer needs, and are quick to develop customer relationships and respond to a market demand.

The technology of today permits a small company to look and act like a large firm; computers, e-mail, and the Internet work the same for a small company as they do for a large one, sometimes better. There has never been a more ideal time to start and grow a small business; never has there been a greater acceptance or a more level playing field. There is a great demand for good specialty work, the very thing that women do well.

Creating a Workplace That Works

Employees are people and they come to your workplace with all of their previous experience, attitudes, and expectations. Learning to supervise each person in a way that builds a team is a skill, a learned set of techniques. When you are a good supervisor—good for the company, good for the employees, and easy on yourself—you will be confident that you can handle any situation that tomorrow might bring.

Good managers focus on results and let the employee have some latitude about how to achieve the results. Know fully the strengths of members of your team and work with those strengths—build on them. Be aware of weaknesses only to be certain that those areas are checked or the work is reassigned.

Employees want to know that they have performed up to expectation. A good supervisor finds ways to tell employees that they have done a good job. Even long-term employees who have done a fine job for years want to know that they are appreciated. You can be leaving the building together and say, "Thanks for another good week; you always hold up your end of the work!"

Equipment, supplies, and even parking spaces become important when you don't have them. We used to joke that we needed another bookkeeper, but they wouldn't have a desk, a chair, or a calculator. When the work was overwhelming, we were willing to share our own desk, chair, and calculator. That's when you know that your staff is really busy–they will share anything. Be sure your employees have the equipment and supplies to get their job done efficiently. It shows that you value their time and energy.

Do you evaluate work and reassign when needed so that experienced, knowledgeable employees are kept busy doing the most difficult work? Not overwhelmed, just a good mix. The more training the employee has, the less he or she wants to do a large amount of entry-level work.

Talk with employees about what they see in their future. With women, talks about the future need to be fairly frequent because their lives change quickly based on circumstances. The woman who didn't want to learn a new job is now interested because her children are all at school or off to college. A woman who didn't ever want to change jobs and earn more money is now asking for the opportunity because she is single again and needs the income.

Be sure to evaluate your employees on a regular basis. Establish a timetable and follow it each year. It is demoralizing for an employee to expect an evaluation annually and have to wait 16 months. Whether or not a raise is part of the review meeting, the communication is essential for a good work environment.

Handle workplace problems faster, not slower. When an employee has a bad habit, like too many personal calls, the other employees usually know it before you do. Soon they resent it that you have not handled the situation. Be on the lookout for workplace problems and arrange meetings with employees who have performance problems or bad habits. Find out what can be done to solve the problem. It will help to keep the morale high.

The New Employee: What to Do First

There is only one first day for a new employee. It's essential that you plan ahead and provide the best possible introduction to the job. This day will set the stage for the beginning of his or her career with your company. If you have carefully screened, selected, and hired an employee that you hope will stay for 10 years—then what should you do to start the first day of that 10 years?

Often, you are not the person who will spend the day with the new employee. Even if you will be with her for an hour or two, usually someone in her department will be helping you to acquaint the new employee with the building, the staff, the way things work. Choose this person very, very wisely. This person will be sharing attitudes with the new employee and you want to expand the good culture in your organization, not the attitude of one person who is still upset about lunch break being changed to 30 minutes instead of one hour.

Decide ahead of time what you want the first day to include. It is a good day to meet and see other departments. Once you start giving them a daily workload, it is difficult for them to see where the work came from or where it goes when it moves to another area. Create an agenda with a good overview of the company. What will the employee think about when they go home that night? Make sure the day included a good overview of all of the right things. I remember arranging the date for a new employee to start based on the vacation return to work date of the employee who would provide the orientation. That's how important the first day can be.

Learning New Things: Some Employees Love It, Some Don't

Some people will want to continually learn new things on their job; others will want to learn how to do a good job and then just keep doing the same thing for 10 years. It is important to know which employee is which. It took me about five years in my corporate position to learn that I needed an appropriate mix of both kinds of employees. I thought that because I wanted to learn every job in the office and then start learning every job in sales that everyone was like that. Not so.

Some employees look forward to the period of time when they excel in their job without learning new things. If you have this situation, you need to be fairly accurate during the hiring process to describe the length of time it will take to learn all of the components of the position.

I hired a wonderful payroll manager, Lyn Brown, and told her that it would take at least a year to learn all of the parts of the salaried, hourly, and contractual wages as well as all of the benefits for each. I was honest so that she would not be concerned at six months when she had not yet learned all parts of the job. I reviewed the completed payroll each week and helped her to continue learning for more than a year until she knew the job as well or better than I did.

Next, you have that group of employees who are interested in learning new jobs and being promoted as fast as the company will permit. This is a wonderful problem to have, but you don't want to have too many of them at the same time. It takes time away from regular work to learn new jobs, and you can afford only a certain number of weeks a year in cross-training.

Find a good schedule that will work for the company and also keep these great employees challenged. I had a college student working for me during her senior year; Cathy Cain was very quick to learn everything I taught her. I was able to arrange for her to supervise someone before she had even graduated. It became apparent to me that she could learn in approximately one year what initially took me five years to learn. Soon she was an assistant controller, then she was promoted to controller in another Pepsi Cola franchise. It took a lot of extra energy to keep up with her, but it was worth every minute of it. She was a great addition to the company, even though I eventually had to watch her leave our franchise.

Time to Train New Managers

If your company grows and you find yourself working 14-hour days, you may need to teach an existing employee to take on some management duties. You may have just learned the skills yourself and now you need to teach another person. Here are some ideas to share with your new manager:

New managers need to sharpen their listening skills. This is not the time to start giving orders, it's the time to ask questions and listen. Employees will share lots of good information when they find out that the new manager wants to learn from them.

Give your new manager information about the near future and let her share it with the employees. While the manager is sharing in an open way, she is building a team.

Suggest that your new manager find a time to talk with each employee. Perhaps it will be over a period of weeks, but a few minutes making a connection with each one will go a long way toward future success.

Help your new manager learn how to share your focus. You have spent years learning how to keep your employees focused and now you need to do it through another person. Explain what to emphasize in meetings. Ask for follow-up.

Here is a way to monitor all of the things that your new manager is doing in your place: keep a checklist of delegated tasks, then choose dates to review each task to be certain that they were accomplished accurately and timely. You can do that by asking, "How did the meeting with Jennifer go?" or by saying, "Did you remember to tell them about the holiday schedule?" Or, you can ask what is going well and what would they like to improve. It's a good way to stay in touch with the old duties without micro-managing—and without taking any duties back.

Meetings—Meetings—Meetings

When you have a very small business, you can communicate by talking from one desk to another. Everyone stays up on all new developments. One person hangs up the phone and announces the change in plans to the other two people in the room. Simple! Then you add more employees, and soon they're not in the same room. New methods to stay in touch become critical to your success. Some information gets traded at the coffeepot; other by a copy of a note distributed to five people. At some point, it becomes necessary to have a weekly meeting to review the past week, discuss the next week's agenda, and to make sure that everyone is on target.

This meeting can become a problem if the meeting leader isn't trained in meeting management. I know a good number of owners who refrain from having a meeting because they know that it may become a free-for-all, with employees wanting to discuss things that should be handled in private, or to complain about whatever is not working well that month. Other owners are oblivious; they schedule a meeting and don't realize that the communication is in worse shape afterward than before. The meeting actually caused more problems than it solved.

It all gets down to understanding the difference between different types of meetings and the planning process.

MEETING TO TELL YOUR EMPLOYEES INFORMATION

In this kind of meeting, you should create an agenda for the items you want to cover. Distribute the agenda, or post it on the board in the meeting room. It should include time to begin, end, any scheduled breaks, and the business topics. If your employees already know the rules around meetings, they'll know how to conduct themselves during the meeting; have policies on late arrival, leaving early, accepting interruptions from pager, phone, or another employee.

You'll probably need time on the schedule to answer questions about the information that you cover. Now, here comes the difficult part: what to do when an employee wants to talk about something else. You have several choices: 1) Put the question on the board to discuss at the end of the meeting if there is time, 2) Put the question on the board to add to a later agenda, 3) Write down the question and tell the employee you will meet with her later to discuss her question. Two important things happen here: First, you didn't let the questions interfere with the flow of the planned meeting, and second, the employee didn't feel ignored because you told them when and how their question will be handled.

MEETING TO GATHER INFORMATION

This meeting needs advance notice because the employees will prepare information to bring to the meeting to share with management and the team. This agenda needs to be distributed with time for good preparation. Be concise about what is expected. Will it be a formal or informal discussion? Will participants talk from notes or bring overhead transparencies? Will you need copies for the group? Are there reports that need to be brought for review? If you are clear about your expectations, employees will have a better chance to fulfill the requirements of the meeting. Follow the guidelines discussed previously for questions that should be covered at another time.

BRAINSTORMING MEETINGS

This type of meeting is a different kind altogether. In this meeting, you may or may not need advance preparation for information to be brought to the meeting. In any case, the rules of the meeting need to be distributed and reviewed at the beginning of the meeting. It is amazing how many brainstorming meetings I have attended and how difficult it is for all individuals to follow the rules. The rule most often broken is "all ideas are good ideas; do not criticize any ideas during the process of the brainstorm."

It's so easy to tell the group why some idea will not work; it's like a dog with a bark—it just comes out. The facilitator or meeting manager can control this by always reminding the group that all ideas are good ideas. Funny ideas lead us to good ideas. Crazy ideas lead us to good ideas.

A good facilitator once brought a bunch of ping-pong balls to the group: every time someone started to say a negative thought, someone in the group threw a ping-pong ball at them. It reminded them to keep the negative thought to themselves, and also was an indication that it was their turn to add another crazy idea to the pot. Find a way to make sure that your group follows the rules and you will have a wonderful brainstorming session.

In all meetings, decide if minutes need to be taken, and who will prepare and distribute them. If there is a to-do list created during the meeting process, be sure it is reviewed at the end of the meeting to add dates and distribute copies. The meeting process can be concise and effective if the meeting manager is clear about the type of meeting and the appropriate process. You will now enjoy your meetings—and that's a good thing, since they are so important to your company.

One last thought about meetings—it is really important that you continue to communicate with your growing staff about the vision of the company. They can't read your mind. Plan every month for the time and place that you will share changes in the company, new plans and opportunities you have decided to incorporate in the business future. Keep your employees in the know as much as is appropriate; they can do a better job for you this way.

Communication: A Key to Management

As the new vice president/general manager for the Pepsi Cola franchise in Akron, Ohio, owned by General Cinema Corporation, I arrived at work in the same location at which I had worked for almost 15 years (after an absence of three years.) But it was a different place, because for the first time I was the person responsible for the franchise.

I put my briefcase in my office, checked in with my secretary, and decided to look for a moment at the information the previous general manager had left for me. But I knew what I had to do next—the thing that would be the most difficult for me, always. I had to walk through the warehouse and the plant and, in doing so, talk with the people working there. Not an easy thing when you are slightly shy and more closely aligned with the introverted group.

I liked the people and knew more than 100 of them by name; I had helped each of them with something or another during those 15 years, and they were supportive of me. Still, I was the one they would look to for the future. They wanted to see by my face and my actions that everything would be okay; they wanted to know that I valued them and their ideas.

It was my job to provide that reassurance—a new duty to be sure. I made that walk, and many others after that day, each time attempting to talk with as many employees as I could reach in the time available. They are wonderful people and their opinions and goodwill were important to me—and to the future of the company.

So, easy or not, remember that all kinds of communications are needed in order to manage your company. Phone, meetings, e-mail, letters, and even a walk around the company will provide connections between you and the other important people in your business.

Recognition: Treat Them Like People Plus

There are a number of ways to recognize people in the workplace. There are some great studies about what people really want in their work and how to provide it. There are plenty of magazine and newspaper articles about companies that take care of their employees in special ways. Be on the lookout for these articles, and keep them in a file. You'll need to have ways to reward people without adding to their wages.

In Akron, Fran Doll, founder of Superior Staffing, found that her employees really appreciated having a free hairstyle or manicure. Her employees enjoyed the boost, and you could hear it in their voices on the phone or in person. General Cinema gave a $25 bond to all families with a new baby. (The cost was only about half of the face of the bond, and it was a great way to recognize a family while keeping the insurance records current.) Pat McKay, president of McKay Insurance Agency, Inc., takes her staff to lunch to celebrate the anniversary of her company every year. From movie tickets to a half-day off before their wedding, employees appreciate small recognitions of hard work.

Managing by the Numbers

When you work in a franchise with direct competitors and you already have all of the customers in town, as we did at Pepsi-Cola Akron, you learn what numbers are important to watch, and the management reports that help you. We talked about some of those management reports in the chapter on money. It's worth further exploration of the value of managing by the numbers; hopefully it will give you some ideas to manage your company even better.

When you manage by numbers you have to create written budgets and written reports. Having this information in writing is a tool—you learn by preparing and reviewing the reports. Looking at the same reports every month provides a consistent method of review, it helps to prevent something from falling out of bed. It also lets you continue to look for and find improvement. Often the reports become a communication tool to use for discussion in meetings. The reports will give you confidence that the important aspects of your business are being monitored, controlled, reviewed, or improved.

My good friend Margaret D'Anieri, former president of Acadia Business Resources, Inc., outlines the process of managing by the numbers like this:

1. Decide what to measure.
   - We get what we measure—deciding what you need to know before you begin will provide the best results.
   - Set your personal and business goals—shape your business in a way to support your choices.
   - Choose the critical numbers—what drives your business?
   - Create key financial reports.
2. Choose performance levels.
   - Derive from your goals—other employee efforts needed to contribute to the goals you have established.
   - Consider changes in market/competition.
   - Base on history—look at the last three years and consider improvements.
3. Observe/measure actual performance.
4. Compare actual against standard performance (variance analysis—what caused the difference and what needs to be done about it?).
5. Learn, communicate, and act!
   - Focus on key issues.
   - What caused the variation? Will it continue?
   - Ask questions, don't guess.
   - How does the variation change your expectations of the future?
   - What changes should be considered?
   - Communicate and ask more questions.

This process can be a valuable addition to your management system. How does it compare with your current method of review? Can you add one new improvement each quarter and make your management system more effective?

Other Management Help

There is free help available to you if you need it. Small Business Administration's Service Corps of Retired Executives, SCORE, is available; find the closest group by calling toll free, 1-800-634-0245. There are 389 SCORE chapters located across the United States and in Puerto Rico. Connect online by clicking on SCORE at the Small Business Administration site *www.sbaonline.sba.gov* and search the online database; send an e-mail message to the counselor of your choice—more than 360 are available to help you online.

These retired men and women help small business owners with difficult challenges at no cost. If you call for help, ask for someone who has experience in your type of industry or your situation. Remember, they won't know everything—there's no magic pill—but they will teach you something you didn't already know. Ask lots of questions, sort out the answers, and try the ones that seem to fit your needs. You'll learn from them and enjoy a new relationship.

The U.S. Small Business Administration (SBA) administers the Small Business Development Centers (SBDC) available in every state. There are 57 business development centers that oversee and coordinate programs located at colleges, universities, vocational schools, chambers of commerce, and economic development corporations. Each center has a director, staff members, volunteers, and part-time workers. They have counselors to help owners or prospective owners start a business or grow a business. Management, marketing, production, organization and technical assistance, and other valuable business information is available, including international trade and government procurement help. Their counseling is free; classes have a small fee. It can be worth it to invest time for an appointment. Learn one thing that you didn't know and put it to good use. At the very least, call and find out exactly what help is available; keep a file within easy reach. Then, the moment that you need help, the phone number will be right there.

The SBDC also offers specialized programs for women business owners. The SBA's Women's Business Center Program, established by Congress in 1988, offers training, counseling, and mentoring services to current and potential women entrepreneurs. With 25 new sites added in 1999, there are now 80 centers nationwide (in 47 states).

These centers receive funding over a five-year period, and each site is required to match federal funds with private contributions, so they are a public/private partnership. They offer great programs including financial management, marketing, technical assistance, mentoring, procurement training, and Internet training. They specialize in assisting socially and economically disadvantaged women. Find out the most current information by calling your local SBA office or checking online at *www.sbaonline.sba.gov* and click on Women's Online Business Center.

The SBA also offers a program for women business owners who want to have a mentor to help them succeed in business ownership. The Women's Network for Entrepreneurial Training Mentoring Program, or WNET, puts together experienced women business owners with women whose business is ready to grow. It is a one-year program in which seasoned owners are matched with less-experienced owners to share experience, knowledge, and support. According to WNET:

You can be a protégé if you:
- Have been in business for at least one year and your business is ready to grow
- Demonstrate strong entrepreneurial skills and show potential for continued success
- Can spend an average of four hours a month with a mentor for at least one year, receiving guidance, training, and counseling
- Show a willingness to apply the advice your mentor gives you

You can be a mentor if you:
- Have three years of experience as a business owner or CEO
- Have a successful business, demonstrated by steady growth
- Can devote an average of four hours per month to your protégé for at least one year
- Can offer your protégé valuable business information and advice in a supportive, one-on-one relationship

The local Women's Network was an early supporter of this program and sponsored one of the pilot groups in Ohio. Marlene Miller was the director, and she helped the first and several other mentor/protégé groups get off the ground.

I remember having the opportunity to help Marlene with the matching process for the first group. What a challenge—to help each protégé be matched with a mentor who would be a good fit, and each mentor with a protégé they would enjoy supporting for a year.

We learned a lot about that process and watched a very successful program take shape. Some protégés in the first group went on to become successful owners, and they became mentors in a later group.

Even today, in Boardroom Groups, I'll hear about the program. Linda Bryant, president of AD DIRECT, was looking at a strategic marketing plan, and told her group that she reviewed the plan with Laurie Zuckerman, president of Zuckerman Consulting Group, Inc. and author of *On Your Own: A Woman's Guide to Building a Business.* Laurie was her mentor from many years ago, and is now a business friend.

The WNET Roundtable provides mentoring and support for women business owners in a group setting. This program is available through the SBA District Offices in cooperation with SCORE.

A Board of Advisors: Can They Really Help?

A board of advisors can be of great help to a small business. They can provide expertise and insight that the owner and management team simply don't have.

How do you find this wonderful help that you probably can't afford?

First let's look at the difference between a board of directors and a board of advisors. A director has legal and fiduciary (financial) responsibility for the organization. Public corporations always have a board of directors and many large companies see the benefit, too. The chairman of the board is the head of the board of directors. The board of directors are responsible for the policy of the corporation and expect to be paid an annual fee, plus fees for meeting attendance. They will expect the firm to have a directors' and officers' insurance policy to protect them from personal liability.

Advisors, on the other hand, are volunteers and do not have legal liability. A board of advisors for a small business may be happy if you treat them to dinner at each meeting and send a holiday gift or a token at the end of each successful year.

You won't want to burden them with ordinary management challenges during these meetings, although they may be quite willing to chat on the phone in between meetings if you are respectful of their time. You wouldn't meet more than two to four times each year, and probably limit each meeting to two hours. These meetings should be well planned. If you have two major opportunities and would like to review them, send the information out ahead of time so that they can be prepared to discuss the alternatives. Be very focused so that you use their time wisely.

Why will these experts be willing to help you? Owners like to meet other owners in a business setting. You may invite other owners to join your board of advisors so that they will enjoy the peer relationship with other board members. Perhaps legal or financial professionals will serve on your board and will easily gain knowledge about your industry and the small business process. This may help them in their own endeavors. The advisory board should be selected carefully; you will trust them with your confidential information, and they need to bring unique information and knowledge that will help you become more successful.

These advisors can help you during difficult times, and they will enjoy celebrating your successes. When you can't talk to anyone else about a challenge or an opportunity, your board will be there for you.

I'll leave you with one bonus secret of success: Behind every successful woman is another successful woman who has opened her heart and shared her story.

The Way We Work: Women vs. Men

In her book, *The Female Advantage: Women's Ways of Leadership*, author Sally Helgesen makes some interesting observations:

Women . . .
- Like to schedule little breaks throughout the day, working a slow, steady pace
- Make their family a priority and are more understanding if subordinates do likewise
- See themselves as being at the center of things rather than at the top

- Are relationship-driven, making themselves available to others for discussion or sharing of information

Men ...
- Collect information rather than share it
- See themselves at the top rather than at the center of business
- Work at a frantic, unrelenting pace without breaks
- Spend less time with family and see their homes as "branch offices"

Styles of Success: the NFWBO Study

According to the National Foundation for Women Business Owners (NFWBO), women and men entrepreneurs have different styles of success. In a study called, "Styles of Success: The Thinking and Management Styles of Women and Men Business Owners," it was discovered that:

- More than half of women business owners (53 percent) emphasize right-brain or intuitive thinking, solving problems creatively, and approaching dilemmas with sensitivity and values-based decision making. Seven out of ten men emphasize left-brain, logical thinking, stressing analysis and processing information methodically. Men are more likely to develop procedures to solve problems.
- Women business owners' style of arriving at decisions is more holistic or whole-brained—evenly distributed between right- and left-brain thinking.
- Two-thirds (66 percent) of women business owners tend to reflect on decisions, weighing options and outcomes before moving to action. Only 56 percent of men business owners tended to do the same; men tended to emphasize swift action over deep thought.

The study also found that women entrepreneurs tended to describe their businesses in family terms, and viewed their business relationships as a resource network. Also, women see men as being more adept at delegating, while men admire the perception and sensitivity that women bring to their businesses.

⊿ BACK TO THE BOARDROOM ⊾

Knowing Where You Stand

Eloise Breiding, president of Snacktime Goodies, Inc., provides vending equipment, great snacks, coffee machines, and supplies for office and factory settings. Eloise and her husband started the company as a second career and thought that it would just be part time. They now have a great business that keeps them both busy full time—and they added a part-time bookkeeper, too. Eloise keeps track of their equipment, the investment, and the return on that investment. One day, as we started the Boardroom Group meeting, everyone around the room was to share one good thing that had happened last month. When it came to Eloise, she said "We finished last month up 15 percent over the prior year."

She knows where she stands and what her goals are; she manages by the numbers and knows when she has accomplished a new level of success. She knows when to celebrate! Congratulations to Eloise.

⊿ IDEA CENTER ⊾

Are You a Great Manager?

1. Do you communicate well with your employees, both as a speaker and as a listener?
2. Do your employees feel that their problems, issues, or concerns are heard by you?
3. Do you set aside plenty of time to talk to your employees or subcontractors, so that no one ever feels rushed?
4. Do you and your employees have fun while doing the work involved in running your company?

5. Are your employees involved in some or many of the key decisions affecting the company?

6. Do you regularly celebrate successes (either of an individual or company nature)?

7. Do your employees seem to like coming to work?

8. Do you enjoy the challenges and joys of managing?

9. Do you enjoy seeking out new opportunities for yourself and your employees to learn and grow?

10. Are your customers aware of how much your employees enjoy working with you?

Getting to the Next Level: How to Position Your Company for Future Growth

Norma J. Rist

—— Secret 9 ——

The future belongs to those who can visualize it into being.

One of the most exciting times in the Boardroom Group is when a woman owner runs into the room and announces, "I've just hired two employees—I'm on a roll and my company's growing!"

But it is a common mistake for owners to think that the addition of employees to the mix is a true statement of your company's growth. It takes so much more than that, because for every employee you add you must cover additional employment costs. Certainly, if your business is in serious money-making mode, you can afford additional help and this could be seen as a sign of growth. But it doesn't always mean that, and all too many women owners have gone on hiring sprees only to discover that they weren't really making enough money to justify it in the first place.

I'm often asked, usually by women who have passed the first-year mark of their business ownership, how to get to the next level—that enviable place where business seems to magically happen and you've truly made something of value from next to nothing.

This "next level" can mean a lot of things to a lot of owners. How will you define it for your company? Will it be based on the number of employees you have, or will it focus squarely on financial figures? Will it be when you perceive you've "made it," or when your phone seems to never stop ringing?

True business growth can be achieved by two basic things: people and technology. Yes, you can add more employees, but you can also build a larger business through innovative strategic partnerships (limited or long term) or on the Internet, where the playing field is on even ground with large, even multinational companies who do the same thing as you. You simply need to find your niche and develop it.

Most of all, good, healthy business growth comes as a result of having a clear vision of your future–a vision that's so clear you can almost touch it.

And just when you thought that you were done planning, after building your business plan and marketing plan–guess what? You'll need another plan to navigate your company's growth. The future not only belongs to those who can see it, but also to those who plan for it.

Seven Steps to Growing a Profitable Business

Growth is the most important issue established business owners face– and 80 percent of women entrepreneurs say that growth-related issues are foremost in their minds.

But where does growth come from? Doing more of the same thing? Working harder? Waiting for a stroke of luck?

No. It starts with looking at your concept, and at your customer base–and with a plan. You must decide which segments or demographics you want to increase. Knowing your desired target market is the first step in a great marketing plan aimed at growth.

Let's look at seven steps to help you increase your customer base and grow those sales statistics profitably–starting today.

Step One: Align Your Business Image

Let's look at this for a minute in a way with which we can all identify: business alignment, simply put, means your "outfit" should match. All of the "accessories" you use to present your business to the world—your company name and tagline, logo, business cards, brochures, letterhead, and envelopes, and even your 20-second commercial—every one of these determine how your customers will perceive you.

As a whole, these outward representations of your business should position or align you naturally to your market. When done correctly, these materials present a cohesive, memorable message and company image.

To best present your business, you must ask yourself: "What makes my business valuable, unique, different?" It's certainly not just your product or service that's at issue here.

The first battle is how your customers perceive you. The best-tasting ice cream in the world can fail if it is not marketed properly. Conversely, an average brand of ice cream can succeed if it is marketed well. How do you want people to perceive you? How do you want to be known? Once you've answered that question, you'll determine how to market yourself with an advantage over the competition, and it will show in everything you say and do. It will absolutely glow in the tone you use, both verbal and written.

The other day, I ran across an elaborate, four-color brochure with a pop-up of a computer. It was unique, but did it sell me? Not really. It was so cute that I neglected to read it. The message got lost in the packaging, because the packaging didn't enhance the product's message. The "outfit" didn't match.

What attracts customers to a product or service like yours? Ask a few customers, and you'll find out. Then, create one dynamic image that tells very clearly what you represent to that customer.

Step Two: Know Your Benefit Statement— from the Customer's Viewpoint

Be able to state the benefit of your product or service in a concise, repeatable, understandable sentence. To do that, you must think from their point of view.

What is it you really do for your customers? Does your product or service give them peace of mind? Or do you save time for busy executives? Know what you ultimately offer your customers, and learn to convey that message as clearly as possible.

If your message is muddy, expect to come across with confusion. Unclear, unfocused messages will yield poor results. Have you ever listened to someone describe their business and, before the third sentence, you're thinking about your to-do list?

Your benefit statement should breathe life into the product or idea you represent. I was once at a networking function and overheard a well-dressed woman say that Weekender clothing takes you from "the beach to the boardroom to the ballroom" in mix-match style. Catchy slogan—and it must have worked or I wouldn't have been able to repeat it to you here.

A simple introduction can work very well, as long as it clearly reflects the value you provide to your customers. Make sure you include the *benefit* in your benefit statement.

Step Three: Create a Healthy Growth Plan

In a start-up business, you're glad to have any customer you can get—but, as your company starts to grow, it becomes harder to run the whole operation, providing services and marketing them, too. But to move forward, you have to add more sophisticated planning to the equation.

Writing your growth plan will force you to focus on where you're going and, best of all, how you can get there. It requires discipline.

Your growth plan should include projected sales income, a marketing plan to achieve those sales, cash-flow projections, talent needed (employees, subcontractors, etc.) and systems/structure (an operating plan).

Your technological support system will most likely be essential to your operation. Recent surveys of women business leaders from 14 countries showed 83 percent currently use computers in their businesses; 51 percent have used the Internet (and that number grows daily) and 26 percent have home pages for their businesses.

How is your technology going to support you in your growth? What kinds of technology do you need now to make your business more efficient? What can wait until later, when you have more money to make the purchase wisely?

Women business owners are taking a more proactive approach than men in adopting new technology and using the Internet to grow their businesses; 17 percent use the Internet to explore new strategies for growth.

Does your growth require capital? Women business owners continue to have less bank credit than their male counterparts; 34 percent with bank credit have $50,000 or more available to them for use in their business, compared to 58 percent of male owners.

If you double your growth, do you have the capital set aside to fund your growth? Don't be afraid to think big—thinking big isn't as scary when you develop your plan in a logical manner.

A colleague told me she was losing time with "stuff" she isn't getting paid for. As part of her next year's plan, she was determined to start billing for those "time-eaters" like follow-through work and extras her customers seemed to keep asking for. She wrote it into her business plan, and her bottom line increased as a direct result.

Document your growth every year. It's a great measuring stick to see where you've come from and determine where you're going.

Step Four: Expect and Enjoy Change

Change—embrace it! Look forward to change and the new benefits it will bring you as you're growing your company. I hope you all enjoy exciting journeys like the ones you're on, even though it's sometimes a bumpy ride. Know that, one day, you will find yourself with a business that looks totally different from the one you started. Why? Because you were open to change and watched the road signs.

When something isn't selling, find out why—and if something else sells better, investigate it. Be on the lookout constantly for new opportunities.

Have you noticed that some businesses are the vanguards for change and others seem to drag behind the times? The Levenger Company, for example, is a vanguard—a company lighting the way for others, literally. What started out as a company that sold small reading lamps became so much more when customers kept asking if they had other products. You know, you only need to receive 50 or so of these kinds of calls before you start thinking, "Am I missing something here?" That's when you create new opportunities—when your current product or service sparks other ideas in the minds of your customers.

Here in Ohio, we had a company called Main Street Muffins. This company made huge, delicious muffins that were so popular that many restaurants requested them for their customers. But every few days, the company's owner received calls from other bakeries that asked if Main Street Muffins sold batter. "Hmmm," thought the owner. "Am I missing something here?" He started a whole other business—supplying batter. The company nailed down a deal with McDonald's and was bought recently by another company. Not a bad way to grow a business profitably.

Be open to change, and don't forget to ask yourself whether you're missing something by not listening to your customers.

Step Five: Meet Challenges Head On

The Girl Scouts taught us to "be prepared." Well, challenges will knock on your door every day. Sometimes, they are opportunities in disguise, and you should let them in because they'll offer you great new ways to be successful.

Learn to work through challenges systematically, like a challenge-processing machine. Build a resource bank of answers and techniques. No one person can know everything, but you can sure collect a lot from other people who know a lot.

There are four ways you can face your challenges with confidence. The first is to keep a backup plan. Ask yourself, "What if sales are down in the first quarter? What if this new product doesn't sell well?" Know what you will do if something doesn't work.

The second way to stay confident in the face of challenge is to keep a growing list of professionals, resources, and other business owners you can call on for help. When in doubt, call someone else who might know the answer or who might have had the same problem. At some point in time, you're going to need advice or assistance in a hurry. So, arm yourself with a Rolodex that's stacked in your favor.

Keeping a sense of humor is your third line of defense. Mistakes are an inevitable part of business. Get comfortable with that; learn to enjoy the journey anyway. You'll have a better chance of hanging in there for the long haul if you can laugh about the things that happen along the way. Anyone can tell you the worst mistakes they ever made. If your progress is error-free, perhaps you aren't trying enough new methods.

The fourth way to stay on top of challenges is to simply keep on going. Good business doesn't come easily, and certainly doesn't happen overnight. The most successful owners I know are the ones who simply kept going—in spite of their fear, in spite of the odds. Keep moving forward, and keep trying new things.

Step Six: Focus on Your Vision

What is your vision for the future of your business? Can you verbalize it or write it down on paper? Get as clear as you can about where you want to be. Are you seeking to build a small empire, or will a specific sales goal do it for now? Decide where you want to see yourself in the next six months to one year.

When you're in this visualization stage, you'll want to imagine all of the following:

- Size
- Structure
- Sales
- Profits
- Location
- Staff
- Market position
- Business culture
- Clients
- Industry changes
- Demands on you, the owner

Are there any conflicts between your personal goals as a business owner and the goals you have for your business? Think about these carefully, then decide which will win out over the other or whether there's a compromise.

Step Seven: Find Your Motivators

Sometimes, everyone else's business appears to be booming, while yours is barely breaking even. That's when you need time with someone who makes you feel like you can do it. A mentor, colleague, friend, family member, or advisor who will listen to your struggles and triumphs while supporting your efforts can be invaluable.

List the reasons business ownership is so important to you. Keep the list near you so that you can see it on the days when everything seems to be falling apart.

Katina has a list like that near her computer. It reminds her to take inventory of all the good things that have happened in the last month; to concentrate on the opportunities she still has; to surround herself with positive people and to never give up. It has a giant "plus" sign at the top to remind her of the ultimate message of positivity.

I have a few friends whom I can call for an emergency tea session. They are business owners, too, so they will likely understand my challenge and may even offer a little advice to me—something I hadn't thought of before, or just a new way of looking at the situation. This is why groups for women business owners are such a good idea—they can form an instant support group for owners with "growing pains."

Find your motivators, then find a way to keep them in front of you for the rough times.

There is one other challenge when you are working on a plan for growth. It's your state of mind. You have to want to succeed in order to wade through the waters and make things happen.

A new client asked me, "What have you found that really makes the difference? Who succeeds and why?" I answered, "The person who continues to try, who puts one foot in front of the other and steps over obstacles. The owner who succeeds is the one who doesn't quit!"

When you've come to the place where you know you can succeed, align your business with materials and messages that consistently reflect who you are and what you offer. When you meet new people, let your benefit statement roll off your tongue with the confidence that you can meet someone's needs. Create a new, comprehensive written plan so that you know where you're going and how you'll get there.

And, when something new is thrown at you or something needs to be changed in your plan, regroup and create a new plan.

Seeing challenges as opportunities for growth will arm you against the stresses they can cause, because your focus is clearly in sight and your motivators are keeping you on task.

Katherine Graham once said, "To love what you do and feel that it matters—how could anything be more fun?" Make your business's growth stage as fun as you possibly can. Make the decision that you will continue to learn from every new experience.

Making Your Business Growth E-asier with E-commerce

—BY KATINA Z. JONES

One of the fastest ways to put your business on the fast lane to success is to load it onto the information highway. According to Banc-America Robertson Stephens, the average Web-head is expected to spend at least $99 per year on Internet transactions—and the number of Web users has grown from 28 million in 1996 to nearly 57 million in 1998. Those figures could represent billions of dollars in Internet business that your business could be a part of if you're ready.

Considering that more women entrepreneurs than men purchase new computers and frequent the Internet, you are probably already familiar with a lot of the technical possibilities and advantages the Web offers.

What should you know about e-commerce? Just that it is the fastest-growing means of selling there is today—and that you probably shouldn't try going it alone. Your best bet is to find a Web site designer locally (or on the Internet) who creates sites like the one you may already have in mind.

On the Internet, you can sell at any moment to just about anyone anywhere in the world. If the user has a valid credit card, your product or service can be purchased online. You would likely need to discuss foreign currency rates and shipping costs with an outside professional such as a banker or accountant, but the fact that you can call your business "global" or "international" as a result will be worth the small headaches and learning curve. (If you want to know how well others on doing with e-commerce, go to *www.computerworld.com/home/Emmerce.nsf/All/stats,* a site that gives you the statistics.)

If you don't feel ready for e-commerce just yet, you should at the very least have a Web page and an e-mail address. Almost all new clients want to know something about your company before committing any dollars to products or services, so you definitely need to have an "online brochure" (Web site) that conveys information about your company and all it has to offer.

Ask yourself how often you've looked at a company's Web site first in order to determine whether they had what you wanted in the way you wanted it. How many books have you purchased from the innovative online bookstore, Amazon.com?

The best thing about doing business on the Internet is its immediacy. You can whip together a virtual storefront in a little more than an hour, and start racking up sales as soon as you've registered your site in all of the major search engines.

But you will need a separate marketing plan for the Internet. Sure, it's easy enough to put together a Web site that sells, but to whom are you selling and why should they buy from you over the hundreds of other online choices they might have? How will your Internet piece fit into your overall marketing strategy? What do you want to accomplish, and why is the Web the way to do it? How will you promote your Web site once it's online—by offering free e-mail newsletters to potential clients, or by posting informative articles as an "expert" on topics related to your business?

Katina's business has a simple but pleasing Web site (*www.ohio.com/jobhunter/starachiever*), and she promotes it by producing free articles for Web sites related to career searches. There's a link in every article that takes viewers back to her company's Web site. This way she can attract potential clients who already see her as an expert—and that's smart positioning.

Norma is even launching her own Web site (*www.smallbizcoach.com*), which will also offer small business owners from the Boardroom Group and beyond the opportunity to house their Web site in a sister site to hers (*www.smallbiztown.com*). E-mail Norma if you're interested—it's a great opportunity, since her business partner (Boardroom Group member Pam Pierce, whose Web development company is called Empowering You!) and she will be doing a lot of work to promote both sites everywhere humanly possible.

What makes a winning Web site? For starters, a well-defined audience. Visitors to your site should know in the first 20 seconds or so whether they landed in the right spot. Tell them up front, on your home page, that they are indeed where they should be.

A big fallacy is the "If-you-build-it-they-will-come" mentality. On the Internet, that's simply not true. You have to work harder than you might in the traditional, local model of marketing, because the world really is your oyster with the Internet. If you don't believe what I'm saying, type keywords pertaining to your business into a major search engine, and count the number of related Web sites the search engine produces. For "women entrepreneurs" and "business coach," there are several hundred thousands "hits," or sites containing all or part of each phrase. This is your competition, because it represents the number of items your potential customers will need to wade through in order to find you. Not an easy proposition, but certainly not unattainable.

Once you are successful in securing visitors to your Web site, you need to constantly feed them new pieces of information. Interactivity works well in the form of online quizzes and contests. One of the best examples I've seen to date is a Web site for women called iVillage.com (*www.ivillage.com*), which offers visitors a new quiz relating to career, home, or family nearly every day. Once you become a member, you get the feeling that you're somehow part of a large community of women—and you feel welcome to return, since the home page recognizes you by name each time you return. A terrific example of what other Web sites, even those for small business owners, could be.

Be careful of trying to put too much into your Web site from the get-go, however. You don't want to overwhelm others with too many things to think about on first contact; instead, let the Web site and its content evolve. One of the beautiful things about the Internet is that you can grow, evolve, and change in just a few minutes, so the opportunity to create fresh, new concepts and products on a regular basis exists in a way that it never has before. Back in what should now be called "the dark ages," you really couldn't add new products or services to your business without the added expense of a newly printed brochure or catalog. That's just not true on the Internet, where you can change and grow every day.

Finally, visit other Web sites constantly in your search for new ideas. Just as you can change your own site on a daily basis, so can others who have innovative sites. Learn as much as you can about what you like and dislike. When you find a site you like, scroll down to the bottom of the home page and look for the site developer's e-mail address. E-mail that designer for quotes on a similar site for you. As long as you feel a creative bond with the designer, it shouldn't matter that you are hundreds, or even thousands, of miles away.

Don't be afraid to expand your business by taking the entrance ramp to the information highway. You'd be surprised how far you can go with just a little effort.

Remember, too, that you can always share expenses by sharing Web space with another business related to your own. Cooperative sites are cropping up everywhere, and they operate more or less like office buildings that lease out individual office space; for a small amount each month, you pay the "host" for sharing space on their main Web site.

The only drawback to an online cooperative venture is that the "host" could someday go out of business—leaving you stranded in cyberspace, since the space was never really yours. Make sure you create an exit plan that covers such unforeseen circumstances.

Joining Forces: Finding Mutually Beneficial Strategic Alliances

The truth is, many women entrepreneurs miss out on great opportunities to expand simply because of a perception that a potentially compatible company is a competitor rather than an opportunity.

A few years ago, I read about a woman who had a personal shopping business. She wanted to expand it, and a mentor had suggested she align herself with a corporate relocation service in town. The woman was so afraid that someone would steal her idea and use it to further develop their own opportunities that she completely missed a terrific chance to gain "instant" business. She turned away from a great opportunity simply out of fear.

Had she developed a written, mutually beneficial plan to illustrate to the company exactly how each service could retain its separateness yet provide their services in a combined manner to busy executives in relocation mode, she might have doubled the sales potential of both companies.

Finding "allies" who can naturally bring their customers to you and vice versa is not as difficult as you might think. Travel agencies and florists can combine packages for honeymoons or anniversaries; pet groomers and pet sitters can help each other by providing cross-referrals.

Think of what other products and services your clients seek out in the course of doing business with you. For Katina's resume service, it was easy to think of other places her clients go: when in a job-search mode, they get a haircut (cross-referral opportunity), buy a new suit (another cross-referral opportunity) and perhaps even talk with a career counselor. So, providing coupons for additional services beyond her resume business is a great way to appear larger—by offering things outside of her normal course of business. It's a win-win for the hair stylist and consignment store she has relationships with, too, since many of the resume clients might not have thought to go to them for their additional needs.

So, becoming advocates and referral bases for each other is another good way to boost business—without laying out too much cash.

As we write this book, Katina is considering aligning her company with two others. Her creative "self-promotion" company nicely complements fellow Boardroom Group member Kathy Baker's The Write Choice public relations firm—and the two companies together can enhance business for a graphic designer who needs to offer Internet public relations services, Web site content building, and creative copywriting. The three businesses plan to share office space and a central administrative support person—keeping their expenses to a minimum and their earning potential higher than it could be separately.

Think of other businesses that could complement yours while remaining a "win-win" situation for both parties. Is there a particular product that might fit nicely as a package with your product or service?

A woman who owns a modeling agency regularly seeks out opportunities to bundle her modeling manual with other products such as lingerie and cosmetics. She makes $25,000 to $50,000 extra per year just doing that—and is building stronger relationships with some of her department store clothing suppliers in the meantime.

So, it's not just about aligning your company with other like businesses in order to grow. You can also grow by offering more opportunities for your customers to grow.

A woman who owns an arts and entertainment newspaper forged an alliance with a local radio station for cross-promotion purposes. Each offers the other free advertising, and they often split the cost of advertising for mutually sponsored events like movie premieres.

The concept of a strategic alliance is not a new one; big corporate players have always joined forces. It's sometimes hard for entrepreneurs like us to see the advantages at first, but once we do, we capitalize on them, too. A 1996 Coopers and Lybrand study found that the majority of the 400 fastest-growing companies in the '90s used some form of creative partnership to get there. These companies grew at an average rate of 37 percent faster than those companies that chose to go it alone—so two heads are better than one!

Commitment to Continual Improvement

Finally, to get your business to grow, you need to be willing to expand your own thinking in order to grow along with it. This will require a commitment to continual self-improvement, as well as practical application of self-improvement principles to your business plan.

Continual improvement, whether for yourself or your business, only happens when you open your willingness to become a lifelong professional at learning new things. With technology changing the way we do business every day, you need to keep your eyes and ears open constantly—and remember that there's a reason God gave us two eyes, two ears, and one mouth. In other words, learn to absorb more than you speak.

Here are some additional tips to keep you focused on your path:

• Write down your plan to learn more. In a journal, you can jot down things you've recently heard about but would like to learn more about. Keep notes in this journal as to what you've learned—and then correlate the lessons to your own business. How does each new item apply to you or your company?

• Break free from the status quo. Know that there is always more to learn about everything—even the things you think you already know inside and out. Get out of your comfort zone and think outside of the box!

• Consider all of the possibilities. I like to do this exercise for my own business's growth: I'll look at a regular household object, such as a dish scrubber, and think about all the thought and planning that went into a product I use every day. Then, I'll ask myself to consider what kind of lesson the dish scrubber can give me about my own business. This may sound like a strange thing to do, but guess what? I start thinking more about how I can make my clients' lives easier in an innocuous way, just as the scrubber does. You see, there are lessons in everything around us.

• Get focused. One of my favorite gifts of all time was a silver star-shaped paperweight with the word "Focus" engraved on it. It was from a Boardroom Group member who attached a note that said, "Thank you for helping me maintain my focus while I chase my star." Staying focused on your business's main objective is key to future plans for growth—you can't grow without focus.

• Use all available resources. When you find something you'd like to learn more about, punch in some keywords and get rolling on the Internet. Use search engines to their fullest capability. If you're still unsure where to look for more, do the old-fashioned thing and call a reference librarian. Librarians have some pretty high-tech tools at their fingertips, and are quite knowledgeable about how to find even obscure bits of information quickly.

⊿ IDEA CENTER ⊾
Dynamic Goal-Setting

If you want to succeed and grow in business, you'll need to start with a good goal-setting program. Seek out professional help in this area if you aren't sure how to identify and set your own goals.

Here are just a few tips to get you started:

- Remember to make your goals specific. The only goals that stand a chance of being achieved are the ones that are clear enough to become part of a mindset and visualization process. The clearer the goal, the easier it will be to accomplish.
- Have a deadline for achievement. You can have a terrific goal, but wander around aimlessly without a drop-dead date for its achievement. Someone once said that a goal is a dream with a deadline.
- Consider and anticipate your obstacles. Know where the pitfalls might occur, and devise a plan to work around such impediments.

Above all else, make sure there is a personal benefit to achieving the goal, or it will not serve to motivate you. You need to reward yourself with a vacation if you sell $1 million worth of product, or you might not be able to focus on the benefit of working so hard to achieve it.

From the *Adams Businesses You Can Start Almanac,* by Katina Z. Jones (Adams Media Corp., 1996).

◿ I D E A C E N T E R ◺

10 Ways to Expand Your Business for Little Cash

1. Get on the Internet. For just a few dollars per month, you can market your services worldwide. Who can beat that?
2. Trade services with a franchisee prospect. You could work a deal where the franchisee's buy-in fee would be cut if the franchisee helped produce the operations manual; this way, you can use one franchisee to get more. The payoff comes later.
3. Hire commission-only sales reps. You only need to pay them a percentage of what they bring in—which keeps them highly motivated to sell for you.

4. Hire interns from colleges and universities. They often work for free or next-to-nothing, and get college credit in return for that work.

5. Participate in business organizations where you can network for free.

6. Find inexpensive ways to advertise your company on a regular basis, such as asking family members to sport your company logo on a sweatshirt, T-shirt, or hat.

7. Join forces with a compatible business. For instance, you could merge with a secretarial service if you have a resume service.

8. Put on seminars, charging a fee for teaching others your own skills.

9. Sponsor trade shows or other events.

10. Develop a program or system for your business that can be marketed and sold to others like it. You could write a book or develop a software program that is key to your industry, then sell it through professional associations.

From the *Adams Businesses You Can Start Almanac*, by Katina Z. Jones (Adams Media Corp., 1996).

◿ BACK TO THE BOARDROOM ◺

Dealing with the Risk Factor

You're trying to get your business to the next level, so what are you afraid of? Probably the risk factor involved. So, here are some ways consultant Annie Russell came up with to deal with the risk factor and fear of failure:

- **Lighten your load.** Don't try to attempt too much at one time.
- **Get support where you need it.** Ask for the help or kind words of others.
- **Protect the relationships you most care about.** Don't leave the people you love out in the cold as you feverishly try to make business growth happen. These are the folks you're doing this for, right?

- **Keep your current world rich and rewarding.** Bloom where you are planted while you plan for future changes.
- **Get clear on what you really want.** Enough said?
- **Plan in phases.** Break your plan into small, workable increments. It might mean setting daily, weekly, biweekly or monthly goals.
- **Get a handle on your money.** You can't spend like a drunken sailor if you want to grow your business. In the early stages of growth, you'll likely be doing the financing, which means your profit will need to be reinvested in the company.
- **Negotiate for what you want.** Don't be afraid to ask for the impossible. Impossible things can become possible for the right price.
- **Have a contingency plan.** Sometimes just knowing that there is a Plan B can make all the difference in your comfort level.
- **Have faith.** This doesn't necessarily have to be in God—it can be in yourself, in your abilities, in your company—whatever will get you through to the next level of your greatest good. Know that the Universe is unfolding perfectly for you. Learn to trust that inner voice.

⊿ IDEA CENTER ⊾

Eleven Rules for Success

(Excerpted from the Online Women's Business Center, a public-private partnership created by the U.S. Small Business Administration.)

1. Work smarter, not harder. It's not how much you do, but what you do and how well you do it. There are better ways to run your business than by brute force.
2. Strive for accuracy first, then build momentum. Since you do not have a second chance to make a good first impression, you must do things right the first time. It is much better to introduce an excellent product a little later than planned than to impetuously release something that you know has problems.

3. Find a niche. Become an expert in your field. Stick to what you do best.

4. Build your reputation on integrity, quality, and value. Don't do anything that might compromise it. Once your reputation is tarnished, it is difficult to redeem yourself in the eyes of your customers.

5. Always better yourself. Constantly strive to improve your products and services.

6. Be creative. Adapt and apply innovative techniques from outside your specific field.

7. Listen and react to your customers' needs. Success comes when you give your customers what they want. Visit your customers and ask them what you can do to improve your product or service. Sell solutions, not products.

8. Plan for success. Know where you are going and how you are going to get there. Too many businesses exist day to day without any long-range plans or goals. Decide where you want your company to be in one, three, and five years, and draw up a plan of action to get you there.

9. Take advantage of change. Changes in your market are inevitable; use them to your advantage. Be a leader, not a follower. It is far better to err on the side of daring than inaction or complacency.

10. Think before you act. There is nothing as useless as doing efficiently that which should not be done at all.

11. Always promise a lot . . . and then deliver even more. Try to provide your customers with more than they expect. Go the extra mile to give exceptional quality, service, or value. Your customers will remember and reward you with their continued business.

◿ IDEA CENTER ◣

Using Your Calendar to Get More Business

There are probably hundreds of great marketing ideas out there, but as far as keeping your current customer base healthy and your expanded market growing, nothing can help you promote your business better than the calendar. Remember, it doesn't have to be limited to just the big holidays; you can even create your own related to your line of business. For instance, a resume service can offer a "Take This Job and Love It" career exploration day, complete with an event or simply a questionnaire that helps job seekers narrow down their choices. Of course, you'd tuck in a coupon for a discount on resume services!

Here are some other ways to use your calendar to build business:

- Hold a contest that relates to a specific holiday. For instance, if you have a small retail shop, you might consider offering a raffle or contest for a gift basket of goodies from your shop at Mother's Day or any other special occasion.
- Use a holiday in your advertising. A local shipping and packaging business runs ads like this one for St. Patrick's Day: "Don't depend on the luck of the Irish to get your package there on time!" It's offbeat enough to get attention.
- Think about why people buy at specific times of year. Are there more weddings in June that you can sell floral goods to? What about June graduations? Would people be likely to want a gift certificate from your business on any occasions like these?
- Publicize your special event or invented holiday. Don't forget to send a press release to your local paper. Stories like these make excellent filler for newspapers, which are always in a pinch to fill space. There's no guarantee it will run, but if you make the event or day sound interesting enough, you will get coverage.

One final tip: Using the calendar to grow more business also works on the Internet. Use a tip sheet format, with a title like, "10 Tips to Get You Through Another Tax Season" (for accountants) or "11 Ways to Promote Your Business on the Internet" (for Web-based marketing/promotion businesses).

⊠ IDEA CENTER ⊠

Six Purchases You Must Make to Move into the Future

- **Accounting software.** Your bookkeeping can still be done in a ledger, but with all the great programs out there, you'll want to get a good program that both you and your accountant can use. Be sure to purchase upgrades when they become available; most money management software programs update their content based on new tax information.

- **Computer system.** You don't necessarily need the newest model with all of the bells and whistles, but a fast and up-to-date computer will save you lots of time. I don't recommend buying a used computer unless you are using the unit for only a few small and specific tasks. You can't realistically depend on older models to give you the flexibility to add upgrades. My six-year-old Compaq is having early-onset Alzheimer's (losing memory), and I know its days are numbered. Good thing I have a newer laptop model as a backup. (P.S. I also wouldn't recommend using a laptop as your main computer unless you back up the hard drive on a daily or weekly basis. Most computer experts I know say they are too easily damaged—it goes with the territory, so to speak, of being highly portable.)

- **Separate fax line.** Handling your orders and other types of business information can be so much easier when clients don't have to call first to see if it's okay to fax. Sure, you cut down on unsolicited faxes this way, but when your business begins to grow, you won't have the time to manage extra phone calls. Unnecessary calls to announce faxes are just not worth it when time is money. Also, if you're planning to do a lot of Internet business, you'd be wise to consider a high-speed modem line—one that runs through your cable television provider instead of depending on phone lines. Access is not only smooth, but the speed at which the information can travel is also faster.

- **Hand-held computer.** These hot little numbers act as portable mini-computers and can hold a surprising amount of data that can be transferred later to your main computer. That's particularly good news for the expanding business owner—who's typically on the road a lot more than in the office.

- **Voice mail system.** At first, you can probably get away with an answering machine. But as you grow, you'll want to add more options, and voice mailboxes (typically available through your telephone service provider) can help your company sound bigger than it is by affording the caller more options. You can usually have up to five "mailboxes," each of which has a name or department. (For instance, you can say, "For customer service, dial one" and the customer will hear your recorded instructions on how to get their problem solved quickly and efficiently.)

- **Internet service and a Web site.** The quickest way to grow big is to equate yourself with other big companies on the Internet.

—KATINA Z. JONES

IDEA CENTER
Creating an E-mail Newsletter That Helps Your Business Grow

The e-mail newsletter is quickly becoming the easiest, fastest, and most economical way of getting your message to thousands of people at one time. It's a great marketing tool because it gives people small pieces of information about your products or services, but does so in a way that doesn't insult their intelligence.

But how do you produce an e-mail newsletter that serves its purpose—mainly, to grow your customer base? Here are some tips that will help:

- Go easy on the eyes. A computer screen is harder to look at for a long period of time. Don't count on everyone printing out your newsletter.
- Use keywords and phrases that will guide the reader instantly to what he or she really wants to know. (Okay, if you're lucky, they'll want to read the whole thing—but don't count on it.)

- Use attractive language. Here, I mean that your newsletter should be magnetic to readers. Just as in traditional forms of advertising, you have only a few seconds to catch their attention. Make them want to read your newsletter with provocative questions and answers to some of their toughest problems.

- Position yourself as an expert. Carve your niche, then stay there. Being a Jill-of-all-trades will not serve you well on the Internet, where a few seconds can make or break you. Be clear and concise in your 20-second commercial. Don't forget to include your tagline about yourself and your business at the end of every issue.

- Make it easy for others to do business with you—straight from the newsletter. Create a hot link to your e-mail address so that, when they're done reading your fascinating history of specialty cakes, they can order one right away. You'd be surprised how many business owners forget this simple—and profitable—item.

- Keep it short, sassy, and irresistible. You know what gets your attention, so why should your e-mail newsletter be any different? Give tips that can be put to immediate use by the reader. Offer a quote or joke of the week (but keep it tasteful).

- Give small snippets of things that appear in larger format on your Web site. For instance, give the first few paragraphs of an article on the newsletter, but offer a link to the full story, which appears on your Web site. The whole idea of the Web is to become spiderlike, right? Don't you want to attract a few flies into the main information center?

- Spend time on your e-mail newsletter. Just because folks can get it for free doesn't mean it's something that should be dashed out in a few seconds. Plan issues on a weekly basis; try to stick to one theme per newsletter.

⊠ IDEA CENTER ⊠

Five Good Reasons to Choose a Creative Partnership

1. To get more clients—especially ones who might not have found you in ordinary ways

2. To offer more services to your established clients—and seem like you have a lot more to offer new customers than your competitors
3. To test the waters of a potential match for a merger later on
4. To enhance your own credibility
5. To save money (co-promotions can save you hundreds or even thousands of advertising dollars)

◁ IDEA CENTER ▷

Keys to Bartering

Bartering—or trading products or services—is a great way to save money and grow your company at the same time.

For instance, if you need the work of a great graphic designer to help with your marketing materials (perhaps a glitzy brochure), you may trade your services for hers if there is some value in what your company can offer to the designer. If you are a writer, you might offer to help the designer with her Web site content, or even with the words for her own brochure.

All you need to have is a verbal agreement between yourself and the other owner involved, and the follow-through ability to actually come through on your side of the bargain. You really don't have much to lose from bartering—you have much more to gain.

◁ BACK TO THE BOARDROOM ▷

How Well Have Your Strategic Alliances Worked?

1. What types of strategic relationships have you tried? What was the plan, and what was the desired benefit from the alliance for both parties?
2. What method or process did you use to implement the new relationship?
3. What worked? What didn't? How did you evaluate the outcome?
4. What do you plan to do in a strategic alliance in the future? What do you see others doing that you would like to do?

⊠ IDEA CENTER ⊠
Thinking about New Technology

1. What technology is important to your business? (Think both now and in the future—i.e., computer, Internet, video conferencing, e-mail, e-commerce, fax, cell phone, pager, scanner, scheduling software, etc.)

2. How do you stay updated on new innovations? What are you currently waiting for in terms of new products on the horizon?

3. How do you budget for changes? How will you decide when and what to buy?

4. What need do you have that technology could fill if you could afford it?

5. What would help you the most in the area of technology (hardware, software, training, knowledge)?

Reinventing Your Business: Knowing When to Make Changes

Norma J. Rist and Katina Z. Jones

—— Secret 10 ——
The best businesses often arise
by accident out of other businesses.

Remember the story we told you in Chapter 5 about Alison Kirby, the owner of Pampered Pals?

Alison had a pet-sitting business, which was successful enough on its own. But Alison always brought treats for her customers—the dogs—so that they would look forward to her visit. The treats available from the store were hard and had little flavor so Alison began toying with the idea of baking her own treats. She tried out numerous recipes until she found one that produces a soft dog cookie that was made from all-natural human food, checked it out with the veterinarian, and then began to offer Pampered Pals treats to her wonderful dog customers. The dogs loved the treats and some of her dog owners wanted to purchase these treats that were great for dogs, young and old alike. This was the beginning of a wonderful new business. Alison sold her pet-sitting business and started a manufacturing company, Pampered Pals, Inc., natural gourmet dog treats, and she is distributing across the United States in health food stores, pet stores, and gift stores.

How do you know when you should make a significant change in your business? If you take the lesson from Alison Kirby, it's when your customers begin to tell you what else they need that you're not currently providing. Perhaps their needs have changed over time, and this is where it pays for you to be in regular communication with your customers because they will give you great ideas for the future.

Or, you can take Katina's lesson about watching your entire industry for signs of change. She started her resume service in a time when downsizing was the norm and people still needed a distinctive printed package to present themselves to potential employers.

But it's not like that anymore. Only smaller, localized companies really require the printed piece of paper as a resume submission. Huge numbers of job-seekers have been posting their resumes on the Internet—and they are getting great responses from all over the world.

It's not always for a happy reason that your business goes through changes. But by staying on top of changing forces in the business world, you can protect your business and capitalize on new opportunities.

Common Entrepreneurial Mistakes

In the Boardroom Groups, we've seen it all. We've seen tremendous successes, heartbreaking changes, and difficult situations.

Why do some businesses simply fail, in spite of what had seemed to be a good idea? There are many reasons, but these seem to be the most common:

- **Sticking to the same way of doing things, or the same old ideas, for too long.** You must be willing to grow and change; you've got to be flexible, especially in a competitive market. Too many owners become wedded to ideas that simply don't serve them anymore.
- **Not being able to "walk the talk."** Many women are terrific at promoting themselves and their businesses, yet unable to

actually deliver what they've promised. You'd be surprised how many women owners have Web sites that gather e-mail they fail to respond to—or phone messages that go unanswered for days.

- **Hiring the wrong people.** Adding staffers just because you like them (or are related to them) isn't necessarily the best idea for small business owners.
- **Overinvesting in the future before it is certain.** This goes back to your planning; did you really think about large purchases before committing to them? Many owners wrap up a lot of money in equipment leases and purchases before they've got a stable enough customer base. You should always start off with the basics, and let your growing business pay for expansion.
- **Putting financial "blinders" on.** Too many entrepreneurs, men and women alike, fail to get a grip on their business's finances. Bills go unpaid (and sometimes unopened), bookkeeping becomes an afterthought, and a lot of questions begin to arise from your suppliers and customers about your stability. Word travels fast in entrepreneurial circles; watch your financial reputation or you could lose business.
- **Giving too much away.** We women are infamous for giving too much of our businesses away for free. Often, we are so afraid of losing a customer that we wind up discounting our products and services in order to keep it from happening. What we wind up with is not enough money to cover our cost of doing business, let alone money for profit. Not a good way to do business, and not good for your self-esteem, either.
- **Not having an exit plan.** As we said in Chapter 1, every business plan should have an exit plan—a detailed passage about your ability to deal with the potential failure of your business and exactly how you intend to handle it should the worst-case scenario present its ugly head. The banks want to know how you'll deal with it, but you should think about it, too, since you'll need to find another source of income if your business doesn't pan out as planned.

Moving On

Closing your business and choosing another way to make a living is not as bad an experience as you might think. Several of the Boardroom Group members have gone on to bigger and brighter futures after making the difficult decision to close a business. There were many valid reasons to close: it wasn't the work that they preferred to do, they had a great opportunity to grow into new competencies or learn about a new industry if they accepted a position, or they had an offer that would double their earning potential in the following year.

Mindy Aleman is one of the best public relations professionals in this region. As an independent public relations and trade show professional, she had an offer to handle events for the John S. Knight Center (trade shows and events) and the Akron/Summit Convention and Visitors Bureau. This was a great fit; they had the benefit of her expertise and she developed a new base of contacts in the trade show industry as well as a new skill—marketing a region instead of a product. More recently, Mindy was appointed marketing and development director for the Kent State Fashion Museum. What a great new challenge—but I see Mindy independent again in the near future, perhaps as an international event planner.

Christy Parvin was president of a start-up computer training company, and she worked full time in computer technology for a hospital. She was starting to build a customer base and to become known in the community as an expert to call for training. She had the opportunity to travel and provide training in health organizations and enjoy a larger compensation package. She decided to accept this opportunity and to put her company on hold. She knows that she can return to her start-up when the timing is right.

Carol Kastelic had a company producing incredible canvas bags—the kind you take to the grocery and everywhere else in your life. They were exceptional in strength—they'd easily hold a watermelon and they fit the trend for environmentally friendly products. Carol found that the grocery stores were primarily interested in buying at a reduced cost, and that was not a style of selling that she enjoyed. She sold her inventory and moved to a different business; she returned to modeling. Now she is a senior model for many senior products in catalogs and television advertising.

As you can see, some women put their business on hold, and some make a permanent change. Still others will make a change in their existing business by altering or updating a product or service, refocusing on a niche market, changing delivery methods, or making a change in size or pricing strategy. Some create a strategic alliance, or explore exporting. They may analyze the competition and move toward the competitive strategy, or move away from it. Others may add new market segments, or try government procurement. Watching trends may reveal a needed change; branding is a great opportunity, or perhaps franchising is possible. We'll discuss some of these options in more depth in the following sections.

Reinvent Your Product or Service

Sharon Klusmann owns Baskets by Sharon. She is a basket designer and weaver and she teaches classes in basket weaving. Each year, Sharon designs a new line of baskets and her customers keep coming back. Several stores carry Sharon's line. But she has only 40 or 50 hours a week to invest in these products and produce wonderful new baskets that will create a profit for her small company. Sharon recently copyrighted her designs and prepared pattern kits for her designs; the patterns can be sold all over the world on her Web site and in stores that handle basket supplies. Making a change in the product she offered expands her ability to earn more income and to become more widely known.

Terrie Bergdorf, president of Bergdorf Productions, Inc., produces audio- and videotapes and major events that use multimedia presentations. Terrie has been in this business for many years and is accustomed to watching changes in technology. Recently it became apparent to Terrie that the new digital equipment would again require a major investment if she wanted to continue to do business in the same way as before.

Terrie looked at all of the segments of her revenue. She earned the most revenue by consulting. Her knowledge of communications, developed over all the years since college, make her a highly valuable consultant. She decided that she didn't really need to own the newest equipment with all of the bells and whistles; she just needed to know how to access all of the resources, equipment, and talent needed to provide a great product for her client. Look at what it is that you really provide and develop new models for delivering that service.

Refocus—Find a Niche

Kathy Wise, president of Wise Nutrition Concepts, Inc., provides a variety of nutrition services for individuals, businesses, and organizations. She has products as well as services to offer. This variety has given her the opportunity to explore the kind of consulting and the type of client she prefers. She creates nutrition programs for restaurants, health product companies, and professional organizations. She provides individual counseling and is known in Northeast Ohio from many appearances on morning television.

After a few years in business, Kathy started looking at the kind of work she loved the most. She decided to market for more business clients in the health product/service arena. She forms a relationship with these businesses to help provide the nutritional expertise as the firms expand their product or service line. She continues to offer her services in other areas, but the niche area is beginning to be a larger part of her business revenue—the area where she uses her education, training, experience, and her entrepreneurial ability, too.

Size Could Be the Key to Profitability

Many women avoid building a larger business. It appears to them that a larger business means more work—perhaps true in some situations, but not true in others. Adding size can not only add to profitability, but adding a management team with higher skills and abilities can actually create a business that is easier to manage.

When you have a functional expert in finance, marketing, sales, and operations, you can work on the future; your team is working on the day-to-day operation. Sometimes growth is the change that is needed in order to build the business of your dreams.

Linda Littler, owner of Carey and Littler Staffing with her partner Laura Carey, is growing a temporary and permanent placement company. After several years of strong business growth, she needs to add other professionals in key positions in order to continue to accomplish their business plan. Adding another trained service professional to interview and match temporaries with positions, adding another sales professional to attract new customers and at some point perhaps an office manager, will help them to grow to the size needed to produce the revenue and profit that they plan.

On the other hand, sometimes the change in size that is needed is really to reduce the number and type of clients needed. One example of this situation may be noticed in the travel business where the commission earned from each flight transaction has been dramatically reduced. In addition, business travelers are able to buy tickets in many new ways due to technology. Travel agencies are concentrating on growing the leisure travel business in order to maintain profitability. This is one example of making your business smaller in order to become more profitable.

Pricing—Pricing—Pricing

If I had to choose one area in which women owners need the most information, it is how to price their service or their product in order to make a profit. It's not that they cannot do the calculations, it's that they want to make sure that their customers are receiving more than a normal value. They want to make sure that the customers are happy with the service and do not believe that they were overcharged. As a result, setting appropriate pricing—pricing that will hold the proper position in the market—pricing that will produce a good profit—is a challenge for many women.

After helping hundreds of women who offer a service to think through their pricing, I came to the conclusion that we could save a lot of time by just writing down the amount they were considering and multiplying it times two. After using good methods to price based on competition, the market or the hourly rate needed in order to earn an annual income needed or wanted, it always turned out that the amount they were considering in the first place could be multiplied by two and it would be right on the mark.

In any event, a change in pricing can put you into a new business. This change may be essential in order to stay in business and thrive. Remember earlier when we talked about the business plan consultant who could charge a number of prices for a plan, from very low to very high. Sometimes, raising your price establishes your new position in the market. When we started Venture Group LLC, with the Business Blast-Off program, we wanted to offer business owners start-up and growth consulting. There are many free programs for this type of consulting, but our price distinguished us from all of the others. For $15,000 we provide a business plan, identity, and collaterals for a start-up or new growth plan. This price was created by calculating the hours required to write a business plan for a new venture at an hourly rate of approximately $75 per hour (plus the fee for the graphic designer to produce an identity package and marketing materials). In addition, we added a full week of training for the start-up owner. After including out-of-pocket costs and profit, the fee was $15,000. It's worth every dollar of the fee for someone who wants to get started quickly—and who realizes that she could earn much more than $15,000 by starting the business a month sooner.

Pricing can be established by analyzing the market—what is already in the market or what the market will bear. It can be calculated by cost, plus a markup for overhead and profit. Or it can be generated by starting with the annual salary you want to earn, add taxes and overhead, divide by the number of hours in a year you believe you can sell and you will have an hourly rate. In any case, women usually start with a price that is low and then are reluctant to raise it. Look at a company you respect. How does that company price its product or service? You need to do the same and it may put you into a new business—having those customers you really want.

When Katina started doing resumes, she received calls from people wanting a bargain basement price. She could not afford to meet with them and let it be known that she would produce a resume for the same price that someone else would charge just for typing it. Katina held her ground and charged more because her resumes "got results" due to the unique style and her great writing. At some point Katina had the opportunity to raise her price, but was reluctant to do so. Clients were readily paying her fee and were exceptionally pleased with the results. This was the time to look at an increase. We were in the Boardroom Group discussing price and I put a model on the board with $250 to $275 for her resume packages. Within six months Katina was marketing her packages at a price exceeding $300, and they are worth every dollar. Katina was in a new business—designer resumes that get results.

The other part of pricing calculations that I notice women omit is the part where you add profit to the equation. Women will start with cost and add overhead and maybe even enough to pay their salary, but that's it. They don't add profit to the business. If you earn only enough to pay yourself a salary, you could get a job. The profit is the reason that you take the risk. Check your calculations—are you adding enough profit to put money in the bank every year?

Strategic Alliances

In the Boardroom Group we talk about strategic alliances many times each year. Even the smallest company of one can create an alliance that provides growth or opportunities for more and ongoing profit. Think about what alliance would be beneficial to your business. If you had a relationship with another organization, or with a large firm, what would it look like? How would you each benefit?

Joan Smith, owner Gallery 143, recently moved to a new retail location and discovered that the other merchants were interested in sharing prospect mailing lists and mailing costs. This is a great strategic alliance.

Judith Snyder, owner of JSM Consulting Group, developed a strategic alliance with another professional in her field of nonprofit development consulting. She and her colleague developed a series of training seminars and delivered them in several states. Together they have now generated hundreds of new prospects, many new clients, and her growing business is strong and successful.

It appeared to me that *Working Woman* magazine may have a strategic alliance with National Association of Female Executives (NAFE). The NAFE bimonthly magazine *Executive Female* can be found inside *Working Woman*. Upon further checking, I found that both NAFE and *Working Woman* magazine are properties of Working Woman Network. This permits them to achieve a number of synergies between the two divisions of the company. (Check out at your newsstands or *www.workingwomanmag.com.*)

Exporting

Jean Rogers, president of Rogers GlassWorks, along with her husband Kevin, started their hand-blown contemporary glass company in Uniontown, Ohio. She told us in a Boardroom Group that she wanted to become known in Northeast Ohio and that their glass would be sold in fine galleries across the United States. After a few short years and much hard work, their outstanding work is found across the country, they are known in art circles everywhere, and their work can be found in many major cities outside the United States. Seeing their work at the Smithsonian Craft Show with other selected artists was breathtaking.

Fortunately, Jean could see how to take the company forward and she never stopped. Building a reputation so that the Rogers Glass-Works color and design would be in demand in the United States and in many other countries, continuing to apply to the best shows, and having a solo exhibition all contributed to building the fine company they now own.

Many women stop short of their real opportunities. Is exporting a possibility for you? Perhaps it will become the largest part of your business. Perhaps it will become your business!

Competition

Some firms need to look at the competitive activity on a regular basis in order to stay in the ball game. Others can check out the competition on occasion, but following their own plan usually brings the best results. Are you in a business that is threatened in some way by the competition? Perhaps you own a small retail book store and a large chain is coming to town. What if you own a kitchen and linen store and a large competitor arrives down the street? Perhaps you are a florist and the large supermarket chain on the next block just opened a new flower and garden department.

If you have a small retail store and competition is a serious threat to your continued existence, check out what it is that your competition is actually doing. Is there a way for you to provide the same products and services that they do? If so, you may need to offer the same stuff to stay in business.

On the other hand, you may need to be different to survive. There are hundreds of articles at the library about retail outlets that survived a large competitor, and mostly they did it by being different. They found a service or a niche of products to offer that were exceptional and developed a public relations campaign to help their customers and prospects know why they were different. They carved out a different reputation, one that people wanted. They reinvented their business and were successful.

This is one case where working harder won't bring success; you need to go to the library and see how other owners accomplished their change. You might even travel to visit a successful store and get good ideas.

New Market Segments

Pam Lahm, president of Lahm & Associates, Interior Design, has a wonderful home-based business of many years. She doesn't need to market at this point because she has been in business long enough to enjoy referrals from prior clients as well as repeat business. Pam has education and training in color psychology and color response. She also has training in feng shui. Recently she has found more prospects who are interested in color psychology and in feng shui—individuals and business owners, including a school for students with attention deficit disorder.

These new market segments could be a whole business on their own. They certainly provide new possibilities for Pam's growth plan. Adding work in these new segments gives Pam the opportunity to choose the combination of work she loves and also to charge a higher rate. She can now bring in other designers to assist her in some of the work; her time can be utilized better with a bigger client base.

Look at the market segments that comprise your customer base. Make a list or a pie chart. What new markets would you like to develop? Do you have markets that you would prefer to hold steady and not grow? If one of your markets is dwindling due to industry change, this is the right time to look for new market segments to develop—and while you are at it, find ones that offer more revenue for the same work, or the same revenue for less work.

Government Procurement

Many owners believe that government procurement is only for manufacturing companies. The SBA will tell you that the government buys everything that any other business or large organization buys—including golf balls.

DeBorah Thigpen-Waller, president of D. Thigpen & ADsociates, an advertising and public relations agency, started her business 11 years ago in Houston. She opened an office in Twinsburg, Ohio, and learned about the opportunity for service companies in the government sector. She secured a million-dollar-plus bid doing work for NASA. After meeting DeBorah, I never again doubted the opportunity for service businesses to do government work.

Perhaps there is an opportunity for you to do work with your state or the federal government. Like anything else, there is a learning curve; but I notice that once a woman owner gets a bid, she usually continues to grow this segment of her business. Look at *www.pro-net.sba.gov* or *www.womanowned.com* for more information.

Branding

Having worked with a Pepsi Cola franchise for so long, branding is one of my favorite subjects. A new owner will come to see me about how to market to start her business, and I can see branding in the future, even though I can't tell her about it for months and months—it can be overwhelming to think about when you are first starting.

What is branding? A product image or a name that represents the value in your product or service is a brand. You are familiar nationally with Pepsi Cola and McDonald's. Other products are known to you by their brand name—Schwinn, Tiffany's, Craftsman, Cover Girl, DK, Microsoft, and Rubbermaid.

Locally, you may be able to think of products or services that carry a name that you recognize. When you associate the name with the product, and even more if you have a belief about value, that is branding. So, you are saying to yourself, "I would never have the money to invest to create and market a brand." Perhaps not if you think that you are competing with Sara Lee. But you could develop a brand locally that your community recognizes and wants to buy because of the value established by the quality of the previous purchases.

Linda Lorkowski, owner of Linda's Kitchen, started baking cookies in her home while her children were all too young for school. She has a great business and has grown so much that she requires two freezers and an assembly line in her basement to accommodate her orders. What if Linda created one particular dessert—how about a lemon bar cookie—and decided to package it and market it to upscale grocery stores and restaurants. The packaging that highlights the name—Linda's Luscious Lemon Bar—would be distinct and recognizable. Soon people would ask the waitress if they had any of Linda's Lemon Bars left. Others would buy six to take home for dessert. It would be superb quality, the tastiest dessert you would every want, light, flavorful, and delicious! That is the value that the brand stands for. That is an example of branding, even in a local community.

If you have a service that could be branded, often it is packaged so that it can be named. Jane Wagner, owner of The Wagner Group, offers training for medium-sized companies; she offers professional development such as team building, facilitation, and meeting management. If Jane packaged a series of three workshops all around running a meeting, named the package Meeting Magic and started marketing this new program to every medium-sized company in the region, soon they will be aware of it. Then, they'll know it by name; an owner will be sitting in a meeting where his time is being wasted and he will say, "We need that Meeting Magic stuff!"

I certainly hope that the name of my Web site will become branded (i.e., Amazon.com). My site *www.smallbizcoach.com* will contain so many resources for small business owners, I hope owners will look at my site first in order to find the information that they need or the referral that I provide to them.

Selling Method/Delivery Method

At Pepsi Cola we delivered our product in more than one way: route truck, semi truck and syrup truck. That was simple. Now, it seems that products are sold and delivered a number of new ways. You can buy your groceries on the Internet and a delivery truck will bring them to your front door.

Services are being delivered in more than one way, too. Look at the Internet "distance learning" opportunities. Take your class directly on the Net and you don't have to sit in the classroom.

If you are in a business where the method of selling or delivery is changing, it will be imperative that you brainstorm new ways to do things.

Cindy Jones and Jan Lorman are owners of Interactive Therapeutics, Inc. They provide products for adults who are regaining their speech following a stroke or accident. These products were distributed by speech therapists all over the United States; their catalog of products and counseling materials were shipped to over 20,000 sites to professionals to order products for their clients.

With changes in health care insurance, many professionals have left these positions. Cindy and Jan now need to distribute their wonderful products directly to families and are starting to do that through their Web site *www.interactivetherapy.com*. They will continue to research other ways to locate families who need the products and new ways to deliver to them.

Watch the trends. Read Faith Popcorn's *The Popcorn Report*. It will help you identify and watch the trends that may affect your business or the business of your suppliers or customers.

Franchising

Is franchising an option for you? How about creating a business opportunity or a distributorship? For the latest trends in these areas, read back issues of *Entrepreneur* magazine. They bring you the Top 500 Franchises and the Top 500 Business Opportunities each year. A dealership/distributorship involves individuals or businesses who are granted the right to buy wholesale and sell retail the products of Business ABC, but are not permitted to use ABC's trade name. Trademark/product licensees receive access to the seller's trade name as well as specific methods, products, technology, or equipment. Other business opportunities include coin-operated businesses, cooperatives, and multilevel/direct sales businesses.

Kay DeBolt, owner of Corporate Gopher, has a great model for a potential franchise, or a business opportunity. The name is catchy, the system has been tested, and she is the expert and can create the instruction training manual.

Chris Perrow, owner of Perrow Organizational Systems, is an organization expert. Her knowledge about the organization of offices and business systems is unbelievable. She also could create a great name, develop a training manual, and market her knowledge to other individuals who want to start the same type of business.

Sherry Huff, owner of Total Office, Inc., provides support services for business owners on the road, home-based owners, and overflow work for large companies. She is planning a Web site to help other people start this type of business in their own city. Check out *www.virtualassistantsnetwork.com*.

If you are really good at something you do, or something you create, how could you develop a system so that others could follow your guidebook and do the same thing that you do? People are interested in an established proven name and a system for making money. Think about your options.

⊿ IDEA CENTER ⊾

Five Life Changes That Will Affect Your Business

1. **Divorce.** In the Boardroom Groups alone, we've seen a rash of divorces—and most often, the emotional drain of the experience is enough to nearly kill the woman's business. Let's face it, unless you have a strong team in place (with two or more employees), it is difficult to sustain business growth when your life is changing so dramatically. This is when you most need a management consultant. It's too hard to remain focused when everything is in transition.

2. **Having children.** Children are not a liability to a business, but they do change the way you do business. You will need to find additional help to care for your kids when you are on a business call—or find creative ways to run your business around your kids' schedule. It's not always easy, but it can definitely be done.

3. **Moving.** Many women choose to move with their husband when a job transfer comes about. Some women are determined to relaunch their businesses in the new location. We've even known of others who have kept the original location and commute between the new one and the old. Anything is possible—you just have to be more creative to figure it out. Certainly if you are in a situation where transfers are a strong likelihood, an Internet-based business would be the ideal solution, since it doesn't rely upon geography as much as traditional businesses do.

4. **Bankruptcy.** For some women entrepreneurs, particularly those already in rocky money situations before launching their businesses, this risk is just too much to take. For whatever reason, their businesses just weren't bringing in enough to support them in their time of greatest financial need. When these women file for personal bankruptcy, it often affects their businesses, too. Many wind up filing for business bankruptcy as well, because it's too hard for the court to separate between personal and business records for sole proprietors or small companies.

5. **Illness.** Any of us could become seriously ill during our tenure as entrepreneurs, but have you really planned for such an event? Probably not, since many of us see ourselves as invincible and would rather not think about worst-case scenarios. But illness does happen, and we've seen a few entrepreneurs step aside to let others run their companies while they're off waging a more important battle against breast cancer. How can you plan for such a disastrous event when you are a sole proprietor, or a small company with just one or two employees? You can plan ahead by talking to your insurance agent about disability coverage. If you think that's too expensive for you to purchase now, imagine how much a six-week recovery period

will cost your business should it become necessary. Who will be working with your customers and bringing in the money you need to cover your bills? For its incredible value, disability insurance too often gets the short end of the stick from all entrepreneurs–both women and men alike.

Of Course You Can Learn the Secrets

The secrets are there for you to learn and relearn as you grow in your role as a business owner. There are many techniques and approaches that work and owners who are willing to share them. There are countless success stories in books and magazines available to you in libraries and on the Web.

But the best news for you is that others will want to help you on your path to success. Women business owners have formed a very close-knit network of support for one another and want to see each other succeed.

From Jill Manda, owner of Manda's Plant Farm in Clinton, Ohio, to Carol Latham, founder, president, and CEO of Thermagon, Inc. (a Cleveland manufacturer of a heat-reducing product used inside high-tech hardware the world over), women are following their hearts and creating organizations for the future. Some of them work 24/7, but they are loving every minute of it. Others find that ownership gives them the independence to work part time or work around their family's needs. They love the flexibility and the opportunity to change their focus when challenges send them off in a new direction.

Their day-to-day business is exciting and the future is theirs for the making. Everything seems more possible than ever before, and they feel confident in knowing that they are in control of their own destiny.

You can have that same feeling of confidence. Take the reins. Read and listen and find friends who know things that will help you. Pull up your bootstraps and decide that you are going to get your arms around this business that you see right out there on the horizon. Learn the secrets and put them into action. You'll be surprised how easy it will be to create the business of your dreams.

Supporting Your Sisters' Businesses: Networking and Informational Resources

---

Web Sites

www.xmission.com/~mcjathan/Century/Century.htm
21st Century Marketing Systems, Inc.
Offers a free marketing evaluation that identifies hidden assets that can grow your business three ways—all with no obligation.

www.dnai.com/~sharrow
Advertising & Marketing Information Resources Center
Named one of the top 10 business Web sites by Point Communications, this site offers a wealth of marketing information and white papers.

www.altavista.digital.com
Alta Vista
This search engine searches Web sites and newsgroups by keyword(s).

www.aahbb.org
American Association of Home-Based Businesses
A nonprofit group out of Maryland with various chapters that offers a bimonthly newsletter with tips for the home-based entrepreneur.

www.americanexpress.com/smallbusiness

In addition to card information, this site offers online tutorials for creating business plans, self-tests, articles, forums, and more.

www.homebusinessworks.com

American Home Business Association

Membership offers benefits in the following areas: communications, insurance services, financial services, professional services, training and support, tools, discounts, buying, and e-commerce tools.

www.anab.com

Association of North American Business

Organization of business owners and managers seeking to better their business skills while reducing costs and increasing their networking or client base.

http://sbc.bus.att.com/small_business

AT&T Small Business Information

This site offers help in data, voice, wireless, Internet, and business solutions categories.

www.bizproweb.com

BizPro Web

This terrific site for small-business professionals provides links to newsgroups, shareware, discussion forums, and more.

www.bizwomen.com

BizWomen

Web site built by Solutions 3000, Inc., offering free membership to women wishing to access the four discussion mailing lists, register an online brochure or business card, or access business information and directory listings.

www.businesscity.com

BusinessCity

Offers an Internet guide for business, a bookstore, and the Ask the Expert article collection.

www.businesstown.com
BusinessTown.com
Features many great links, including Associations, Business Directories, Internet, Time Management, and others.

www.Demographics.caci.com
CACI: Marketing Systems
Provides data on demographics, businesses, lifestyles, consumer spending, purchase potential, and other statistics.

www.ceo-express.com
CEO Express!
Created by a busy executive for a busy executive.

www.claritas.com
CLARITAS
Provider of marketing informational resources for firms engaged in consumer and business-to-business markets.

www.connect.claritas.com
Claritas Connect: Online Precision Marketing Services
Marketing reports are available for browsing.

www.accra.org
Comparative Cost of Living Index
A great site if you're thinking of relocating. Offers relative price levels for goods in six areas: housing, utilities, grocery items, transportation, health care, and a miscellaneous category.

www.copyright.com
Copyright Clearance Center
A resource for people who own or need to use copyrighted information. Allows for the exchange of rights and royalties with ease.

www.dejanews.com
Deja News Research Service
This site searches a Usenet news archive by keyword(s). Use it to find Usenet newsgroups relevant to your area of interest.

www.directmarketing-online.com
Direct Marketing On-line
An online resource for direct marketers, with a focus on educating them on how to apply traditional methods of direct marketing to the Internet.

www.dnb.com
Dun & Bradstreet
Their resource center offers not only a site for small business but also valuable tips and advice in eight other areas.

www.sec.gov/edgarhp.htm
Edgar Database: Corporate Information
Provides detailed annual 10-K reports on publicly held companies.

www.elibrary.com
Electronic Library
An online research center with a 30-day free trial. Allows you to choose the sources you wish your information to come from like books, newspapers, or magazines.

www.edgeonline.com
Entrepreneurial Edge
Market Planning—how to prepare a market analysis business toolkit.

www.en-parent.com
Entrepreneurial Parent
An entrepreneurial parent is someone trying to balance work and family. Offers free membership, free newsletter, and free expert advice on both home and job fronts.

www.entreworld.org
Entreworld.Org: Competitive Intelligence
Identifies Web sites and articles regarding competitive intelligence.

www.fasttrac.org
Fast Trac
Provides high quality, innovative educational programs that help entrepreneurs improve their business skills and succeed as self-sufficient people in healthy communities.

www.nypl.org/research/sibl/market/ficonsum.htm
Finding Consumer Information: How to Find Market Research Information
Identifies a variety of print directories and source books that provide consumer information on: demographics, tastes, and spending; geographic market characteristics; and lifestyles.

www.forbes.com/growing
Forbes Small Business Center
Offers a forum, audio center, database, and current as well as archived articles of interest to small business owners.

www.inter800.com/freelist.htm
Free Listing (Internet 800 number directory)
List your 800 or 888 number free on the Internet in this directory

www.thefreesite.com
The Free Site
Home of the Web's best freebies.

www.fuld.com/index.html
Fuld & Company: Competitive Intelligence Guide
An excellent source of industry/competitive information available on the World Wide Web.

www.gale.com
Gale Research, Inc.
This company publishes *Small Business Sourcebook*, which lists state and federal government programs.

www.geocities.com/wallstreet
General Business Services
Offers a business chat room and a business message board.

www.metacrawler.com
The Go2Net Network
Search engine resource.

www.hbiweb.com
Home Business Institute
As a member you get benefits in the following areas: credit card processing, financial planning experts, business and health insurance, marketing and advertising specialties, legal and accounting services, dental, prescription drugs, seminar workshops, debt collection, and more.

www.hoaa.com/main.htm
Home Office Association of America
The national organization for full-time, home-based professionals home page. Offers information on how to look for business information, capital opportunities, and advertising information.

www.smalloffice.com
Home Office Computing Magazine
Online version offers reviews, news, management, and a free weekly newsletter.

www.homestead.com
Homestead
Free online Web creation service with over 40 templates. A great site to use.

www.homeworks.com
HomeWorks
Home page of Paul and Sarah Edwards, who have written numerous home-based business books. Offers free lists and reviews.

www.hoovers.com

Hoovers Online

Subscribe to the service to get detailed reports on companies—offers a free trial run that is well worth it.

www.hwg.org/resources/faqs/ratesFAQ.html

HTML Writer's Guild: How to Set Rates FAQ

Help for Web technicians to ensure they are competitively priced.

www.businesscenter.ibm.com

IBM Small Business Center

Support site for small businesses offers a useful mix of articles and links along with related IBM product information.

www.IdeaCafe.com

Idea Café: The Small Business Channel

Money and business communications are only two of the areas worth checking out here.

www.ibaonline.com

Independent Business Alliance

Membership offers services in the following areas: legal services, accounting, marketing services, Internet services, business and personal development, and incorporation services.

www.osha.gov/oshstats/sicser.html

Industrial Classification System

Enables the user to search the SIC manual by keyword to access descriptive information for a specified four-digit SIC and to examine the manual system.

www.infind.com

Inference Find

Simultaneously searches through six search engines and gives you the results clustered for easier reading.

www.go.com/wedir/business/small_business
Infoseek: Start a Business
List of Web sites for the budding entrepreneur included in the following categories: business technology, home business, small business, and research.

www.insiderreports.com/cla.html
Insider Reports
Stop in here for valuable information on home-based business financing and credit.

www.interbiznet.com
Interbiznet
Founder and CEO John Sumser has compiled an easy-to-navigate site that, in addition to rating the top job-listing sites, also provides regular newsletters about recruiting online.

www.ustreas.gov/treasury/bureaus/irs/irs.html
Internal Revenue Service
Tax law information, help for your taxes, and tax forms are just the tip of the iceberg at this user-friendly site.

www.icsb.org
International Council for Small Business
Offers an opportunity to attend the World Conference, a journal, and a newsletter among other benefits.

www.isbc.com
International Small Business Consortium
Services include a business discussion group, marketing tips, business issues, business sites, and funding sources.

www.tig.com:80/IBC
Internet Business Center
Provides information about conducting business on the Internet, including Internet user demographics, marketing, and business sites on the Web.

www.barbaraling.com
Internet Recruiting Edge
Well-written and realistic overview of Internet recruiting.

www.financehub.com
Intersoft Solution's FinanceHub
Offers information on venture capital, banks, small business, the
stock market, and law links.

www.labelco.com
Interstate Label Company Label Catalog
Your source for labels of every size, shape, and type!

www.irs.ustreas.gov/cover.html
IRS Small Biz Site
More than just taxes, designed to be friendly, fast, and efficient.

www.liveprint.com
Kinko's
Check out what this state-of-the-art office center can do for you.
For example, you can electronically transmit documents from your
home office to Kinko's using Kinkonet, thus saving both time and
money.

www.lessonsinleadership.com
Lessons in Leadership: Blanchard, Peters, and Covey
Lets you learn from leaders Martha Rogers, Ken Blanchard,
Stephen Covey, Tom Peters, Robert Cooper, and Peter Senge.

www.ltbn.com
Let's Talk Business Network
Home of the *Let's Talk Business* syndicated radio program.

www.lcweb.loc.gov
Library of Congress
Provides an extensive list of Web-searching and index resources.

www.liszt.com

Liszt

Search engine that indexes subscription mailings lists by topic area—also provides subscription instructions and links to information documents and FAQs.

www.lycos.com

Lycos

An index of Web sites that allows users to query by keyword(s).

www.whowhere.lycos.com

Lycos WhoWhere

Where to go when you are looking for a phone number and an address.

www.marketingsource.com

Marketing Resource Center

Includes sections for classified ads, links to marketing associations, and an assortment of marketing statistics.

www.nsns.com/MouseTracks

Mouse Tracks

This site provides a list of marketing resources, including marketing mailing lists, marketing service firms, and links to information about marketing publications.

www.nafe.com

National Association of Female Executives

Benefits of membership include: career services, travel, personal services, finance, business services, legal services, insurance, and the corporate program.

www.nape.org

National Association of Private Enterprise

Membership benefits include seminar scholarships, legislation watch, and publications.

www.nase.org

National Association for the Self-Employed

Benefits include many discounts in business, personal, and health areas.

www.nawbo.org

National Association of Women Business Owners

Benefits from member partners such as: AT&T, Wells Fargo, Mass Mutual, Wyndham Hotels & Resorts, Lucent Technologies, IBM, *Working Woman*, Continental, New England Financial, *Inc. Magazine*, Jaguar, and Kemper.

www.nationalbusiness.org

National Business Association

Members enjoy benefits and discounts in the following areas: business, lifestyle, education and health, software, entertainment, and scholarships.

www.nfibonline.com

National Federation of Independent Business

Members vote on policies and then NFIB representatives go to all 50 state capitals as well as Washington, D.C. to speak to policy makers as advocates of the small business community.

www.npr.org

National Public Radio

Get news on the hour, programs, and find the NPR station nearest to you.

www.nsbu.org

National Small Business United

Member benefits include: insurance protection, discounts on foreign currency exchange, overnight delivery discounts, and a resource guide.

www.nebs.com

NEBS Checks, Forms, and More

Provider of imprinted checks and much more, like free catalogs, free sample packs, free product samples, and a free e-mail newsletter.

www.networksolutions.com
Network Solutions
Allows you to register your domain name.

www.nytimes.com
New York Times on the Web
The great thing about this site is that it is updated every 10 minutes so you have the most up-to-date news there is.

www.nolo.com
Nolo.com Self-Help Law Center
Online legal advice for more than just small business. Other categories include patents, employment, and debt.

www.census.gov
North American Industry Classification
This is the system that will replace SIC codes.

www.osha.gov
Occupational Safety and Health Administration
Offers a forum, special publications, training resources, and advisors.

www.pleiades-net.com/voices/entrepr/entrepr.html
Pleiades Women Entrepreneur Forum for Women in Business
Forum for women starting their own business.

www.corporateinformation.com/uspriv.html
Privately Held Company Information
Provides a rich source of information regarding privately held firms.

www.pro-net.sba.gov
Pro Net
Database of information on more than 171,000 small, disadvantaged, and women-owned businesses. Businesses profiled can be searched by SIC code, key words, location, etc.

www.brennerbooks.com/realpricesgd.html
Real Prices: Graphic Design
Contains easy to use formulas to help professionals keep themselves priced right.

www.roadway.com/shippers/sbrc.html
Roadway's Small Business Resource Center
Lists many useful sites, only a few of which are mentioned here. Featured sites include American Express Small Business Exchange, *Business Week*, Dow Jones Interactive Publishing, and the State Web Locator.

www.webcom.com/seaquest/sbrc/welcome.html
Seaquest's Small Business Resource Center
Resource topics include Finding and Starting a Business, Sales and Marketing, Internet Marketing, and Self-Improvement.

www.calafia.com/webmasters/major.htm
Search Engine Guide: The Major Search Engines
Discusses the major search engines and directories and provides links to all of them.

www.sec.gov/smbus1.htm
Securities and Exchange Commission
Features Q & A's, links to resources, as well as news on forums.

www.silverfox.org
Silver Fox Advisors (Seasoned Business Pros)
Free initial meeting with a professional who can help you build a profitable business.

www.bizoffice.com
Small and Home-Based Business Links
Article libraries, Web listing tools, merchant status tips, and an online bookstore are just a few of the things you'll find.

www.sbaonline.sba.gov
Small Business Administration Online
Find information on starting, financing, and growing a business, plus information on other topics of interest.

www.sbba.com
Small Business Benefits
Over 35 benefits in these seven areas: discount buying, publications, education and training, insurance, communications, financial support, and professional services.

www.smallbizsmarts.com
SmallBiz Smarts: Home Page
Monthly newsletter whose subscribers get benefits like low long-distance rates.

www.smallbizcoach.com
SmallBizCoach
Marketing and management information for business owners; homepage for Norma J. Rist, CEO Consulting, Inc.

www.entrepreneur.com
Entrepreneur.com
Search engine with a business-to-business directory and categories like management and computers that indexes pages of information geared to the small business owner.

www.smartbiz.com
Smart Business Supersite
Offers a free newsletter, over 60 categories to browse, trade show information, and a search engine.

www.mcgraw-hill.com/businesses/finser/index.html
Standard and Poors
Over 15 different lists that help make sense of the financial markets.

www.stat-usa.gov
Survey of Current Business
Subscribers get access to State of the Nation, a site with economic and financial resources and economic data, and GLOBUS & NTDB, a site with trade-related releases, international marketing research, country analysis, and trade opportunities.

www.tap.mills.edu
The Ada Project
While this is a site devoted to women in computer science, it has articles on notable women and women starting computer businesses.

www.asbaonline.org
The American Small Business Association
Members receive health, business, educational, and personal benefits.

www.doc.gov
U.S. Department of Commerce
This publication lists more than 180 federal and 500 state business assistance programs and provides information on funding, assistance finding, free management consulting, and more.

www.edwardsresearch.com
The Edwards Directory of American Factors
This book lists a number of different companies that offer factoring.

www.delta.com/prog_serv/exec_womens_travel
The Executive Woman's Travel Network
Offers discounts on travel to members.

www.prosavvy.com
The Expert Marketplace
The industry resource for technical and consulting services.

www.sleeter.com
The Sleeter Group
Seminars, software, and books for people who use the Quick Books systems.

www.tsbj.com
The Small Business Journal
Features articles on management, tax and legal, time management, and customer service.

www.so-ho.org
SOHO America–The Small Business Benefits Association
Members enjoy business benefits, personal benefits, and health benefits.

www.usps.gov
The United States Postal Service
Offers a zip code finder, rates, mail classes, and where to find the nearest post office.

www.thomasregister.com
Thomas Register of American Manufacturers
Simple search of over 150,000 companies, 7,700 online supplier catalogs, 135,000 brand names, and 63,000 product and service categories.

www.toolkit.cch.com
Business Owner's Toolkit
Offers business tools, online services, power tools, news and advice, business services, SCORE counseling, a bookstore, and a free e-mail newsletter.

www.tscentral.com
Trade Show Central
A listing of trade shows for most industries.

www.travelocity.com
Travelocity Travel Guide
Find/book a flight, rental car, hotel, vacation, or cruise.

www.business.gov
U.S. Business Advisor
Five ways to get information: Common Questions, How to . . . , Search, Browse, and News.

www.access.gpo.gov
U.S. Government Printing Office (GPO)
There are a variety of publications, ranging from starting a business to securing funding.

www.future.sri.com/vals/valsindex.shtml
VALS Segmentation System
VALS categorizes U.S. consumers into mutually exclusive groups based on their psychology (lifestyles, attitudes, interests, and opinions) and several key demographics.

www.voiceofwomen.com
VOWworld–Voices of Women Online
There are articles, a calendar of events, links to other sites, a directory of women-friendly businesses, and an online shop at this site.

www.wsj.com
Wall Street Journal
The *Wall Street Journal* Web effort gives you access to past and current articles.

www.webcrawler.com
Webcrawler
A large index of World Wide Web sites and their contents that users can search by keyword(s).

www.web-search.com/women.html
WebSearch, The Business of Women
An enormous database of women-owned businesses—each with a link to its own Web site. Entrepreneurial women who have their own Web sites can list them free of charge.

www.womenconnect.org
Women CONNECT: Women's news, etc.
Offers information in the following areas: Arts, Books/Authors, Boards and Chats, Business, Career, Communities, Education, Gender Equity, Health, Law/Safety, Politics, Sports/Fitness, Technology, Travel, History, and a 30-day index.

www.womeninc.com
Women Incorporated
Benefits can be found in the areas of communications, insurance, health care, business products and services, money matters, travel, and home and family.

www.witi.com
Women in Technology, International
Geared for women in high-tech, science, and technology-related fields, this site offers discussion forums, advice articles, and business information in a wide range of topics. Use the pull-down search menus on the home page to locate resources.

www.womenswire.com
Women's Wire
Light-hearted news as well as information on money and work.

www.workingsolo.com
Working Solo Online
Special sections include starting a business, a free newsletter, business book center, and small business resources.

www.wowfactor.com
WOWFactor—Women on the Web
Proclaims itself to be the world's largest online directory for women business owners.

www.wwwomen.com
WWWomen.Com! The Premier Online Directory for Women
Features many of the same categories that the other search engines boast like Arts and Entertainment but also has special areas targeted to women like Personal Time for Women.

www.xlibris.com
Xlibris: The Power to Publish
A site definitely worth looking into if you want to get published. Their electronic database means your book will never be out of print and authors retain the rights to their works and collect up to 50 percent of the gross profits.

www.yahoo.com
Yahoo!
An index of World Wide Web sites and their contents, with very specific site descriptions compiled by the service. Also includes a hierarchical topic index, allowing users to choose increasingly more specific categories to narrow a search.

www.yahoo.com/Business_and_Economy
Yahoo's Business Resources
This site has too many categories to list here, each with its own subcategories and linked Web sites. A few examples of the categories include Business Libraries, Consumer Economy, Conventions and Conferences, Management Science, and Small Business Information.

www.onlinewbc.or/resourcedatabase.html
Online Women's Business Center Resource Directory
Contains a comprehensive database of women's business resources. Also includes links for state-by-state information on several Small Business Administration programs.

www.onlinewbc.org/docs/wbcs/NHPortsmouth.html
Women's Business Center, Inc.
A collaborative organization designed to encourage and support women in all phases of enterprise development. They provide access to educational programs, financing alternatives, technical assistance, advocacy, and a network of mentor, peer advisors, and business and professional consultants.

www.onlinewbc.org
Online Women's Business Center
Entrepreneur business development information for starting and expanding women-owned businesses sponsored by SBA, IBM, JCPenny, NationalBank, GTE, and Avon.

www.oxygen.com
A blend of Web sites and TV that's designed to serve women better than they've ever been served before.

www.womenentrepreneurs.com
A business-friendly environment dedicated to the support and empowerment of entrepreneurial mothers and businesswomen.

Books

Aburdene, Patricia, and John Naisbitt. *Megatrends for Women*. Santa Monica, CA: Ballantine Books, 1992.

Adams, Bob. *Adams Streetwise Complete Business Plan*. Avon, MA: Adams Media, 1999.

Adams, Bob. *Adams Streetwise Managing People*. Avon, MA: Adams Media, 1997.

Adams, Bob. *Adams Streetwise Small Business Start-Up*. Avon, MA: Adams Media, 1997.

Ailes, Roger. *You Are the Message*. New York, NY: Doubleday, 1988.

Alarid, William. *FREE HELP From Uncle Sam to Start Your Own Business or Expand the One You Have*. Willits, CA: Bell Springs Publishing, 1997.

Alarid, William. *Money Sources for Small Businesses: How You Can Find Private, State, Federal, and Corporate Financing*. Santa Maria, CA: Puma, 1997.

Albrecht, Steven. *Service, Service, Service*. Avon, MA: Adams Media, 1997.

Allen, Kathleen. *Launching New Ventures: An Entrepreneurial Approach*. Chicago, IL: Upstart Publishing Company, 1995.

Allen, Mark. *Visionary Business: An Entrepreneur's Guide to Success*. Novato, CA: New World Library, 1996.

Angowski, Lisa. *1001 Ways to Market Yourself and Your Small Business*. Gilbart, AZ: Perigee, 1997.

Applegate, Jane. *201 Great Ideas for Your Small Business*. Princeton, NJ: Bloomberg Press, 1998.

Applegate, Jane. *Succeeding in Small Business*. New York, NY: Penguin Group, 1992.

Arden, Lynie. *Working at Home Sourcebook*. Woodland, CA: Live Oak Publications, Annual.

Arkebauer, James B. *Golden Entrepreneuring: A Mature Person's Guide to Starting a Successful Business*. New York, NY: McGraw-Hill, 1995.

Artz, Nancy. *301 Great Customer Service Ideas from America's Most Innovative Small Companies*. New York, NY: Inc. Pub, 1998.

Baker, Sunny, and Kim Baker. *Million-Dollar Home-Based Businesses*. Avon, MA: Adams Media, 1997.

Balter, Neil. *Closet Entrepreneur: 337 Ways to Start Your Successful Business with Little or No Money*. Franklin Lakes, NJ: Career Press, 1994.

Bangs, David H., and Andi Axman. *Work at Home Wisdom*. Venice, FL: Dearborn, 1998.

Bangs, David H. *Business Planning Guide*. Chicago, IL: Upstart, 1998.

Bangs, David H. *Market Planning Guide*. Chicago, IL: Upstart, 1998.

Bangs, David H., and Andi Axman. *Launching Your Home-Based Business*. Chicago, IL: Upstart, 1997.

Bangs, David H. *Smart Steps to Smart Choices: Testing Your Business Idea*. Chicago, IL: Upstart, 1996.

Bangs, David H. *Creating Customers*. Chicago, IL: Upstart, 1992.

Blechman, Bruce, and Jay Conrad. *Guerrilla Financing: Alternative Techniques to Finance Any Small Business*. New York, NY: Houghton Mifflin, 1992.

Blum, Laurie. *Free Money from the Federal Government for Small Businesses and Entrepreneurs*. New York, NY: John Wiley & Sons, 1996.

Blum, Laurie. *Free Money for Small Businesses and Entrepreneurs*. New York, NY: John Wiley & Sons, 1995.

Bowker, R. R. *Literary Marketplace*. New Providence, NJ: Reed Reference Publishing Co., Annual Volume.

Brabec, Barbara. *Homemade Money: Your Home-Based Business Success Guide for the '90s*. Willits, CA: Bell Springs Publishing, 1997.

Brattina, Anita F. *Diary of a Small Business Owner*. New York, NY: AMACOM, 1995.

Brennan, Gregory. *Successfully Self-Employed*. Chicago, IL: Upstart, 1996.

Brodsky, Bart, and Janet Geis. *Finding Your Niche . . . Marketing Your Professional Service*. Willits, CA: Bell Springs Publishing, 1991.

Bromley, D. B. *Reputation, Image & Impression Management*. New York, NY: John Wiley & Sons, 1993.

Burke, Charles E., and Charles H. Burke. *How to Build an Internet Service Company*. Menlo Park, CA: Peer-to-Peer Communications, 1997.

Burnes, Kent J. *Secrets to Small Business Success*. San Francisco, CA: SMART Resource Center, 1996.

Card, Emily. *Business Capital for Women: An Essential Handbook for Entrepreneurs*. New York, NY: Macmillan General Reference, 1996.

Chant, Ben. *How to Start a Service Business (The 21st Century Entrepreneur)*. New York, NY: Avon Books, 1995.

Chapman, Elwood N. *Human Relations in Small Business*. Menlo Park, CA: Crisp Publications, 1994.

Chickadel, Charles. *Building a Profitable Business: The Proven Step-By-Step Guide to Starting and Running Your Own Business.* Avon, MA: Adams Media, 1994.

Clifford, Dennis & Warner, Ralph. *Partnership Book.* Willits, CA: Bell Springs Publishing, 1997.

Cochrane, Patrick. *Kitchen Table Millionaire: Home-Based Money Making Strategies to Build Financial Independence Today.* Rocklin, CA: Prima Publishing, 1997.

Cohen, William A. *Entrepreneur and Small Business Problem Solver: An Encyclopedia and Reference Guide.* New York, NY: John Wiley & Sons, 1990.

Consumer Law Foundation. *Complete Small Business Loan Kit.* Avon, MA: Adams Media, 1997.

Cook, Marshall. *Adams Streetwise Time Management.* Avon, MA: Adams Media, 1999.

Cook, Mel. *Home Business, Big Business: The Definitive Guide to Starting and Operating On-Line and Traditional Home-Based Ventures.* New York, NY: Macmillan General Reference, 1998.

Daily, Frederick W. *Tax Savvy for Small Businesses: Year Round Tax Advice for Small Businesses.* Berkeley, CA: Nolo Press, 1995.

Darnay, Arsen J. *Statistical Record of Older Americans.* Farmington Hills, MI: Gale Research, 1996.

Davidson, Jeff. *Market Yourself and Your Career.* Avon, MA: Adams Media, 1999.

Davidson, Jeffrey P. *Marketing for the Home-Based Business.* Avon, MA: Adams Media, 1997.

Davis, Will. *Start Your Own Business for $1000 or less.* Chicago, IL: Upstart, 1994.

Dayton, Doug. *Total Market Domination.* Avon, MA: Adams Media, 1999.

Debelak, Don. *Marketing Magic.* Avon, MA: Adams Media, 1997.

Deems, Richard S. *More Than a Gut Feeling.* Franklin Lakes, NJ: Career Press, 1995.

Dickey, Terry, and Tony Hicks. *Basics of Budgeting: A Practical Guide to Better Business Planning.* Menlo Park, CA: Crisp Publications, 1992.

Dickey, Terry, and Beverly Manber. *Budgeting for a Small Business.* Menlo Park, CA: Crisp Publications, 1994.

Dicks, J. W. *How to Incorporate and Start a Business Series.* Avon, MA: Adams Media, 1997.

Dicks, J. W. *Small Business Legal Kit.* Avon, MA: Adams Media, 1997.

Doswell, A. *Office Automation: Context, Experience and Future.* New York, NY: John Wiley & Sons, 1990.

Dove, Kent E. *Generation E <Entrepreneur>: The Do-It-Yourself Business Guide.* San Francisco, CA: Jossey-Bass Publishers, 1988.

Dragoo, Bob. *Real Time Profit Management.* New York, NY: John Wiley & Sons, 1995.

Dugan, Ann. *Franchising 101.* Chicago, IL: Upstart, 1998.

Dvorak, Robert R. *Productivity at the Workplace.* Menlo Park, CA: Crisp Publications, 1995.

E-Z Legal Forms. *E-Z Legal Guide to Limited Liability Company.* Boise, ID: E-Z Legal Forms, 1997.

Edwards, Paul. *Teaming Up: the Small Business Guide to Collaborating with Others to Boost Your Earnings and Expand Your Horizons.* New York, NY: Jeremy P. Tarcher, 1997.

Edwards, Paul, and Sarah Edwards. *Best Home Businesses for the 90s.* E. Rutherford, NJ: Jeremy P. Tarcher/Putnam Publishing Group, 1995.

Edwards, Paul, and Sarah Edwards. *Making Money with Your Computer at Home.* E. Rutherford, NJ: Jeremy P. Tarcher/Putnam Publishing Group, 1996.

Eis, Arlene L. *Newsletters in Print.* Teaneck, NJ: Infosources, 1999.

Elias, Stephen. *Patent, Copyright and Trademark: A Desk Reference to Intellectual Property Law.* Berkeley, CA: Nolo Press, 1996.

Elster, Robert J. *Small Business Sourcebook.* Farmington Hills, MI: Gale Research, 1998.

Entrepreneur Magazine. *Entrepreneur Magazine: Guide to Raising Money.* Willits, CA: John Wiley & Sons, 1997.

Entrepreneur Magazine. *Entrepreneur Magazine: Starting a Home-Based Business.* Willits, CA: John Wiley & Sons, 1996.

Erffmeyer, Robert, Gretchen Hutterli, and Peter Smith. *Marketing: Mastering Your Small Business.* Chicago, IL: Upstart, 1996.

Evanson, David R. *Where to Go When the Bank Says No: Alternatives for Financing Your Business.* Princeton, NJ: Bloomberg Press, 1998.

Fallek, Max. *Finding Money for Your Small Business.* Chicago, IL: Upstart, 1994.

Federal Trade Commission. *Franchising and Business Opportunities: Rules and Guides.* Washington, D.C.: Federal Trade Commission, Annual Publication.

Fishman, Stephen. *Software Development: A Legal Guide.* Berkeley, CA: Nolo Press, 1994.

Flanagan, Lawrence. *Raising Capital: How to Write a Financing Proposal.* Grant's Pass, OR: Psi Research—Oasis Press, 1994.

Flescher, John. *Online Market Research.* Indianapolis, IN: Addison-Wesley, 1995.

Fleury, Robert E. *Small Business Survival Guide.* Naperville, IL: Sourcebooks, 1996.

Floyd, Elaine. *Marketing with Newsletters: How to Boost Sales, Add Members, Raise Donations & Further Your Cause With a Promotional Newsletter.* St. Louis, IL: E. F. Communications, 1991.

Fournies, Ferdinand F. *Coaching for Improved Work Performance.* Blue Ridge Summit, PA: Liberty Hall Press, 1987.

Frey, Robert S. *Successful Proposal Strategies for Small Businesses: Winning Government, Private Sector, and International Contracts.* Cambridge, MA: Artech House, 1997.

Friedman, Robert. *Upstart Small Business Legal Guide.* Chicago, IL: Upstart, 1998.

Fritz, Roger. *Small Business Troubleshooter.* Franklin Lakes, NJ: The Career Press, 1995.

Fry, Fred L., and Charles R. Stoner. *Strategic Planning for the New and Small Business.* Chicago, IL: Upstart, 1995.

Garner, D., R. Owen, and R. Conway. *Ernst & Young Guide to Financing For Growth.* Willits, CA: John Wiley & Sons, 1994.

Gerber, Michael E. *E-Myth Revisited.* New York, NY: HarperCollins, 1995.

Godfrey, Joline. *Our Wildest Dreams.* New York, NY: HarperCollins, 1993.

Godin, Seth. *If You're Clueless About Starting Your Own Business.* Chicago, IL: Upstart, 1997.

Goldstein, Arnold S. *Starting on a Shoestring: Building a Business without a Bankroll.* New York, NY: John Wiley & Sons, 1995.

Goltz, Jay, and Jody Oesterreicher. *Street Smart Entrepreneur: 133 Tough Lessons I Learned the Hard Way.* Omaha, NE: Addicus Books, 1998.

Gumpert, David E. *How to Really Start Your Own Business: A Step-By-Step Guide Featuring Insights and Advice from the Founders of Crate & Barrel, David's Cookies, etc.* New York, NY: Inc Publishing, 1996.

Harding, Ford. *Rain Making.* Avon, MA: Adams Media, 1994.

Harper, Stephen C. *McGraw-Hill Guide to Starting Your Own Business: A Step-By-Step Blueprint for the First-Time Entrepreneur.* Burr Ridge, IL: McGraw-Hill, 1992.

Hawken, Paul. *Growing a Business.* Cambridge, MA: Simon & Schuster, 1987.

Hiam, Alexander. *Adams Streetwise Motivating and Rewarding Employees.* Avon, MA: Adams Media, 1999.

Hicks, Tyler Gregory. *199 Great Home Businesses You Can Start (And Succeed in for Under $1000).* Rosaville, CA: Prima Publishing, 1992.

Holden, Greg. *Small Business Internet for Dummies.* Dallas, TX: Paperback, 1998.

Huff, Priscilla Y. *101 Best Home-Based Businesses for Women.* Rocklin, CA: Prima Publishing, 1995.

Janson, Robert L. *Handbook of Inventory Management.* Ramsey, NJ: Prentice Hall, 1987.

Jones, Katina Z. *The 150 Most Profitable Home Businesses for Women.* Avon, MA: Adams Media, 2000.

Jones, Katina Z. *Easy to Start, Fun to Run, and Highly Profitable Home Businesses.* Avon, MA: Adams Media, 1998.

Jones, Katina Z. *Adams Businesses You Can Start Almanac.* Avon, MA: Adams Media, 1997 (CD-ROM).

Kahn, Sharon. *101 Best Businesses to Start.* New York, NY: Doubleday, 1992.

Kamoroff, Bernard B. *422 Tax Deductions for Businesses & Self-Employed Individuals.* Willits, CA: Bell Springs Publishing, 1998.

Kamoroff, Bernard. *Small Time Operator: How to Start Your Own Small Business, Keep Your Books, Pay Your Taxes, and Stay out of Trouble!* Willits, CA: Bell Springs Publishing, 1999.

Keeler, Len L. *Cyber Marketing.* New York, NY: AMACOM, 1995.

Kintler, David. *Adams Streetwise Consulting.* Avon, MA: Adams Media, 1997.

Koehler, Dan M. *Insider's Guide to Small Business Loans.* Grant's Pass, OR: Psi Research-Oasis Press, 1996.

Kremer, John. *1001 Ways to Market Your Books—Fifth Edition.* Tempe, AZ: Open Horizons, 1998.

Kushell, Jennifer. *No Experience Necessary: Young Entrepreneur's Guide to Starting a Business.* New York, NY: Princeton Review, 1997.

Langhoff, June. *Telecom Made Easy.* Middletown, RI: Aegis Publishing Group, 1996.

Larson, Richard, and David Zimney. *White Collar Shuffle: Who Does What in Today's Computerized Workplace.* New York, NY: AMACOM, 1990.

Lesko, Matthew. *Free Money to Change Your Life.* Foster City, CA: Information USA, 1997.

Lesonsky, Rieva. *Start Your Own Business: The Only Start-Up Book You'll Ever Need.* Atlanta, GA: Entrepreneur Media, 1998.

Levine, Mark. *Field Guide to Starting a Business.* New York, NY: Fireside, 1990.

Levinson, Jay Conrad. *Guerrilla Negotiating: Unconventional Weapons and Tactics to Get What You Want.* New York, NY: John Wiley & Sons, 1999.

Levinson, Jay Conrad. *Guerrilla Marketing with Technology: Unleashing the Full Potential of Your Small Business.* Reading, MA: Addison-Wesley, 1997.

Levinson, Jay Conrad. *Guerrilla Trade Show Selling: New, Unconventional Weapons and Tactics to Meet More People, Get More Leads, and Close More Sales.* New York, NY: John Wiley & Sons, 1997.

Levinson, Jay Conrad. *Way of the Guerrilla: Achieving Success and Balance as an Entrepreneur in the 21st Century.* Boston, MA: Houghton Mifflin, 1997.

Levinson, Jay Conrad. *Guerrilla Marketing Online Weapons: 100 Low-Cost, High-Impact Weapons for Online Profits.* Boston, MA: Mariner Books, 1996.

Levinson, Jay, and Seth Godin. *Guerilla Marketing for the Home-Based Business.* Boston, MA: Houghton Mifflin, 1995.

Levinson, Jay Conrad. *Guerrilla Advertising: Cost-Effective Techniques for Small Business Success.* Boston, MA: Houghton Mifflin, 1994.

Levinson, Jay Conrad. *Guerrilla Marketing Excellence: The 50 Golden Rules for Small-Business Success.* Boston, MA: Houghton Mifflin, 1993.

Levinson, Jay Conrad. *Guerrilla Marketing for the Nineties: The Newest Secrets for Making Big Profits from Your Small Business.* Boston, MA: Mariner Books, 1993.

Levinson, Jay Conrad. *555 Ways to Earn Extra Money; Revised for the '90s.* New York, NY: Henry Holt and Company, 1991.

Levinson, Jay Conrad. *Earning Money Without a Job.* New York, NY: Henry Holt and Company, 1990.

Levinson, Jay Conrad. *Guerrilla Marketing Weapons: 100 Affordable Marketing Methods for Maximizing Profits from Your Small Business.* New York, NY: Plume Books, 1990.

Levinson, Jay Conrad. *Guerrilla Marketing Attack: New Strategies, Tactics, and Weapons for Winning Big Profits for Your Small Business.* Boston, MA: Houghton Mifflin, 1989.

Levinson, Jay Conrad. *Quit Your Job! Making the Decision, Making the Break, Making It Work.* New York, NY: Dodd Mead, 1987.

Lindsey, Jennifer. *Entrepreneur's Guide to Capital.* Seattle, WA: Probus Publishing, 1990.

Lonier, Terri. *Working Solo Sourcebook: Essential Resources for Independent Entrepreneurs.* New York, NY: John Wiley & Sons, 1998.

Lumpkin, James R. *Direct Marketing, Direct Selling and the Mature Customer: A Research Study.* Westport, CT: Greenwood Publishing Group 1989.

Maddox, Rebecca. *Inc Your Dreams—for Any Woman Who Is Thinking about Her Own Business.* New York, NY: Viking Penguin, 1995.

Malburg, Christopher R. *Accounting for the New Business.* Avon, MA: Adams Media, 1997.

Malburg, Christopher R. *All-In-One Business Planning Guide.* Avon, MA: Adams Media, 1997.

Mancuso, Joseph A. *How to Prepare and Present a Business Plan.* Ramsey, NJ: Prentice Hall, 1992.

Manning, Marilyn. *NAFE Guide to Starting Your Own Business: A Handbook for Entrepreneurial Women.* Burr Ridge, IL: Irwin Professional Publishing, 1995.

Mariotti, Steve. *Young Entrepreneur's Guide to Starting and Running a Business.* New York, NY: Times Books, 1996.

McCoy, Thomas J. *Creating an "Open Book" Organization.* New York, NY: AMACOM, 1996.

McGaulley, Michael T. *Selling 101.* Avon, MA: Adams Media, 1997.

McKeever, Mike. *How to Write a Business Plan.* Berkeley, CA: Nolo Press, 1999.

McWhirter, Darien. *Entrepreneurial Growth Strategies.* Avon, MA: Adams Media, 1997.

Meyerowitz, Steven A. *An Ounce of Prevention: Marketing, Sales & Advertising Law for Non-Lawyers.* Farmington Hills, MI: Gale Research, 1993.

Milano, Carol. *Hers: The Wise Woman's Guide to Starting a Business on $2,000 or Less.* New York, NY: Allworth Press, 1998.

Milling, Bryan. *Cash-Flow Problem Solver.* Naperville, IL: Sourcebooks, 1992.

Miner, Lynn E. *Proposal Planning and Writing.* Phoenix, AZ: Oryx Press, 1998.

Minter, Scott, and Sheri Moore Humphrey. *Business and the Legal System: Mastering Your Small Business.* Chicago, IL: Dearborn Trade, 1996.

Montgomery, Vickie. *Smart Woman's Guide to Starting a Business.* Franklin Lakes, NJ: The Career Press, 1994.

Morgan, C., and D. Levy. *Segmenting the Mature Market.* Riverton, NJ: American Demographics Marketing Power Series, 1993.

Morrison, Deborah. *Building a Better Website.* Irvine, CA: IDG Books, 1995.

Morrison, Terri, Wayne A. Conaway, and George A. Borden. *Kiss, Bow, or Shake Hands: How to Do Business in Sixty Countries.* Avon, MA: Adams Media, 1997.

Moulton, Susan. *Bond's Franchise Guide.* Naperville, IL: Sourcebook Publications, Annual Publication.

Muckian, Michael, and John Woods. *Business Letter Handbook.* Avon, MA: Adams Media, 1997.

Nelson, Bob. *1001 Ways to Reward Employees.* New York, NY: Workman Publishing, 1994.

Nicholas, Ted. *Complete Book of Corporate Forms.* Carmel, CA: Enterprise Publishing, 1994.

Olins, Wally. *Corporate Identity: Making Business Strategy Visible Through Design.* New York, NY: McGraw-Hill, 1992.

Paulson, Ed, and Marcia Layton. *Complete Idiot's Guide to Starting Your Own Business.* New York, NY: Macmillan General Reference, 1998.

Perlstein, David. *Solo Success: 100 Tips for Becoming a $100,000 a Year Freelancer.* Three Rivers, MI: Three Rivers Press, 1998.

Pfaffenberger, Bryan & Wall, David. *10 Secrets for Web Success: What It Takes to Do Your Site Right.* Inverness, CA: Ventana Press, 1996.

Phillips, Michael, and Salli Rasberry. *Marketing Without Advertising.* Willits, CA: Bell Springs Publishing, 1997.

Pinson, Linda. *Steps to Small Business Start-Up: Everything You Need to Know to Turn Your Ideas into a Successful Business.* Chicago, IL: Dearborn Trade, 1996.

Pinson, Linda, and Jerry Jinnett. *Keeping the Books.* Chicago, IL: Upstart, 1998.

Pinson, Linda, and Jerry Jinnett. *Anatomy of a Business Plan.* Chicago, IL: Upstart, 1996.

Pinson, Linda, and Jerry Jinnett. *Home-Based Entrepreneur.* Chicago, IL: Upstart, 1996.

Pinson, Linda, and Jerry Jinnett. *Target Marketing: Out of Your Mind . . . And Into the Marketplace.* Chicago, IL: Upstart, 1996.

Pinson, Linda, and Jerry Jinnett. *Woman Entrepreneur.* Chicago, IL: Upstart, 1996.

Plachy, Roger J., and Sandra J. Plachy. *Results-Oriented Job Descriptions.* New York, NY: AMACOM, 1993.

Popcorn, Faith, and Lys Marigold. *Clicking.* New York, NY: HarperCollins, 1996.

Popcorn, Faith. *Popcorn Report: Faith Popcorn on the Future of Your Company, Your World, Your Life.* New York, NY: HarperCollins, 1992.

Popell, Steven B. *Big Profits from Small Companies.* Mountain View, CA: Lomas Publishing, 1985.

Pressman, David R. *Patent It Yourself.* Berkeley, CA: Nolo Press, 1995.

Putman, Anthony O. *Marketing Your Services.* New York, NY: John Wiley & Sons, 1990.

Rachlin, Robert, and Allen Sweeny. *Accounting and Financial Funding for Non-Financial Executives.* New York, NY: AMACOM, 1996.

Reierson, Vickie. *Start Your Business: A Beginner's Guide.* Grant's Pass, OR: Psi Research–Oasis Press,1995.

Rice, Craig S. *Marketing Without a Marketing Budget.* Avon, MA: Adams Media, 1997.

Rice, Craig S. *Strategic Planning for the Small Business,* 2nd ed. Avon, MA: Adams Media, 1997.

Rich, Stanley R., and David E. Gumpert. *Business Plans That Win $$$.* New York, NY: HarperCollins, 1987.

Ries, Al, and Jack Trout. *Positioning: The Battle for Your Mind.* New York, NY: Warner Books, 1981.

Ross, Marilyn, and Tom Ross. *Big Marketing Ideas for Small Business.* Homewood, IL: Dow Jones-Irwin, 1990.

Rossiter, Jill A. *Human Resources: Mastering Your Small Business.* Chicago, Il: Upstart, 1996.

Rubin, Charles, and Jay Levinson. *Guerrilla Marketing Online: The Entrepreneur's Guide to Earning Profits on the Internet.* Boston, MA: Houghton Mifflin, 1997.

Rubin, Richard, and Philip Goldberg. *Small Business Guide to Borrowing Money.* Willits, CA: Bell Springs Publishing, 1980.

Rye, David E. *Starting Up: An Interactive Adventure That Challenges Your Entrepreneurial Skills.* Upper Saddle River, NJ: Prentice Hall Trade, 1997.

Rye, David E. *Winning the Entrepreneur's Game.* Avon, MA: Adams Media, 1997.

Salmon, Bill, and Nate Rosenblatt. *Complete Book of Consulting.* Ridgefield, CT: Round Lake Publishing, 1995.

SBA, New Orders. *Minority Small Business and Capital Ownership Development Program.* Washington, D.C.: Superintendent of Documents, Annual Publication.

Schaefer, David. *Surefire Strategies for Growing Your Home-Based Business.* Chicago, IL: Upstart, 1997.

Schiffman, Stephan. *25 Most Common Sales Mistakes and How to Avoid Them,* 2nd ed. Avon, MA: Adams Media, 1997.

Schiffman, Stephan. *25 Sales Habits of Highly Successful Salespeople,* 2nd ed. Avon, MA: Adams Media, 1997.

Schiffman, Stephan. *Closing Techniques (That Really Work!).* Avon, MA: Adams Media, 1997.

Shaw, Lisa. *Telecommute! Go to Work Without Leaving Home.* New York, NY: John Wiley & Sons, 1996.

Sheldon, Betsy, and Joyce Hadley. *Smart Woman's Guide to Networking.* Franklin Lakes, NJ: The Career Press, 1995.

Sher, Barbara. *Wishcraft.* New York, NY: Ballantine Books, 1986.

Siegel, Joel G., and Jae K. Shim. *Keys to Starting a Small Business.* Hauppauge, NY: Barron's Educational Series, 1991.

Silver, David A. *Enterprising Women: Lessons from 100 of the Greatest Entrepreneurs of Our Day.* New York, NY: AMACOM, 1994.

Simon, Neil. *Franchise Sales Compliance Guide.* Newark, NJ: Reed Smith Shaw & McClay, 1994.

Sinclair, Carole. *Keys for Women Starting and Owning a Business.* Hauppauge, NY: Barron's Educational Series, 1991.

Smith, Cynthia S. *A Woman's Guide to Starting Her Own Business.* Seacaucus, NJ: Carol Publishing Group, 1995.

Smith, Brian R. *How to Become Successfully Self-Employed,* Revised 2nd ed. Avon, MA: Adams Media, 1997.

Spiegel, Jill. *Flirting for Success: The Art of Building Rapport.* New York, NY: Warner Books, 1994.

Spiro, Herbert T. *Finance for the Non-Financial Manager.* New York, NY: John Wiley & Sons, 1996.

Stack, Jack. *Great Game of Business.* New York, NY: Doubleday Currency, 1992.

Standard & Poors Corp. *Industry Surveys.* Chicago, IL: Standard & Poors, Annual Publication.

Steingold, Fred S. *Small Business Legal Guide (series).* Willits, CA: Bell Springs Publishing, 1998.

Steingold, Fred S. *Legal Master Guide for the Small Business.* Upper Saddle River, NJ: Prentice Hall, 1983.

Stephens, Nancy J. *Adams Streetwise Customer-Focused Selling.* Avon, MA: Adams Media, 1999.

Stephens, Nancy J. *Adams Streetwise Selling.* Avon, MA: Adams Media, 1997.

Stern, Linda. *Money-Smart Secrets for the Self-Employed.* New York, NY: Random House, 1997.

Stolze, William J. *Start-Up Financing: An Entrepreneur's Guide to Financing a New or Growing Business.* Franklin Lakes, NJ: Career Press, 1997.

Stolze, William J. *Start-Up: An Entrepreneur's Guide to Launching and Managing a New Business.* Franklin Lakes, NJ: Career Press, 1996.

Superintendent of Documents. *Franchise Opportunities Handbook.* Washington, D.C.: U.S. Government Printing Office, Annual Publication.

Swiss, Deborah J. *Women Breaking Through.* Princeton, NJ: Peterson's/Pacesetter Books, 1996.

Tabet, Joseph, and Jeffrey Slater. *Financial Essentials for Small Business Success.* Chicago, IL: Upstart, 1994.

Tompkins, Nevile C. *A Manager's Guide to OSHA.* Menlo Park, CA: Crisp Publications, 1995.

Tuller, Lawrence W. *Entrepreneurial Growth Strategies.* Avon, MA: Adams Media, 1997.

Tuller, Lawrence W. *Independent Consultant's Q & A Book.* Avon, MA: Adams Media, 1997.

U.S. Department of Commerce. *U.S. Industrial Outlook.* Washington, D.C.: International Trade Association. (Usually about five years' worth of data.)

U.S. SBA. *Avoiding Patent, Trademark, and Copyright Problems.* Washington, D.C.: SBA Publications, Annual Publication.

U.S. SBA. *Women and the Small Business Administration.* Washington, D.C.: Office of Women's Business Enterprise, Annual Publication.

U.S. SBA. *Women's Handbook: How the SBA Can Help You Go Into Business.* Washington, D.C.: Office of Women's Business Enterprise, Annual Publication.

Ventura, John. *Small Business Survival Kit.* Chicago, IL: Dearborn Financial Publishing, 1994.

Weinstein, Grace. *Financial Savvy for the Self-Employed.* New York, NY: Henry Holt, 1995.

Weiss, Alan. *Money Talks: How to Make $1 Million as a Speaker.* New York, NY: McGraw-Hill, 1997.

Weiss, Alan. *Our Emperors Have No Clothes.* Franklin Lakes, NJ: Career Press, 1995.

Weiss, Alan. *Million Dollar Consulting.* New York, NY: McGraw-Hill, 1992.

Weiss, Alan. *The Innovation Formula: How Organizations Turn Change into Opportunity.* Minneapolis, MN: Las Brisas Research Press, 1988.

Wesman, Jane. *Dive Right In, the Sharks Won't Bite.* Chicago, IL: Upstart, 1995.

White, Sarah, and John Woods. *Adams Streetwise Do-It-Yourself Advertising.* Avon, MA: Adams Media, 1999.

White, Sarah, and John Woods. *Adams Streetwise Advertising, Direct Mail, & Publicity.* Avon, MA: Adams Media, 1997.

Wilbur, L. Perry. *Money in Your Mailbox.* New York, NY: Wiley Press, 1985.

Winter, Barbara. *Making a Living Without a Job: Winning Ways for Creating Work That You Love.* New York, NY: Bantam/Doubleday, 1993.

Yudkin, Marcia. *Marketing Online: Low Cost, High Yield Strategies for Small Businesses and Professionals.* New York, NY: Plume, 1995.

Zarozny, Sharon, ed. *Federal Database Finder.* Farmington Hills, MI: Gale Research, 1995.

Zbar, Jeffery D. *Home Office Know How.* Chicago, IL: Upstart, 1998.

Zobel, Jan. *Minding Her Own Business: The Self-Employed Woman's Guide to Taxes and Recordkeeping.* Oakland, CA: Easthill Press, 1998.

Zuckerman, Laurie B. *On Your Own: A Woman's Guide to Building a Business.* Chicago, IL: Upstart, 1990.

Pamphlets and Workbooks

ACCRA Community Profile. American Chambers of Commerce Researchers Association, Annual Publication.

Comparative Cost of Living Index. American Chambers of Commerce Researchers Association, Quarterly Compilation.

Directory of Franchising Organizations and Franchising Investigation and Contract Negotiation. Pilot Books, Annual Publication.

Franchise Annual Directory. Info Franchise News, Inc., Annual Publication.

IMS Ayer Directory of Newspapers, Magazines, and Trade Associations. Ayer Press.

International Franchising Law. International Franchise Association.

National Directory of Minority-Owned Business Firms. Business Research Services, Inc.

SMART Steps to Small Business Success. SMART Resource Center, 1995.

Start Up Marketing: An Entrepreneur's Guide to Advertising, Marketing and Promoting Your Business. Career Press, 1996.

Words to the Wary: 10 Rules to Remember When Borrowing Money from a Bank. Cappello & McCann. Send a SASE to receive a free copy: Cappello & McCann, 831 State Street, Santa Barbara, CA 93101.

Small Business Financial Resource Guide. U.S. Chamber of Commerce Center for Small Business. Call 202-463-5500 to get a copy.

Government Organizations

The Chamber of Commerce USA
202-659-6000

This organization provides data on all types of businesses nationwide. Ask for sources of state information and state industrial directories. Local chambers can supply information for a specific region.

Internal Revenue Service
800-829-3676

The IRS provides a publication list addressing the tax issues of concern to the entrepreneur.

The Library of Congress
202-707-5522

The Library's Telephone Reference Service can be of great help in locating information you are trying to find.

The Library of Congress Duplication Service
202-707-5640

The photoduplication service will find materials and send you photocopies. Turnaround time runs from six to eight weeks.

Minority Business Development Agency
202-482-4547
This is a training center supported by the SBA, in which minority businesses are given technical guidance.

Minority Business Development-Procurement Assistance
202-482-4547
This SBA agency provides specialized services to disadvantaged businesses.

National Minority Supplier Development Council
212-944-2430
This agency gives information about procurement opportunities.

Office of Women's Business Ownership
U.S. Small Business Administration
409 S. W. 3rd Street
Washington, D.C. 20416
202-205-6673
This agency has pamphlets and other resources of value for women. Be sure to ask for the new guide *Blueprint for Success: A Guide for Women Entrepreneurs.*

SBA Publications
817-355-1933 or 817-885-6500
SBA offers free and low-cost booklets to help you plan your budgets, personnel policies, and business plans. A list is available.

SCORE
800-827-5722
The 800-number answer desk provides information on government agencies.

Service Corps of Retired Executives
202-205-6600
SCORE provides free individual counseling, courses, conferences, and workshops.

Small Business Administration
1-800-8-ASK-SBA

The SBA was created in 1953 as an independent agency of the federal government to aid, counsel, assist, and protect the interests of small business concerns, to preserve free competitive enterprise, and to maintain and strengthen the national economy.

Small Business Development Centers
1-800-8-ASK-SBA

www.smallbiz.suny.edu/roster.htm

Sponsored in part by the SBA and administered by the State University of New York.

Statewide networks of experts assisting small businesses in business planning, development, and problem solving. Call the SBA for the number of the nearest office in your home state.

U.S. Patent and Trademark Office
703-308-4357

Contact this office for information about patents and trademarks. You can obtain an index of patents and order printed copies of patents at $3 each or faxed copies at $25 each. There are also many depository libraries around the United States.

Women and Money

Black Enterprise/Greenwich Street Corporate Growth Partners
388 Greenwich Street
New York, NY 10013
212-816-1308

$60 million fund with its focus on minority- and/or women-owned or managed companies. The average investment is $5 million to $15 million.

Capital Across America
414 Union Street, Suite 2025
Nashville, TN 37219
615-254-1515
fax: 615-254-1856
capxam@aol.com

$28 million fund, including funds from the Small Business Investment Company program, which partners the SBA and venture funds in the private sector. Although its primary focus is on women-owned businesses, the fund will look at any established small company that fits its investment criteria. The average investment is $500,000 to $1.5 million.

First USA VISA Credit Card
1-800-347-7887
Call and ask about First USA's special credit card for NAFE members. It offers no annual fee and a 3.9% introductory rate.

Inroads Capital Partners
1603 Orrington Avenue
Suite 2050
Evanston, IL 60201
847-864-2000
847-864-9692
carrington@inroadsvc.com
$50 million fund with a target company that is owned or led by women and/or minorities, although this is not the only focus. The average investment for this fund is $3 million to $5 million.

Isabella Capital LLC
312 Walnut Street
Suite 3540
Cincinnati, OH 45202
peg@fundisabella.com
Target of $25 million fund. Once formed it will focus primarily on women-owned or women-led businesses. The typical investment will range from $500,000 to $3 million, usually given in more than one round.

NAFE
1-800-634-NAFE
www.nafe.com
The National Association for Female Executives provides the resources and services—through education, networking, and public advocacy—to empower its members to achieve career success and financial security. American Express Financial Advisors, Inc., offers NAFE members an initial consultation free. The organization also offers *Executive Female* magazine to its members.

Viridian Capital
220 Montgomery Street
Suite 946
San Francisco, CA 94104
415-391-8950
fax: 415-391-8937

$24 million fund including SBIC contributions. Its target base is companies that were founded or cofounded by women, are led by women, or sell products or services targeted primarily at women. The average investment ranges from $500,000 to $2 million.

Wells Fargo
800-577-4990

Offers *BusinessLine*, an unsecured line of credit that's an excellent source of the cash your business needs. It offers you a range of services tailored to the needs of the small business owner—like more ways to access your funds and more flexibility.

Women's Growth Capital Fund
1054 31st Street NW
Washington, D.C. 20007
202-342-1431
fax: 202-342-1203
info@womensgrowthcapital.com
www.womensgrowthcapital.com

$30 million fund, including funds from the Small Business Investment Company program, which partners the SBA and venture funds in the private sector. Targets women-owned businesses or companies with at least one top female executive. The average investment is $500,000 to $2 million.

Organizations

9 to 5 National Association of Working Women
655 Broadway Suite 300
Denver, CO 80203
800-522-0925
www.quikpage.com/9/9to5naww

An inclusive membership organization using advocacy, education, activism, leadership development, and support to improve the workplace for women and to strengthen the ability of low-wage women to win economic justice.

American Agri Women
aagriwomen@aol.com
www.americanagriwomen.com
Women's agricultural organizations and individuals uniting to communicate with one another and with other consumers to promote agriculture for the benefit of the American people and the world.

American Association of Black Women Entrepreneurs
301-585-8051
Founded in 1982, BWE is a national nonprofit membership organization that is designed to increase the success rate of African American women engaged in business ventures geared toward the government and major corporate markets.

American Association of Home-Based Businesses
301-963-9153
This nonprofit association provides a network of home-based businesses through local chapters.

American Association of University Women
111 16th Street, N.W.
Washington, D.C. 20036
800-326-AAUW
info@aauw.org
www.aauw.org
AAUW is composed of three corporations: the Association, a 150,000-member organization with more than 1,500 branches nationwide that lobbies and advocates for education and equity; the AAUM Educational Foundation, which funds pioneering research on girls and education, community action projects, and fellowships and grants for outstanding women around the globe; and the AAUW Legal Advocacy Fund, which provides funds and a support system for women seeking judicial redress for sex discrimination in higher education.

American Business Women's Association (ABWA)

816-361-6621

ABWA is a large organization that supports professional women and women who own their own businesses.

American Franchisee Association

800-334-4232

The AFA is a national organization aimed at improving the investment climate for potential and existing franchisees. It publishes a quarterly newsletter and provides consulting services.

American Medical Women's Association

801 North Fairfax Street, Suite 400

Alexandria, VA 22314

703-838-0500

info@amwa-doc.org

www.amwa-doc.org

National organization of women physicians and medical students. They are dedicated to promoting women's health, improving the professional development and personal well-being of their members, and increasing the influence of women in all aspects of the medical profession.

American Nurses Association

600 Maryland Avenue, S.W.

Suite 100 West

Washington, D.C. 20024

1-800-274-4ANA

www.nursingworld.org

They give their members easy access to sources of substantive information on ANA, on the nursing profession, and on health care issues of the day. This information is available to you in newspapers, journals, and books; on the phone, and on the Internet.

American Society of Women Accountants

800-326-2163

60 Revere Drive, Suite 500

Northbrook, IL 60062

www.aswa.org

The mission of ASWA is to enable women in all fields of accounting and finance to achieve their personal, professional, and economic potential and to contribute to the future development of the profession.

American Women's Economic Development Corporation
800-222-2933

This nonprofit organization assists women in realizing their business potential. It has assisted or trained more than 100,000 women during the past 15 years.

Association for Women in Communications
1244 Ritchie Highway
Suite 6
Arnold, MD 21012-1887
410-544-7442
www.womcom.org

The Association for Women in Communications is a professional organization that champions the advancement of women across all communications disciplines by recognizing excellence, promoting leadership, and positioning its members at the forefront of the evolving communications era.

Association for Women in Science
202-326-8940
1200 New York Avenue
Suite 650
Washington, D.C. 20005
www.awis.org

Dedicated to achieving equity and full participation for women in science, technology, and engineering.

Capital Rose
1-800-678-7930

Capital Rose is a company created by women, for women who choose self-employment as their vehicle for personal and professional fulfillment. They are in the business of putting women into business for themselves, and enabling them to be successful.

Financial Women International

200 North Glebe Road

Suite 820

Arlington, VA 22203

703-807-2007

www.fwi.org

Financial services professionals rely on Financial Women International for professional growth, information sharing, peer networking, mentoring, leadership development, and career advancement.

Home-Office Association of America

909 Third Avenue

Suite 990

New York, NY 10022-4731

Write about subscribing to Home-Office Connections, a monthly newsletter with news, ideas, opportunities, and savings for those who work at home.

Latin Business Association

213-721-4000

The Latin Business Association is a nonprofit organization that promotes the economic growth of the Latino business community.

Licensing Industry Merchandisers' Association

212-244-1944

This association strives to establish standards of professional and ethical marketing of licensed properties. It is a leading source of information through publishing, public speaking, and an open line.

National Association for the Cottage Industry

P.O. Box 14850

Chicago, IL 60614

NACI is an organization that supports home-based entrepreneurs by providing specialized information, resources, and support to its members. Ask about the newsletter. Contact by sending a SASE.

National Association for the Self-Employed (NASE)

800-232-6273

The self-employed members of this association have access to a
business-consultant hotline, group health insurance, and disability insurance.

National Association of Black Women Entrepreneurs (NABWE)

313-559-9255

NABWE supports black women who are thinking of starting their own businesses and those who already own businesses.

National Association of Home-Based Businesses

410-363-3698

The NAHBB provides seminars and educational materials for home-based entrepreneurs.

National Association of Insurance Women

contact@NAIW.org

www.naiw.org

Originally created to help women gain enough industry knowledge to be competitive after WWII, today the association offers leadership opportunities, publications, and discounts to its members.

National Association of Negro Business and Professional Women's Club, Inc.

NANBPW

P.O. Box 91226

Pittsburgh, PA 15221

www.realpittsburgh.com

NANBPW is a nonprofit community-based volunteer organization composed of business and professional women devoted to community service projects. The organization also takes great pride in honoring men, women, and youth in their area who have demonstrated outstanding success in their professions and/or an exceptional commitment to the community.

National Association of Women in Construction

327 S. Adams Street

Ft Worth, TX 76104-1081

817-877-5551

nawic@onramp.net

NAWIC is an international association that promotes and supports the advancement and employment of women in the construction industry.

National Coalition of 100 Black Women, Inc.
Houston Chapter
P.O. Box 273071
Houston, TX 77277-3071
713-659-NCBW (6229)
NCBW_Houston@yahoo.com
www.fhpw.org/ncbw

This organization provides forums to promote awareness of African-American culture, networking, and career development in the social, economical, political, and educational arenas.

National Federation of Business and Professional Women
2012 Massachusetts Avenue NW
Washington, DC 20036
202-293-1100
www.women.co.jp/directory/data/40.html

This organization works to improve equity for all women in the workplace through advocacy, education, and information.

National Federation of Independent Businesses
800-634-2669

This association represents the interests of independent and small businesses to federal and state legislative bodies.

National Association of Women Business Owners (NAWBO)
301-608-2590

Various chapters across the country make this one of the most popular professional networking groups there is.

National Foundation of Women Business Owners
301-495-4975
www.nfwbo.org

NFWBO is dedicated to promoting the growth of women business owners and their enterprises through gathering and sharing of knowledge.

National Women's Hall of Fame
315-568-8060

The hall was established in 1969 and stands as a proud monument to the nation's heroines. Past women honored include Amelia Earhart, Rosa Parks, and Eleanor Roosevelt.

Society of Women Engineers
120 Wall Street
Eleventh Floor
New York, NY 10005-3902
212-509-9577
hq@swe.org
www.swe.org
Stimulates women to achieve full potential in careers as engineers and leaders; expands the image of the engineering profession as a positive force in improving the quality of life, and demonstrates the value of diversity.

Women Business Owners' Corporation
310-530-7500
www.wboc.org
WBOC is a national not-for-profit corporation that was established to increase competition for government and large corporate contracts by implementing a pioneering economic development strategy for women-owned businesses.

Women's Council of Realtors
www.wcr.org
webmaster@wcr.org
The Women's Council of REALTORS is a community of real-estate professionals creating career opportunities, promoting success strategies, and inspiring leadership and individual achievement. All 50 states have a chapter.

Women Inc.
800-930-3993
Women Incorporated was created as a response to women's growing need for business loans, lines of credit, health insurance, and discounts on commonly used business products and services. Their mission focuses on improving the business environment for women.

Women's World Banking
212-768-8513
wwb@igc.apc.org
WWB is committed to taking a leadership role in documenting and disseminating innovations by financial institutions that effectively address the needs of low-income entrepreneurs.

Magazines

Black Enterprise
Monthly
Earl G. Graves
Publishing Company
212-242-8000

Brand Marketing
Monthly
800-289-0273

Business Geographics
Monthly
847-427-2024

Business Marketing
Monthly
888-288-5900

DMNEWS
Weekly
609-786-4780/4781

Enterprising Women
Bimonthly
919-460-8282

Entrepreneur
Monthly
800-274-6229

**Entrepreneur's
Business Start-Ups**
Monthly
Entrepreneur
Magazine
800-274-8333

**Entrepreneur's Guide
to Franchise Business
Opportunity**
Annual
Entrepreneur Media, Inc.
800-421-2300

Executive Female
Bimonthly
National Association of
Female Executives
800-634-6233

Fast Company
Bimonthly
800-688-1545

**Home Office
Computing**
Monthly
800-288-7812

HR Magazine
Monthly
Society for Human
Resource Management
703-548-3440

Inc.
18 Issues/yr
800-234-0999

**Managing Small
Business**
Quarterly
216-671-1534
tsperic@penton.com

**Self-Employed
Professional**
Bimonthly
Business Media Group
LLC
978-887-7900

**Selling Power
Magazine**
Bimonthly
800-752-7355

**Small Business
Success**
Annually
800-848-8000

Success
Monthly
800-234-7324

TeleServices News
Weekly
201-445-2205

Working Woman
Monthly
Carol Anderson Taber
800-234-9675

Index

$15.95 ($24.95 Canada)

How to capitalize on the biggest trend in business!

Building a small business can be a major challenge for anyone. In today's modern workplace, women continue to have a unique set of obstacles to overcome as small business owners: skepticism from friends and family, difficulties obtaining credit and financing, and, generally, more scrutiny than male competitors.

Whether you're about to build a business from the ground up—or buy an existing one—*Small Business Savvy* shows you how to succeed. Authors Norma J. Rist and Katina Z. Jones are entrepreneurial pioneers who have successfully launched their own small businesses, as well as worked as consultants to more than 500 women-owned businesses across the country. These two incredible mentors are your guides through the process of creating, launching, and expanding your business. They've seen it all, and understand the issues you face every day as a female small business owner.

The authors show you all the ropes of small business ownership, including:

- **How to thrive in even the worst economic times**

- **When it's worth taking a risk—and when to sit tight and await the "right" moment**

- **How women can crack any market**

- **Whom to turn to for advice in making pivotal de**

- **How to b 18th money w**

- **How to k change yo**

Whether you're opening a small boutique or running your own public relations firm, *Small Business Savvy* has the facts, figures, and, best of all, the advice you need. Take it from your mentors, Norma and Katina, who've already "been there and done that"— if you believe in yourself, you, too, can succeed as a small business owner.

Norma J. Rist is president of Norma J. Rist CEO Consulting, Inc., and founder of Boardroom Groups In 1999, she received the U.S. SBA Business Advocate of the Year award. She on, Ohio.

Jones owns Going Places Self-Promotions, gner resume service. She is author of nesses You Can Start Almanac and *Easy to Start, Fun to Run & Highly Profitable Home Businesses*. She lives in Akron, Ohio.

ISBN 1-58062-568-1

51595

9 781580 625685

ADAMS
M E D I A
C O R P O R A T I O N

adamsmedia.com